lacrosse

BOB SCOTT

Lacrosse

technique
and tradition

The Johns Hopkins University Press
Baltimore and London

The Johns Hopkins University Press
701 West 40th Street
Baltimore, Maryland 21211
The Johns Hopkins Press Ltd., London

Originally published, 1976
Second printing, 1977

Johns Hopkins Paperbacks edition, 1978
Second printing, 1982
Third printing, 1985

Library of Congress Cataloging in Publication Data

Scott, Bob.
    Lacrosse: technique and tradition.

    Includes index.
    1.   Lacrosse.   I.   Title.
GV989.S36   796.34'7   76-17223
ISBN 0-8018-2060-X

THE GAME AND ITS HISTORY

contents

foreword

It is a privilege to introduce this book about a graceful sport by a graceful man. Bob Scott knows lacrosse so well because most of his life has been involved with the game, and he personifies its best qualities. Disciplined control marks the great athlete. It also marks the great gentleman. Calmness under pressure, graciousness in victory, dignity in defeat, cool skill in the heat of the contest, the use of emotion as incentive rather than diversion—these are not born in us but bred by disciplined control. Bob Scott achieved these qualities as a player and coach, and he commands them as a man. We at Johns Hopkins are proud of him.

Lacrosse as a collegiate sport delights not only in its excitement but also in its purity. Collegiate lacrosse is not contaminated by commercialism. Those who play lacrosse as undergraduates are truly scholar-athletes. They play for love of the game and its skills, without the lure of a future professional contract.

The Johns Hopkins University and collegiate lacrosse have been so long and so closely intertwined that they have become almost synonymous. The game is loved and played with distinction at sister institutions, but ours is the only university at which lacrosse is the dominant intercollegiate sport. Perhaps nothing brings the Johns Hopkins community together as much as each lacrosse season. Many alumni would paraphrase Browning to say, "Oh, to be at Homewood, now that April's there."

So here is a book about lacrosse that instructs all friends of the game, from those who have loved it long to those just making acquaintance with it. No one could be better qualified to have written it for you than Bob Scott.

STEVEN MULLER
President
The Johns Hopkins University

preface

In this book, Bob Scott has assembled material
invaluable to all lacrosse enthusiasts. The book is
divided into three sections. A description of the
game of lacrosse, its rules, and its history com-
prises the first section, while the second part de-
lineates the techniques and tactics of the game.
The final section is devoted to lacrosse at the
Johns Hopkins University.

A masterly presentation of the principles of individual and team play, the second section of the
book will appeal to players, coaches, and students of lacrosse. Rarely have the fundamentals
and tactics of the game been described so
clearly and competently. Eighty-seven years of
Johns Hopkins lacrosse are explored in the third
part of the book, which will interest not only those
who feel in some way close to Hopkins but all
who enjoy the game, since the history of lacrosse
at Hopkins is intimately related to its development in other institutions where the game has
achieved prominence.

The book is informative and instructive and
will be enjoyed by everyone who is interested in
lacrosse or in athletics in general.

G. WILSON SHAFFER
Dean Emeritus, Homewood Schools
The Johns Hopkins University

acknowledgments

I wish to acknowledge the assistance and support of the many people who have helped me with this book. John R. Riina, who sparked the idea several years ago, was primarily responsible for laying the groundwork for this volume. John's encouragement and friendship have been especially meaningful to me. I am also indebted to Henry Jarrett, who, as my manuscript editor, worked closely with me. Not only is Henry an expert editor, but he also has a great enthusiasm for lacrosse that began fifty years ago, when he was assistant manager of the 1926 Hopkins championship lacrosse team. His help has been invaluable.

Special thanks go to Milton R. Roberts, who is the authority on the history of lacrosse. He and Alexander M. Weyand wrote *The Lacrosse Story,* which is the most complete volume on the history of the game. This book was the only reference source used in my writing, and I relied heavily on it in my two chapters on the history of lacrosse. Milt's personal involvement with my book—in particular, with the historical data—was most significant.

For the artwork, which is such an integral part of the book, I am especially grateful to Robert G. Rothgaber, who is responsible for all the instructional photographs and many of the action pictures, including the one on the front cover. Bob has worked endless hours with many aspects of the book and should get the credit for suggesting its title; his contribution has been outstanding. Other action photographs have been furnished by Willard R. Bonwit (a long-time expert in lacrosse photography), John E. DiCamillo, Richard Linfield, and Jeff Wagner. Credit for the fine artwork in the diagrams goes to Thursby S. Pierce and his son, Robert S. Pierce.

George M. Chandlee, Jr. was my technical adviser, and he spent many hours reading the manuscript in its formative stage. His suggestions were a tremendous help, and it has been reassuring to know that my book has been reviewed by a real student of the game. The proofreading of the completed manuscript was another important job, ably performed by Henry Ciccarone, Mickey Cochrane, Doyle Smith, and Walter Herman. The office secretaries played a key role—Catherine Colman typed the manuscript and Jane Smoot handled much of the office business while I was writing.

A special word of gratitude is due the staff members of the Johns Hopkins University Press. Everyone has been most cooperative and helpful —in particular, Theresa Czajkowska, who directed the copy editing of the book and was assisted by Mary Lou Kenney; Patrick Turner, who did an excellent job handling all the details of book design; and Jim Johnston, who provided sound advice in many areas of concern.

Finally, I want to express my thanks to the people who gave me the opportunity to play and coach lacrosse at Johns Hopkins University. It was Howdy Myers who encouraged me to attend Hopkins. Kelso Morrill, Gardner Mallonee, Fred Smith, and Wilson Fewster coached me as a student. Wilson Shaffer and Marshall Turner hired me as the Hopkins coach and gave me direction during my years in that position. And during those twenty years it was my good fortune to have outstanding men working with me on the sidelines: Henry Ciccarone, Fred Smith, Wilson Fewster, Kelso Morrill, Bill Logan, Buzzy Budnitz, Jerry Schnydman, Joe Cowan, Duane Levine, Alex Sotir, Hal Grosh, Willie Scroggs, Geoff Berlin, Michael Hanna, and Dennis Townsend.

To all of these people and to the members of my twenty Hopkins teams, I say, "Thanks."

R. H. S.

the game and its history

the game of lacrosse

Lacrosse is one of the great team games on the American sports scene. Nearly everyone who has played it or watched it as a spectator loves the game. Lacrosse gets in your blood because it is such a fast-moving and exciting sport. It has been accurately characterized as "the fastest game on two feet" (ice hockey, a potential claimant, is played on skates).

It is a beautiful game, too—above all, for the skill of the stick handlers in throwing and catching either long, looping passes or bulletlike shorter ones. But that is just the beginning. There are frequent changes in the action when the defensive team gets possession of the ball and dashes downfield; the dodging and the stick checking; the quick pass to an attackman on the crease and his equally quick shot at the goal; the amazing saves of a good goalie (but he can't stop them all); and the sudden body checks that are so different from the constant pounding of bodies in football. Also in contrast to the often obscured contact in football, all action takes place in the open, so that the knowledgeable spectator can follow and appreciate fine points of strategy and tactics.

This wide-open, action-packed game presents many scoring opportunities. In fact, one of the foremost reasons for the popularity of lacrosse is the high number of climactic plays that occur during a game. In a typical college game, a combined total of seventy-five to eighty-five shots will be taken at the goal by the two teams, and fifteen to twenty-five goals will be scored. This makes for excitement, geared to the action-loving player and fan of today.

Practices are more fun in lacrosse than in many other sports because a major portion of each session is devoted to scrimmaging. Although most athletes realize the need for drills on basic skills and techniques, they prefer the game itself. Fundamentals are certainly stressed in every lacrosse practice, but scrimmaging is the only way to learn the various phases of the team game. The athlete who plays both football and lacrosse will almost always say that lacrosse practices are much more enjoyable than football practices. Jim Brown, thought by many to be the greatest all-round athlete of modern times, is best known for his accomplishments in football both at Syracuse University and with the Cleveland Browns. But he was also an All-American lacrosse player and has been quoted as saying that on game day football was his favorite but overall, when considering both practices and games, he liked lacrosse better because it was more fun.

Lacrosse is played in the springtime, and in most areas this means green grass, budding leaves on the trees, and blooming flowers. Except in the few areas that have year-round warm climates, this provides a refreshing change from the winter season, when most sports are played indoors. How invigorating it is to leave the heated gymnasiums and get outside in the beautiful spring weather of April and May to play or watch lacrosse! There is a certain magic to springtime, and those who have been exposed to lacrosse know there is a touch of magic in this great American game.

Lacrosse was originated by the American Indians many centuries ago. The white man took up the game in the nineteenth century and introduced many refinements. Today lacrosse is played extensively in many sections of the United States and Canada and to a more limited degree in England and Australia.

Although the Canadians play both field and box lacrosse, the box game is considerably more popular there. It is played in ice-hockey arenas with six players on a team, compared with ten in the field game. Continuous action and physical contact highlight the box game, and in its general makeup it is more similar to ice hockey than to field lacrosse.

Modern lacrosse has a definite set of rules, similar to those that govern team sports like football, soccer, basketball, and ice hockey. A neophyte can learn the important ones easily by watching a game or two with a veteran player or spectator who can give a running commentary on the action. Spectators become as addicted to lacrosse as the players. In Baltimore and at Johns Hopkins University, the sport has had strong support for almost a century. Although many other

cities and college campuses now have deep roots in the game, I am sure that a larger number of expert spectators have been developed at Homewood Field on the campus of Johns Hopkins University than anywhere else. Over the years Hopkins students have been quick to learn the rules, even as entering freshmen who never before saw the game played. After watching their first game or two, they start to get the "feel" for the sport, and by midseason they are knowledgeable fans. I know, because as the coach on the sidelines of Homewood Field for twenty years, I have heard their negative reactions to the officials' calls against Hopkins (which in their opinion are always wrong) and positive reactions to clever maneuvers by our players. By the end of the freshman year they can be considered veteran spectators, and by graduation time, "All-American" spectators.

In the United States today lacrosse is played at 168 colleges and is the most popular spring sport at the great majority of them. Just check attendance figures at any of the lacrosse-playing schools, and you will find very few places where any other spring sport comes close to having as many spectators. Over the years crowds of 12,000 to 20,000 people have seen the big games of each season. In recent years, over 20,000 saw the 1973 Maryland-Hopkins game at College Park, Maryland; 14,000 saw the 1974 NCAA championship game between Maryland and Hopkins at Rutgers University in New Brunswick, New Jersey; 13,500 saw the 1975 Cornell-Hopkins game at Cornell University in Ithaca, New York; and 12,000 packed every inch of Homewood Field for the 1975 NCAA championship game between Navy and Maryland.

Sports are an integral part of American life, and lacrosse is one of the fastest-growing sports. As long as they are kept in the proper perspective, sports provide a beneficial outlet for both players and spectators, but it is the athlete who reaps the greatest satisfactions from being in the playing arena. He learns to live with victory and with defeat, and these experiences are basic to daily living. The opportunity for growth in personal character traits is as great in athletics as it is in any other area—possibly even greater. Self-discipline is vital to a person's development, and athletic competition demands complete commitment. Learning to say "no" to cutting corners, to cheating, and to telling white lies and learning to put the good of the group above personal ambitions are perhaps the most important factors in an individual's character growth. Respect for others (teammates, coaches, opponents, and referees) helps the individual to appreciate the necessity of getting along with people. When the athlete respects other people, he gains self-respect as well.

Lacrosse has provided these opportunities to so many young men that in the final chapter I shall give a few examples from my own experience as coach at Hopkins.

2

a brief history

Early North American explorers found different forms of lacrosse widely played by the Indians. The French settlers gave the game its present name because the sticks the Indians used had a resemblance to the crosier (*la crosse*) carried at ceremonies by a bishop as a symbol of pastoral office.

The first use of the word "crosse" in reference to the game was made in 1636 by a Jesuit missionary, Jean de Brébeuf, who saw the Hurons play it near Thunder Bay, Ontario, and mentioned it in a report to his ecclesiastical superiors. He said nothing of the technique of the game, and it was left for another Jesuit, Pierre de Charlevoix, to describe it as played by the Algonquins in 1721.

The Indians used a stick 3 or 4 feet long with a netted loop at one end (in some areas two smaller sticks were used, one in each hand). Even in day-long contests, early reports say, the ball rarely touched the ground. The ball was about the size of a modern tennis ball and was made either of wood or of deerskin stuffed with deer hair.

Indian lacrosse was a mass game. Most teams were made up of about a hundred players and sometimes of more than a thousand. Distance between goals usually was between 500 yards and a half mile, but on occasion the goals were several miles apart. Some tribes used a single pole or tree or rock for a goal, and scores were made by a hit with the ball. Other tribes used two goal posts, 6 to 9 feet apart, and the ball had to pass between them. There were no sidelines, and play ranged over the countryside in all directions.

Games lasted as long as two or three days, starting at sunup and ending at sundown. If a brave seemed to be playing below top pace, the squaws of his tribe would rush to him on the field and beat him with switches. Players wore only breechcloths and some decorative paint; they usually played barefoot.

Lacrosse was played not only for recreation but also as a means of training warriors. The roughness of the game served to accustom players to conditions of close combat, and its length to develop endurance for war and hunting parties. The historian Francis Parkman tells how in 1763, during the Conspiracy of Pontiac, an intertribal game of lacrosse, then called "baggataway," was cover for an Indian massacre of the British garrison at Fort Michilimackinac.

In early colonial days, the Jesuits labored in the New York State area among the Six Nations of the Iroquois Confederacy and the Huron tribe. Members of these tribes who converted to Christianity found it prudent to move to Canada, because they feared reprisal from the more savage tribes. They settled at Caughnawaga, near Montreal, or at St. Regis, near Cornwall. It was among these people that the prototype of the modern lacrosse stick was developed.

After the Revolutionary War, the Canadian Indians lived peacefully as wards of the British Crown. Lacrosse, as played around Montreal in the 1790s, underwent a number of changes. Teams were limited to sixty men, and fields took on a specific size—the goals were about 500 yards apart. The pure sport of the game replaced the warrior-training aspects of play. By 1825, Indians were playing with seven-man teams on fields 50 yards long. To make the tribal team had become a great honor.

As early as 1740, some reports have it, a group of French pioneers met the Indians at their own game. If this is true, the occasion must have been a monumental fiasco from the settlers' point of view, for it took another hundred years for white men to work up any enthusiasm for playing lacrosse again. Even then it was the general opinion that no group of whites could match a good Indian team.

In 1834 a group of Montreal gentlemen arranged for the Caughnawaga Indians to play an exhibition in Montreal. The game was well reported in the newspapers, and it is probable that experiments with the game started among settlers as a result of these reports. In 1844, as part of an athletic program conducted in Montreal, a team of five Indians easily defeated seven white men. In 1851, a group of seven white players finally succeeded in defeating an Indian team of the same size.

The Montreal Lacrosse Club was formed in 1856, and its members introduced some changes that improved the style of play. They used a longer stick with a wide triangular netting that was tightly strung with gut. This stick encouraged passing and teamwork, as compared with the bagged net that the Indians used to mass-attack the goal. The white man was successful with this style of attack, and the Indians eventually adopted it, too. Montreal thus became the cradle of modern lacrosse.

On the same day in 1867 that the Dominion of Canada was created, lacrosse was declared its national sport. At the beginning of the year there were only six clubs in Canada; at the end of the year there were eighty. Among the clubs formed in 1867 was one representing Upper Canada College of Toronto, which thus became the first college to play lacrosse.

Dr. W. George Beers, a Montreal dentist, formed the Canadian National Lacrosse Association in 1867 and drew up the first set of written rules. The following is a summary of the more important of them:

The crosse: any length, netting must be flat when ball is not in it.

The ball: India-rubber sponge not less than 8 inches and not more than 9 inches in circumference.

Goals and length of field: agreed upon by the captains. (Dr. Beers advised 200 yards.) The goal posts were 6 feet high, with a flag on top of each, and were 6 feet apart.

Goal crease: line 6 feet in front of goal posts. No opponent could cross the line until the ball had passed it.

Coach: Each team had a "field captain" to supervise the play. If he was not a player, he could not carry a crosse or dress in playing garb.

A team: consisted of twelve men. Positions: goalkeeper, point, cover point, center, home; the remainder, fielders. No substitution was permitted after a match was started, not even if a player was disabled.

Match: decided by three goals or "games" out of five, unless otherwise agreed upon by the captains. If, because of darkness or other reasons, neither side won three games, the match was considered unfinished and called a draw, unless the captains had agreed that, should one side score two goals and the other none, the former would be declared the match winner. Teams changed goals after each "game," and rested at least five minutes, and not more than ten, between "games."

Not authorized: touching ball with hands (except by goalkeeper, who might block the ball with a hand), wearing spiked shoes, throwing a crosse at a player or at the ball, holding another player with the crosse or hands, striking, tripping, or threatening.

In 1867 an Indian team went to England, Ireland, France, and Scotland. As a result of the interest aroused in England, clubs were formed at Blackheath and Richmond, near London, and at Liverpool. In 1868 an English Lacrosse Association was formed. It adopted a code of laws that differed from the Canadian in several respects. One change prescribed a time limit for a game. That was well in advance of the game's eventual development; a time limit was not used in championship club play in the United States until 1883, or in Canada until 1888. Another important new rule provided for a tape across the tops of the goal posts, which were 7 feet apart. That definite target was the forerunner of the goal net.

A troupe of Indians from Canada demonstrated lacrosse at the Saratoga Springs fairgrounds during racing season in 1867. This event brought the first mention of lacrosse in the United States by American newspapers. Soon after this, an exhibition was played in Troy, New York, between eight Canadian Indians and eight Americans. The Indians won, but an offshoot of the game was the formation of the first lacrosse club in the United States, the Mohawk Club of Troy. In 1868 the Mohawk Club played and lost four games to good Canadian clubs. Soon there were clubs in the Midwest, North, and East.

When the game was first played in New York City in 1868, the New York *Tribune* said, "Lacrosse may be called a madman's game, so wild it is." The *World* called it the "most exciting and at the same time the most laughter provoking among the whole range of outdoor sports." The *Times* rated it as "a noisy game and one of much excitement."

In 1874 the sport was introduced into Australia, and in 1878 it spread to New Zealand. Dr. Beers took a club team and an Indian group to the British Isles in 1876. On June 26 the teams played before Queen Victoria at Windsor Castle. The Queen was quite pleased with the game and presented each of the players with an autographed picture of herself.

On their return to North America, the teams that had appeared before the Queen were invited by the Westchester Polo Club to visit its grounds at Newport, Rhode Island, and demonstrate lacrosse for the vacationers at that exclusive resort. The game was played before a crowd of 8,000. The New York *Herald* reported that "the immense popular success of the game caused lacrosse to be the talk of Newport. The universal verdict is that lacrosse is the most remarkable, versatile, and exciting of all games of ball."

In New York City, in the fall of 1877, intercollegiate lacrosse had its beginning. New York University played Manhattan College. When the game was called for darkness, NYU was ahead 2–0.

John R. Flannery was so active in promoting lacrosse in Boston and New York that he is sometimes called "the father of American lacrosse." He initiated the movement that resulted in the formation of the United States National Amateur Lacrosse Association, in 1879. Harvard and New York University joined the association along with nine clubs: Ravenswood, New York, Brooklyn, Westchester, and Bay Ridge from the metropolitan area of New York; Elmira and Osceola from Elmira, New York; Union from Boston; and Bradford from Bradford, Pennsylvania.

The Baltimore Athletic Club did not join the association until 1880 but had gotten its start in lacrosse more than a year earlier as a result of a trip by a Baltimore track and field team that traveled to Newport to compete at the three-day sports carnival of the Westchester Polo Club. They saw the exhibition lacrosse game played there and liked it. They brought sticks back to Baltimore and resolved to master the sport. The first formal lacrosse exhibition conducted by the Baltimore Club was at old Newington Park in Baltimore on November 23, 1878. About 4,000 turned out to get what was, for many, their first view of lacrosse. The first interclub game to be played in Baltimore took place on May 29, 1879, when the Ravenswood Club beat the Baltimore Athletic Club 3–1. By the spring of the following year the Monumentals and the Ivanhoes were also playing lacrosse in Baltimore. Many of the players on these club teams, especially the Monumentals, who later became the famous Druids, were high-school students.

During the spring of 1881 Princeton and Columbia fielded lacrosse teams. Lawrason Riggs, a Baltimorean and a football star for Princeton, started the sport there and was the Tigers' first captain. Princeton, Columbia, Harvard, and New York University competed in the first intercollegiate tournament sponsored by the National Association. In the final game of the tournament Harvard beat Princeton for the first intercollegiate championship.

The Intercollegiate Lacrosse Association was formed in March 1882. Harvard was voted the title, although both New York University and Harvard had identical records and their game ended in a scoreless tie. Yale fielded its first varsity team in the fall of 1882 and formally joined the association in 1883. The Johns Hopkins Club was organized in the fall of 1882 and played its first game, against the Druid Club, the following spring. However, the team disbanded and was not officially reorganized until 1888.

Stevens Institute and Lehigh began playing in 1885 and joined the association in '86 and '88 respectively. Prior to 1900, several other colleges took up lacrosse: Rutgers, 1887; Union, 1887; City College of New York, 1888; University of Pennsylvania, 1890; Lafayette, 1890; Cornell, 1892; and Hobart, 1898. None of these schools was a member of the association.

The association championship was dominated by Harvard and Princeton in the 1880s and by Lehigh, Stevens, and Hopkins from 1890 to 1903. Swarthmore began the sport in 1891, joined the association in 1902, and won championships in '04 and '05.

Two of the original members of the association withdrew, Columbia in 1883 and Harvard in 1890, but joined with Cornell to form the Inter-university Lacrosse League in 1899. The University of Pennsylvania joined the next year. This organization continued through 1905, with Cornell, Columbia, and Harvard taking turns as champions.

Around the turn of the century several innovations greatly improved the game. During the 1897 season, Rossiter Scott, Stevens' captain, conceived the idea of fastening a tennis net to the goal posts. He passed on this idea to his friend Ronald Abercrombie, the Hopkins center. Hopkins adopted that primitive form of goal net in 1898 and was soon followed by other colleges and by the Crescent Athletic Club. That same season, Abercrombie, a short man, cut a piece from the handle of his stick, which was long, in the custom of the day. Other Hopkins players liked the modification, and the team, after some experimenting, ordered special sticks. The following year Hopkins used shorter, lighter sticks with smaller nets for attackmen in order to present smaller targets to opposing defensemen. The goalies' sticks were shorter and, while defensemen continued to use long sticks, these were made lighter. These sticks, which increased maneuverability, gave rise to the short passing game that was installed by coach and captain William H. Maddren. This change was considered by many to have been Hopkins' most important contribution to the tactics of lacrosse.

William C. Schmeisser entered the collegiate picture in 1900. Not only was he a great player at Hopkins; he was also an outstanding coach and a pioneer in the development of the game for many years. He was instrumental in the early organization of the Mount Washington Club and in 1904 wrote a book on the coaching of lacrosse, which became the standard textbook for coaches.

The Crescent Athletic Club of Brooklyn was formed as a football club in 1884 but reorganized as an athletic club two years later. A lacrosse team was organized in 1893. The Crescents were a dominating factor in American lacrosse for over forty years. The club played most of the leading college and club teams annually and was rarely beaten. The revitalizing of lacrosse in the United States was due mainly to the efforts of that club.

Along with the rise of the Crescents, the game unfortunately lost another famous team, the Druids. On May 7, 1894, the Druids closed their distinguished career with a 3–1 victory over Hopkins.

Baltimore moved back into a place of prominence in club lacrosse ten years later, when the Mount Washington Lacrosse Club was organized. Dr. Ronald T. Abercrombie, the former Hopkins star and coach, was chairman of the lacrosse committee, and he captained the first team to represent Mount Washington. In 1904 the team played only one recorded game—with Johns Hopkins—but it soon was contesting supremacy with the Crescents, and ultimately it replaced them as perennial national open champions.

There were interesting developments among the colleges after the 1905 season. Since the dissolution of the National Association in 1888, the Intercollegiate Association had made its own rules. When the Inter-university Lacrosse League came into existence in 1899, it played under a code of its own, which differed slightly from the rules of the older association. Cyrus C. Miller proposed combining the two organizations in order to standardize the rules. The plan was favorably received, and on December 22, 1905, the United States Intercollegiate Lacrosse League was founded. Each of the two merging groups maintained its identity within the structure of the league by the formation of northern and southern divisions. A champion was selected for each division, but in some years it was difficult to determine the nation's best team because the division champions did not play each other.

The following rules were accepted to cover the more important points on which the two organizations had differed. The dimensions of the crease were fixed at 18 by 12 feet. Substitutes could be used at any time, but a player once removed could not return. Halves of thirty-five minutes were prescribed. The penalty for a foul was suspension for three minutes or until a goal was scored. For a second offense, the offending player was suspended for the remainder of the game.

During the first four years of the new league arrangement, Johns Hopkins, under the tutelage of Bill Schmeisser, not only won the Southern Division championship but probably had the best college team in the country. It did not lose to another college team during that period and beat the Northern Division champions three times—Cornell in 1906 and Harvard in '08 and '09. Hopkins did not play the northern champions, Cornell, in '07, or the cochampion, Columbia in '09.

The service academies began playing lacrosse within a year of each other. In 1907, the U.S. Military Academy played its first game and beat the Stevens freshman team. Army continued to field a team for four years, but the sport was dropped after the 1910 season. It was revived in 1921. Navy's beginning was more auspicious. In 1908 Navy accepted a challenge from Harvard to play a game. James M. Irish, who had learned the game at Hobart, was appointed captain and coach. With some assistance from Frank Breyer and other Hopkins players, he assembled and

trained a team. Navy's first game was with its instructors on April 4, and the instructors won 6–1. In the challenge game, Navy lost to Harvard, but in the next year in its first season under an official coach, L. Alan Dill from Hopkins, it beat the Crimson 6–3.

The year 1910 was interesting. Navy turned on its mentors and defeated Hopkins 7–6. Swarthmore gained the Southern Division title by soundly trouncing Hopkins 13–3. Harvard lost to Hopkins but won the Northern Division title for the third straight year. Maryland Agricultural College (now the University of Maryland at College Park) organized a team with Edwin E. Powell, former Mount Washington Junior player, as captain and coach. Glenn "Pop" Warner, athletic director at the Carlisle Indian School at Carlisle, Pennsylvania, substituted lacrosse for baseball. He was quoted as saying, "Lacrosse is a developer of health and strength. It is a game that the spectators rave over once they understand it." In 1910, Carlisle's first year in the game, it rose to great heights in defeating Navy and Mount Washington, but the school lost to Swarthmore, Lehigh, and Stevens.

The next ten years were eventful, although World War I did curtail lacrosse activity. Hopkins and Harvard repeated as sectional champions in 1911, but Hopkins edged the Crimson 3–2 in a bitterly contested game in the early part of the season. The same story was repeated in 1913 and 1915, with Hopkins winning by 6–3 and 8–1 scores respectively. In 1912 Navy pulled the upset of the year when it defeated the previously unbeaten Crescents. For the first time a formal postseason playoff was attempted between the intercollegiate division champions, Harvard and Swarthmore. The Crimson won by a 7–3 score. Navy, coached since 1911 by George Finlayson from Canada, was tied by Carlisle but won all other games and compiled the best collegiate record in 1914. However, Navy was not a member of the United States Intercollegiate Lacrosse League and therefore could not be considered for the league championship. Lehigh and Cornell were division champions and played to a 1–1 tie during the season. These same schools again won their division championships in 1916, but Lehigh edged Cornell 5–4 in the regular season.

World War I caused many cancellations in 1917, 1918, and 1919. In abbreviated schedules, Stevens and Lehigh were division champions in

1917, and Navy was undefeated in its two-game schedule. This began a unique period in college lacrosse annals, as the Midshipmen did not lose a game for seven seasons. George Finlayson coached them during that period of glory. But Navy was not in the league and unfortunately could not be identified as champions. In 1918 Stevens and Hopkins were the champions. Hopkins was champion again in 1919, but a Northern Division champion was not named.

After the war, conditions got back to normal. Syracuse and Lehigh were division champions in 1920, but Lehigh won its postseason game 3–1. However, Navy defeated both of them and was the best of the nation's college teams. Its defense, built around two football All-Americans—Eddie Ewen and Emery "Swede" Larson—was superb in allowing only six goals in nine games. Navy's next-door neighbor, St. John's College, ventured into lacrosse competition for the first time and was defeated by Maryland.

The year 1921 brought two major changes in lacrosse—one technical, the other historical. An offside rule, which was instituted for the first time, divided the field in half by a center line. Each team was required to keep at least three men, exclusive of the goalies, in each half of the field. This relieved the problem of defense players massing in front of the goal and preventing a wide-open offense. Penalty for violation of that rule was suspension for from three to seven minutes. The other change was the Crescents' first loss to the Mount Washington Club in their fifteen-year rivalry. Captain Fenimore Baker led the Mounts to a 4–3 victory, but the Crescents rebounded by winning the second game 10–3 later in the season.

Navy continued its unbeaten ways in 1921, '22, and '23. Lehigh, the southern champion, beat northern champion Syracuse 3–1 in a playoff game in 1921. Irving B. Lydecker captained the 1922 Syracuse team to an undefeated seventeen-game season, which included victories over the Crescents and the University of Pennsylvania, the southern champion. Victor Ross of Syracuse led the nation in scoring for the second year in a row. In 1922 an All-American lacrosse team was first selected. Hopkins won the Southern Division championship in 1923, but Army, Navy, and Syracuse shared the limelight as the top teams in the country.

Laurie Cox's 1924 Syracuse team was unde-feated in fourteen games, with impressive wins over Navy and the Crescents. Navy's first loss after forty-six consecutive victories came at the hands of the University of Maryland, which made an impressive debut in the association under the leadership of Dr. Reginald V. Truitt. Maryland also knocked Hopkins, the southern champ, from the unbeaten ranks with a 4–2 victory. The first Army-Navy game was played in 1924 at West Point, and Navy won 5–0.

In 1925 Navy bounced back with another unde-feated season, led by its captain, Fred Billing, who scored two goals against Army and gave the Cadets their only loss for the season, 3–2. Harold "Soft" Wood and Walt Townsend guided Syracuse to a Northern Division championship, and Maryland won in the South by virtue of a 3–1 victory over Hopkins. Doug Turnbull captained the Blue Jays and became the first player ever selected for the first All-American team for four straight years. Mount Washington, captained by Edward Allen and coached by F. Gibbs LaMotte, ended the long reign of the Crescents by beating them 5–3 and winning the national open championship for the first time. The University of Virginia fielded a team for the first time in twenty years, and Brown University took up the sport.

Most of the colleges that had adopted lacrosse desired membership in the United States Intercollegiate Lacrosse League, which was not in a position to accommodate them. Thus a reorganization of that governing body was in order. As of March 1, 1926, the league was replaced by the United States Intercollegiate Lacrosse Association (USILA), with unlimited membership. The northern and southern divisions of the old league were merged. Rutgers, Navy, Union College, New York University, Colgate University, and St. Stephen's were admitted to full membership. Playing for the first time or resuming play that year were Dartmouth, Lafayette, City College of New York, University of Georgia, St. John's of Annapolis, and Randolph-Macon College.

It is interesting to note that for the next fifty years collegiate lacrosse was dominated by teams from the state of Maryland—Johns Hopkins, Navy, Maryland and St. John's. Some attention should be given to the reasons for this. Lacrosse was the major spring sport at the two largest public high schools of Baltimore, Poly and City, and at almost all of the Baltimore private high schools. Players from these schools stocked the teams of the four collegiate lacrosse powers in the state. During the early years of the USILA, if one drew a wide circle around the Johns Hopkins and Mount Washington areas, one would find most of the children with lacrosse sticks in their hands in the springtime, but around the rest of Baltimore youngsters were seen with baseballs and gloves. In the fifties this circle began to widen, and today most of the high schools in Baltimore's outlying areas are playing the game.

Besides the Maryland teams, Army and Princeton won a number of championships during this fifty-year period. Their teams were coached by men who had a strong Baltimore lacrosse background—William Logan and Ferris Thomsen at Princeton, and Morris Touchstone and James Adams at Army. Most of their key players were also Baltimoreans. When Howard Myers, Jr., moved from Hopkins to Hofstra University in 1950, he joined forces with William Ritch of Sewanhaka High School, Jason Stranahan of Manhasset High School, and Joseph "Frenchy" Julien, the president of the Lacrosse Officials Association, to spread the game among the Long Island high schools. Today these schools rival the Baltimore high schools in developing the largest number of outstanding players in collegiate lacrosse.

In 1926 the association decided to rate the teams officially and award medals to the leaders. Although Navy was undefeated (8–0) and Syracuse lost only to the Crescents, Johns Hopkins, coached by Ray Van Orman to a 9–0 record, won the gold medal. In 1927 the Blue Jays were again victorious over all opponents, and their only close game was a thrilling come-from-behind win over Navy 6–5. But in 1928 it was a different story. Gold medals were given to four teams—Johns Hopkins, Maryland, Navy, and Rutgers—as each finished its regular season with only one loss to an association rival. Army was not a member of the association, but the Cadets had an excellent record, which included a 5–3 victory over Hopkins and a 4–4 tie with Navy. Rutgers gave Army its only loss, 8–3. Army's "Light Horse Harry" Wilson achieved the distinction of being selected to the All-American team in football, basketball, and lacrosse. At the conclusion of the season, Hopkins won the playoff series to determine the United States representative to the Olympic Games in Amsterdam. The Blue Jays won all three playoff games (Mount Washington 6–4, Army 4–2, and Maryland 6–3). In the Olympic Games, the Blue Jays beat Canada 6–3 but lost to Great Britain 7–6. Canada downed the Englishmen 9–5.

St. John's of Annapolis moved into the limelight for the next three years under the leadership of coach William H. ("Dinty") Moore III. Although the team was not a member of the association in 1929, it was undefeated in thirteen games. The offense was led by Ferris Thomsen, formerly of Swarthmore, and Clem Spring and the defense by "Long John" Boucher. The Johnnies gave Maryland its first defeat on its home field in thirteen years. Navy and Union, both undefeated, were awarded goal medals that year by the association. In 1930, St. John's joined the association and was voted the gold medal with a 10–1 record. Its only loss was to Hopkins after twenty-one consecutive victories. The next year the Johnnies won all ten of their games, scoring 108 goals and giving up just 7. Goalie Bill Armacost and defensemen Ed and Phil Lotz spearheaded the defense, which registered six shutouts, five in a row. Bobby Pool was outstanding on the attack and Bill Ziegler and Ernest Cornbrooks, Jr., in the midfield. In international competition St. John's represented the United States and beat Canada in two of three games to bring the Lally Trophy to America. This was the last time for the competition, because the amateur clubs of Canada were to play field lacrosse no longer.

The year 1932 was another Olympic year. Hopkins was undefeated in the regular season as well as in the playoffs, beating St. John's 5–3, the Crescents 10–2, and Maryland 7–5. Jack Turnbull and Don Kelly were the offensive leaders of the team. In the Olympic Games in Los Angeles, Hopkins beat the Canadians in two of three games for the world championship.

The end of the celebrated career of the Crescent Club was nearing as the New Yorkers lost their home in Brooklyn in 1932. They combined with the Hamilton Club of Long Island and competed as the Crescent-Hamilton Club until the late thirties.

Although no champion was selected by the association from 1932 to 1935, Hopkins was considered by many as the leading team in '32, '33, and '34, as the Blue Jays did not lose to a college team during that period. In 1935, St. John's, Maryland, and Navy each won all of its games but one. However, Princeton was undefeated for the third straight year under the expert coaching of Albert B. Nies and had an important 4–3 victory over Navy to boost its claim for the championship.

Probably the most drastic rule changes in the history of modern lacrosse were enacted in 1933. They were to speed up the game and give it more wide-open play. The changes were somewhat influenced by the popularity of box lacrosse. The number of players on a side was reduced from twelve to ten. The distance between goals, which had been 110 yards since 1922, was reduced to 80 yards, and the playing area in the rear of each goal was fixed at 20 yards. It had been as much as 35 yards in 1930. Playing time was still sixty minutes, but it was divided into four quarters, with teams changing goals after each quarter.

Lacrosse lost a devoted friend and an influential supporter when W. Wilson Wingate, a Baltimore sportswriter, died in 1936. He had been one of the most talented writers on lacrosse that this country ever produced. He had edited the Official Lacrosse Guide in 1931 and had been appointed an official to accompany the Johns Hopkins teams to the Olympic Games in both 1928 and 1932. A group of his friends, desirous of perpetuating his memory, placed in competition a silver trophy to be awarded each year to the team voted the intercollegiate championship by the executive board of the United States Intercollegiate Lacrosse Association.

The University of Maryland, under the leadership of Dr. John E. Faber, won the first Wingate trophy in 1936. In 1937 the Terps shared the trophy with Princeton, coached by William F. Logan and captained by C. M. Dering. Both were undefeated in collegiate play. Jack Kelly (goal) and Charles Ellinger (attack) starred for the Terps as first-team All-Americans in both years. John Christhilf and Bobby Neilson were the leading Terp scorers in '36 and '37 respectively.

The year 1937 was a great one for the Baltimore Athletic Club, which won the national open championship in the sport that the fathers of their club had brought to Baltimore in 1878. Benny Boynton coached the team, and cocaptains Ed Lotz and Don Kelly led the team to an undefeated season, including a 7–5 victory over Mount Washington.

Dinty Moore, who had coached St. John's College to national championships had moved to the Naval Academy in 1936. His '38 Navy team, captained by Frank Case, was undefeated in collegiate play and the unchallenged winner of the Wingate Trophy. The University of Maryland won the championship in '39, with Jim Meade and Rip Hewitt leading the way, and again in 1940, when Milton Mulitz (defense) and Oscar Nevares (attack) were the top Terp players. After the 1939 season St. John's College discontinued participation in all forms of intercollegiate athletics. At the end of the 1940 season a new feature was introduced, partially to take the place of the international games with Canada, which had been discontinued since the adoption of box lacrosse in the Dominion. The first annual North-South All-Star game, which highlighted the best players from each area in the association, was played in Baltimore Stadium. The North won the game 6–5. In 1941 Kelso Morrill and Gardner Mallonee coached Hopkins to an undefeated season that was climaxed with a 7–6 victory over Mount Washington. Hopkins' first-team All-Americans were John Tolson and Nelson Shawn on defense and Charlie Thomas on attack.

The World War II years curtailed lacrosse activity. However, Princeton's veteran team in 1942 was undefeated in college ranks and was the first northern team to defeat the "big three" of the South (Maryland, Navy, and Hopkins) in the same year. Captain Elmer Weisheit had a hand in ten of the goals scored in a 12–10 victory over Maryland, and Ty Campbell's play in the goal was outstanding throughout the season. Navy won the Wingate Trophy in 1943 and Army in 1944. This was the Cadets' first national championship and came under the fine coaching leadership of F. Morris Touchstone, who had transferred to West Point in 1928 after having met with considerable success at Yale. In 1945 Army and Navy shared the championship after they had battled through two extra periods in a driving rainstorm to a 7–7 tie.

With the war over, lacrosse returned to full-scale competition. Navy, although beaten by Hopkins, compiled the best record and won the Wingate Trophy in 1946. Navy, behind at one point by six goals, rallied to beat Army 12–10.

The years 1947 through 1950 were dominated by Hopkins; the Blue Jays did not lose a collegiate game during those four years. The 1949 Navy team, led by All-Americans Richard Seth (goal), Philip Ryan (defense), and Lee Chambers (attack), also went undefeated and shared the championship that year with Hopkins. Howard

THE GAME AND ITS HISTORY

Myers, Jr., was responsible for organizing and coaching those Blue Jay teams the first three years. However, Howdy then left Hopkins and went to Hofstra University. Dr. W. Kelso Morrill directed the 1950 Hopkins team. Quite a few players were outstanding during that period. Two of the best were Brooke Tunstall, a two-year captain and first-team All-American attackman, and Lloyd Bunting, a three-time first-team All-American defenseman.

Princeton, coached for the first time by Ferris Thomsen and led by Captain Don Hahn (attack) and Reddy Finney (midfield), shared the championship with Army in '51. Finney was an All-American in both football and lacrosse, as was West Point's Dan Foldberg. Bruno Giordano combined with Foldberg to give Army an excellent defense. Ray Wood of Washington College established a new national record by scoring 187 goals in four years of varsity play. Mount Washington's reign of club lacrosse was halted when the Maryland Lacrosse Club beat the Mounties 6–5. William P. Wittelsberger had organized the club in 1941, and his son Ray coached and captained the team to this upset victory. Lou Kimball scored four goals, and Bob Stocksdale was outstanding in the goal.

Cochampions were again named in 1952. Robert "Pic" Fuller coached Virginia to a 7–1 collegiate season, and Ned Harkness directed Rensselaer Polytechnic Institute to a 10–0 record, although its opposition did not include any of the traditional collegiate powers. The offensive leaders were Gordon Jones and Dick Godine for the Cavaliers and Lester Eustace and Ken Martin for RPI.

A new rule went into effect in the 1953 season. It allowed free movement of players when play was stopped. Since the adoption of the initial rules in 1867, a player was required to "freeze" in position at the sound of a whistle, or if he moved, had to leave his stick to mark his place.

Princeton, led by All-American attackman Ralph Willis, won the Wingate Trophy in 1953 but gave way to an undefeated Navy team in 1954. The Navy defense, headed by goalie John Jones and defenseman Stanley Swanson, limited Navy's opponents to an average of 3.1 goals per game. The 1954 season marked the last at Mount Washington for Oster Norris, who since 1938 had piloted the Wolfpack to an amazing record of 110 victories, 8 defeats, and one tie. Before becoming

coach, "Kid" had been a star Mount Washington player for fifteen years. His last team, captained by the great attackman Billy Hooper, won all its games.

The University of Maryland, coached by Dr. Jack Faber and Albert Heagy, dominated the game for the next two years with identical 11–0 seasons. Its only close games were with Navy (9–8) in '55 and Mount Washington (12–11) in '56. The Terps had a powerful team with one exceptional player at each position: Charles Wicker (attack), James Keating (midfield), John Simmons (defense), and James Kappler (goal).

Bill Morrill, Jr., and Mickey Webster led Hopkins to two unbeaten collegiate seasons the next two years. The Blue Jays won the Wingate Trophy in '57 but were denied a share of it in '58, when Army, under the fine leadership of Jim Adams, who took over the coaching reins at West Point after Morris Touchstone's death, was also undefeated and selected as the champion.

In 1959 Army, Maryland, and Hopkins shared the championship, since each had one collegiate loss on its record. Don Tillar (defense) and Robert Miser (attack) were Army's top players for both championship teams, and Robert Schwartzberg and Roger Goss led the '59 Maryland team at defense and attack respectively. William Keigler directed Mount Washington to its first unbeaten season since 1955. Emil Budnitz, Jr., was the leader of the Wolfpack's potent offense.

The Lacrosse Foundation (originally founded as the Lacrosse Hall of Fame Foundation in June 1959) is a nonprofit organization dedicated to the support and development of the game of lacrosse throughout the country. Its offices and museum are located on the campus of Johns Hopkins University. In addition to operating the Lacrosse Hall of Fame Museum, the foundation functions as a clearing house of information for the entire sport.

In 1959 Willis P. Bilderback replaced W. H. Moore III as the Navy coach. Dinty retired after a brilliant career at both St. John's College and Navy. In his first season, Bildy guided Navy to a 6–3–1 record, but from 1960 through 1967 it was all Navy in collegiate lacrosse. The Middies lost only three college games during this eight-year period, and two were upsets to Army in games played at Annapolis in '61 and '63. The 10–8 loss to the Cadets in '61 caused the national championship to be shared by the two service academies. A 9–6 loss to Hopkins in '67 gave Navy a three-way share of the crown with Maryland and Hopkins. During this golden era in Navy lacrosse, there were a number of outstanding players. The most acclaimed attackmen were Karl Rippelmeyer, '60; Tom Mitchell, '61; George Tracy, '62 and '63; and one of the greatest of all time, Jimmy Lewis in '64 to '66. The top defensemen were Neal Reich, '61; Michael Coughlin, '63 and '64; James Campbell, '64; Pat Donnelly, '65; and Carl Tamulevich, '67. Leaders in the midfield were Roger Kisiel, '62, and John Taylor III, '64, and faceoff specialists Neil Henderson, '65, and John McIntosh, '67. Dennis Wedekind, '65, was considered by many as the best of the Navy goalies during this period.

Mount Washington's domination of the club ranks was interrupted in the early sixties. In 1961 the Baltimore Lacrosse Club, coached by Thomas Gough, who was assisted by Robert Proutt, gave the Mounties their first club loss (13–11) since 1951. Two years later the University Club of Baltimore, coached by Robert Bonsall in its first lacrosse season, conquered the Wolfpack 8–6. The Mounties returned to the top of the club ranks under Ben Goertemiller's direction from 1964 through 1967.

Hopkins was involved in championship play from 1967 through 1970. After sharing the Wingate Trophy in '67 with Navy and Maryland (led by its high-scoring attackmen, Jack Heim and Alan Lowe), the Blue Jays won sole possession of it in '68 with a 10–0 collegiate record. In 1969 Hopkins shared the championship with Army. Pete Cramblet and Tom Cafaro were the Cadet's one-two scoring punch. Joe Cowan was the offensive leader of the Blue Jays from '67 through '69; Hank Kaestner, the number-one defenseman in '67; and Mike Clark in '68 and '69. Virginia, Navy, and Hopkins shared the championship in 1970, when each had only one loss on its record.

Club lacrosse was at its peak in the seventies. The Long Island Athletic Club organized a lacrosse team in 1966 through the efforts of Al Levine and soon became the reigning power. Richie Moran coached the Islanders to their first of four consecutive championships in 1968 and was followed by Cliff Murray in '69 and Bill Ritch in '70 and '71. Among the top players during this period were attackmen Jim Martone, Bruce Cohen, Jack Heim, and Alan Lowe; midfielders Ron Fraser, Dick Finley, and Tom Postel; de-

fenseman Jack Salerno; and goalie Bob Ricci. Arlyn Marshall's Carling Club edged the Islanders 9–8 for the '72 championship as Gene Fusting scored the winning goal on a pass from Charles "Chooch" Turner with twenty-eight seconds remaining in the game. Long Island won the title again in '73 and '74 under Jack Kaley's leadership. After a seven-year lapse, Mount Washington regained the championship in 1975 by beating Long Island 18–9. Coach Joe Seivold's key players were Dennis Townsend, Skip Lichtfuss, and Don Krohn.

The year 1971 marked the first year of NCAA lacrosse championship tournament play, and Cornell University was the first champion. After losing the season opener to Virginia 10–9, Richie Moran's Big Red team won thirteen straight games, including a 17–16 thriller with Army in the NCAA semifinals and a 12–6 victory over Maryland for the championship. Outstanding players for Cornell were Robert Rule (goal), John Burnap (defense), Robert Shaw (midfield), and Al Rimmer (attack).

Glenn F. Thiel directed Virginia to an undefeated regular season in 1971, but a loss to Navy in the opening round of the NCAA tournament knocked it out of championship contention. However, in 1972, after suffering three regular-season collegiate losses, the Cavaliers were primed for the NCAAs and beat Army 10–3, Cortland State 14–7, and then Hopkins 13–12 in the action-filled finals at College Park, Maryland. Pete Eldredge scored the winning goal, his fourth, with four minutes remaining in the game. Jay Connor and Tom Duquette were the offensive guns for the Cavaliers, and Bruce Mangels led the defense.

The United States Intercollegiate Lacrosse Association sponsored its first College Division Tournament in 1972. Jerry Schmidt's Hobart team went through the regular season with a 14–1 record, including an 11–10 victory over Cornell. In the tournament, Hobart beat Adelphi 14–13 in sudden death, Massachusetts 13–2, and Washington College 15–12 in the finals. Rick Gilbert was the team's offensive leader, and Dave Creighton was outstanding in the goal.

The University of Maryland, coached by Buddy Beardmore, won the 1973 NCAA championship by beating Hopkins 10–9 in overtime at the University of Pennsylvania's Franklin Field. Freshman Frank Urso scored the winning goal in the second overtime period after Doug Schreiber had tied the score with three minutes remaining in regulation time. Pat O'Meally (attack) and Mike Thearle (defense) joined midfielders Schreiber and Urso on the first All-American team. Five Terps were also selected to the second All-American team—this gives an indication of the overall depth and strength of their team.

In his first season as a head coach, Chuck Winters directed Cortland State to the College Division championship. His 1973 Red Dragons beat Washington College 13–8 in the finals, after having won playoff games with Adelphi 11–5, Massachusetts 9–3, and Hobart 14–8. Dominating factors in Cortland's success were great midfield speed and a veteran defense headed by Bob Ernst and goalie Peter Graham.

After losing in the NCAA finals by one goal two years in a row, Johns Hopkins came through with the gold championship plaque in 1974, defeating Maryland 17–12. This game climaxed outstanding careers by Jack Thomas, Rick Kowalchuk, and nine other seniors.

In 1974 the NCAA inaugurated a Division II–III championship, which replaced the USILA tournament. Carl Runk's Towson State team edged Hobart 18–17 to win it in overtime. While Beaver Draffen scored eight goals for Hobart, it was Wayne Eisenhut, Jim Darcangelo, and Bob Griebe who directed the high-powered Towson offense.

The only undefeated team in the country in 1974 was Bowling Green State University, which coach Mickey Cochrane directed to a 12–0 season. Also of note was the third straight Middle Atlantic Conference championship won by Ross Sachs's Franklin and Marshall College team.

A banner year for lacrosse came in 1975. Tournament interest was at an all-time high. Maryland and Cortland State became the first schools to repeat as tournament champions. The Terps were the NCAA champions in 1973, and the Dragons were the USILA's college-division champions the same year. The Terps beat Navy 20–13 in the '75 Division I finals, with Frank Urso, Doug Radebaugh, and Mike Farrell leading the way. Cortland was the underdog in each of its Division II–III NCAA tournament games but won all three, including a 12–11 victory over Hobart in the finals. Judson Smith, Jim Tarnow, and Ernie Olson were the key Cortland players throughout the season.

Intercollegiate lacrosse has grown from 4 schools playing the game in 1881, to 32 in 1926, to 84 in 1965, to 168 in 1975. The doubling of the number of participants in the last ten years is a significant fact.

Interest continued to rise, expressed in club teams in the Southeast, Southwest, and Far West. The U.S. Club Lacrosse Association added eighteen new members to its organization—ten in the Texas Lacrosse Association and eight in the Northern California Association. The total membership in the association is fifty-nine. Compared with the twelve members in 1968, this shows tremendous growth of the game on the club level.

The expansion of the game on the high-school level is equally impressive. Thirty-eight high schools were playing lacrosse twenty-five years ago and 416 are playing today, with the greatest growth in Long Island—from 5 schools in 1951 to 76 schools in 1975. High-school lacrosse is flourishing in Maryland, New York, New Jersey, Pennsylvania, Massachusetts, and Connecticut. It is being played to a lesser degree in several other New England states, as well as in Delaware, Virginia, Georgia, Ohio, Illinois, Michigan, Colorado, California, and Washington, D.C.

Little-league lacrosse for youngsters aged nine to fifteen got under way in Baltimore in 1959. Three teams were involved in competition that first year, and over fifty teams are playing in three separate leagues today—a phenomenal increase in seventeen years. Long Island also has a large number of teams playing, and so do quite a few of the other lacrosse areas throughout the country.

Lacrosse is flourishing in the United States on all levels, and continued growth is anticipated.

A BRIEF HISTORY

the rules

THE FIELD AND GOALS

The playing area of a lacrosse field is bigger than that of a football field. It is 110 yards long and from 53⅓ to 60 yards wide. Most fields are 60 yards in width, but to facilitate the conversion of a football field, which is 53⅓ yards wide, to a legal lacrosse field, the Rule Book allows the narrower dimension. The goals are 80 yards apart, and there is a playing area of 15 yards behind each goal, which permits considerably more behind-the-goal action than in ice hockey. The length of the field is divided in half by a center line. A circle with a 9-foot radius is drawn around each goal and is known as the "crease." A rectangular box, 35 yards by 40 yards, surrounds each goal and is called the "goal area." It is formed by marking a line 40 yards in length, centered on the goal, parallel to and 20 yards from the center line. A line connects the terminal points of this line with the end line. A wing area is formed on each side of the field by marking a line parallel to the sideline and 20 yards from the center of the field. The line extends 10 yards on each side of the center line. A point on the center line, equidistant from each sideline, is marked with an "X" and is designated the center of the field. There is a special substitution area on the sideline, next to the timer's table and marked by two lines that are 2 yards from the center line. See Figure 3–1 for markings of the field.

The goal consists of two vertical posts joined by a top crossbar. The posts are 6 feet apart, and the top crossbar is 6 feet from the ground. A line is drawn between the goal posts to indicate the plane of the goal, and it is designated as the goal line. Attached to the goal is a pyramidal-shaped cord netting, which is fastened to the ground at a point 7 feet in back of the center of the goal. A goal is scored when a loose ball passes from the front, completely through the imaginary plane

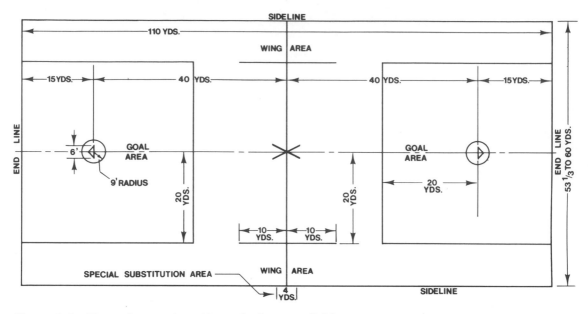

Figure 3–1 Dimensions and markings of a lacrosse field.

formed by the rear edges of the goal line, the goal posts, and the top crossbar. If a defending player causes the ball to pass through the plane of the goal, it counts as a goal for the attacking team. A goal counts one point.

THE PLAYERS

There are ten players on a team, plus a number of substitutes for each of the four positions: goal, defense, midfield, and attack. The goalkeeper, or goalie, mans the goal and receives primary support from three defensemen. Since they are normally in the proximity of the goal, they are known as the "close defense." The defender whose man plays primarily on the crease is called the "crease defenseman." Three midfielders cover the entire field, operating as both offensive and defensive players. One of the midfielders handles the faceoffs and is called either the "center" or the "faceoff man." Three attackmen spend most of their playing time around the opponent's goal and are referred to as "the close attack." The one who plays on the crease is called the "crease attackman."

It is not unusual for a defenseman or attackman to play the entire game, because his activity is confined mainly to only one half of the field, although the fast pace at which the game is played today often requires a substitute or two, if but for a few minutes, to give the regular player a chance to catch his breath. Obviously the goalie does not need a substitute during a close game as long as he is performing capably. However, with almost continuous action between the goals, midfielders cannot be expected to play an entire game. The physical demands placed upon them require substitution approximately every three or four minutes. Although two or three midfield units will share the playing time in most games, the best unit will probably be in the game 60 to 70 percent of the time.

THE BALL AND STICKS

The lacrosse ball is solid rubber and white or orange in color. It is slightly smaller than a baseball and just as hard. When dropped from a height of 6 feet on a solid wooden floor, it must bounce 43 to 51 inches. The ball may not be touched by the hands except by a goalie while he is in the crease. Although it is legal to kick the

toward the narrower head on the defense because the stick work is so advanced. However, only defensemen who are very skillful at stick handling should be allowed to use an attack-sized head. Figure 3–2 shows the various types of sticks.

The stick is made of wood, plastic, or any other synthetic material. Before the late 1960s, when the machine-made plastic-headed stick was first introduced, all sticks were hand-crafted wooden sticks. The uniformity, balance, and lightness of the plastic stick gave it a decided advantage over the wooden stick, and since the early 1970s the plastic stick with either a wooden or aluminum handle has dominated the market. The net of the stick is constructed of gut, rawhide, clock cord, linen, nylon, or any other synthetic material and is roughly triangular in shape. A guard stop, which is made of a rubberized material, is located at the throat of the stick and a minimum of 10 inches from the outside edge of the head. The pocket of the stick may not sag to such a depth that it becomes unreasonably difficult for an opponent to dislodge the ball. This is determined by placing a ball in the pocket: if the top surface of the ball is below the bottom edge of the wall, the pocket is too deep and must be adjusted. This ruling does not apply to the goalie's stick. The end of the handle is known as the "butt." Figure 3–3 identifies the parts of a lacrosse stick.

Figure 3–2 Types of lacrosse sticks: from left to right—attack, midfield, goal, and defense.

ball with the foot or bat it with the stick, most of the action takes place with the ball being controlled in the pockets of the players' sticks.

The lacrosse stick—or crosse, as it was originally called—may be of an overall length between 40 and 72 inches, with the exception of the goalie's stick, which may be of any length. The inside measurement of the head of every stick, except the goalie's, is between 6½ and 10 inches. Attackmen normally use sticks with the smallest heads, 6½ to 7 inches, to aid them in ball control and dodging. Most midfielders will also use the small-headed stick. Close defensemen usually prefer the 8-inch head, and it is the recommended size for them. The trend today is

PERSONAL EQUIPMENT

The Rule Book requires all players to wear a pair of gloves and a helmet equipped with a face mask. A chin pad is secured to the mask and acts as a cushion to keep the mask from being pushed into the face. A cupped chin strap must be fastened on both sides of the helmet to keep it in the proper position. A lacrosse helmet is considerably lighter than a football helmet because the amount of physical contact in lacrosse is minimal compared with that in football. The lacrosse helmet mainly provides protection from the ball and from blows by the opponent's stick. Gloves are worn for the same reason. They are similar to ice-hockey gloves but more flexible. Although the gloves are manufactured both with and without the palms, most experienced players will cut out

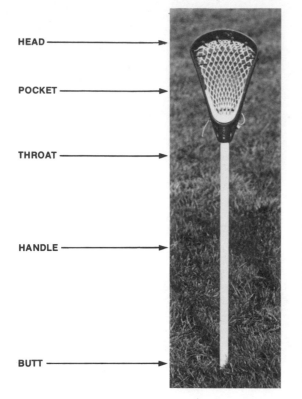

HEAD

POCKET

THROAT

HANDLE

BUTT

Figure 3–3 Parts of a lacrosse stick.

the complete palm and the inside part of the fingers to give them better control of the stick with their hands.

Although arm pads and a shoulder pad, or collar, are not required equipment, most players will wear these items for protection from illegal stick checks. Although some attackmen prefer not wearing the collar, the coach should make it mandatory that every attackman wear these pads, because attackmen are exposed to so many checks from aggressive defenders. The coach can be less demanding of his midfielders, defensemen, and goalies, but there is still the chance of their being hurt if they play without the collar. In most cases the goalie wears neither collar nor arm pads because he wants, above all else, complete freedom of movement. Elbow pads are not as cumbersome and often can be used by the goalie as a suitable replacement for

arm pads. Midfielders and defensemen can also get by with elbow pads, although it is safer for them to wear the regular arm pads.

The remaining pieces of equipment worn by the lacrosse player are shoes, a jersey, and shorts. The cleated shoes worn for football or soccer are used for lacrosse. The jerseys are similar to football jerseys, and the shorts are similar to those worn in soccer or basketball.

PLAY OF THE GAME

The regulation playing time of a college varsity game is sixty minutes, divided into four periods of fifteen minutes each. High-school teams play ten-minute periods. In the event of a tie score at the end of a regulation game, play will continue with eight minutes of overtime, in two periods of four minutes each. High-school teams play two periods of three minutes each. If the score is still tied at the conclusion of the overtime, then sudden-death play will begin, with the winner being the team that scores the first goal.

The game is controlled by two officials: a referee and an umpire. If both teams agree, a third official, who is designated the field judge, may be used. The referee has the final word in all decisions. The officials start the play at the beginning of each period and after each goal with a faceoff. The players on each team are assigned to a specific area on the field for the faceoff. Figure 3–4 shows their alignment with the goalie and three players in the defense-goal area, three players in the attack-goal area, one player in each of the wing areas, and the faceoff man at the center of the field. The particulars of faceoff play are covered in detail in Chapter 16. The top left picture in Figure 16–1 shows the ball placed between the sticks of the opposing faceoff men. When the whistle sounds to start play, the players in the wing areas are released, but all other players are confined to their areas until a player on either team gains possession of the ball, the ball goes out of bounds, or the ball crosses either goal-area line. After gaining control of the ball, the team moves it toward the goal and tries to score.

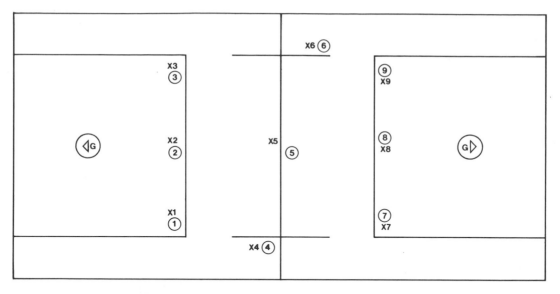

Figure 3–4 Alignment of players for a center faceoff.

The offside rule, which is peculiar to the game of lacrosse, requires each team to have three players located on its attack half of the field (between the center line and end line) and four players on its defensive half of the field (between the center line and end line). This rule prevents all ten players from jamming in front of the goal in an effort to prevent a score, as is done at times in the game of soccer. It enables lacrosse to be a more wide-open, freewheeling game with ample opportunity for scoring attempts.

When a player throws or carries the ball out of bounds, the opposing team gets possession. This is a basic rule for all team sports. However, in lacrosse there is one exception to this rule: when a loose ball goes out of bounds as a result of a shot taken at the goal, it is awarded to the team whose player is closest to it at the exact time it crosses the boundary line. This gives the offense the opportunity to maintain control of the ball after a missed shot goes out of bounds. An attack player is normally responsible for backing up a shot at the goal.

There are two methods of substituting players in lacrosse. The regular method follows that used in basketball, with a player entering the game whenever play has been suspended by the official blowing his whistle. The other method is similar to ice hockey's substitution of players while the game is in progress. One player at a time may enter the game when a teammate leaves the playing field. This takes place at the special substitution area at the center line.

Although the uninitiated spectator often thinks lacrosse is a wild, stick-swinging game, it is not nearly as rough as it appears. There is physical contact in lacrosse but not nearly as much as in football, with its continuous hitting on every play. Injuries in football are more numerous and more serious. Even though body and stick checks are part of lacrosse, there are definite limitations on them, which prevent injuries. In addition, the protective equipment worn by the lacrosse player minimizes injuries. Body checking of an opponent is legal as long as he either has possession of the ball or is within 5 yards of a loose ball and the contact is from the front or side and above the knees. A player can check his opponent's stick with his own stick when the opponent has possession of the ball or is within 5 yards of a loose ball. The opponent's gloved hand on the stick is considered part of the stick and can be legally checked. However, no other part of his body may be checked.

Lacrosse is similar to ice hockey in that players who violate the rules must spend time in the penalty box. This forces the violator's team to operate with one less player than its opponent, or even more if other penalties occur at the same time or while a player is already in the penalty box. The team that has been fouled is then operating with one man more than the other team and usually ends up taking a close-range shot at the goal. There are two types of fouls: personal and technical.

Personal fouls are the more serious and consist of the following:

1. Illegal body checking—hitting an opponent from the rear, at or below the knees, or when he is not in possession of the ball or within 5 yards of a loose ball.

2. Slashing—striking an opponent on his arms, shoulders, head, or any other part of his body except the gloved hand holding the stick.

3. Crosse checking—using the portion of the handle between the player's hands to check or push the opponent.

4. Tripping—obstructing an opponent below the knees with the stick, hands, arms, feet, or legs.

5. Unsportsmanlike conduct—using threatening, profane, or obscene language to an opposing player or official, or any act considered unsportsmanlike by the official.

The penalty for a personal foul is suspension of the offending player from the game for one to three minutes, depending on the official's diagnosis of the severity and intention of the foul. Most personal fouls call for only a one-minute suspension. An expulsion foul can be levied against a player who deliberately strikes or attempts to strike an opponent with his stick or fist. Such a player receives a three-minute penalty and is not allowed to return into the game. His substitute may enter the game after the three minutes have elapsed.

Technical fouls are those of a less serious kind in the game and consist of the following:

1. Interference—interfering in any manner with an opponent who does not have possession of the ball and thus preventing his free movement on the field. If the ball is loose, a player may interfere with an opponent only if he is within 5 yards of the ball.

2. Holding—grasping an opponent's stick or any part of his body in any manner.

3. Pushing—pushing an opponent with the hand, arm, or any other part of the body unless he has possession of the ball or is within 5 yards of a loose ball. A player may never push an opponent with his stick or push him with any part of his body from the rear.

4. Illegal action with the stick—throwing his stick under any circumstances or taking part in the play of the game in any manner without his stick.

5. Withholding the ball from play—lying on a loose ball on the ground or trapping it with his stick longer than is necessary for him to control the ball and pick it up with one continuous motion.

6. Illegal procedure—checking the goalie's stick when he has possession of the ball in the crease; an offensive player stepping in the opponent's crease when the ball is in the attacking half of the field; a defending player with the ball in his possession running through the crease.

7. Offside—a team having less than three men in its attack half of the field or less than four men in its defensive half of the field.

The penalty for a technical foul is suspension from the game for thirty seconds if the offending team does not have possession of the ball at the time the foul is committed. If the offending team has possession of the ball at the time of a technical foul, it simply loses possession to the opposition. This is also the case if neither team has possession when the foul is committed.

A player who has committed a violation of the playing rules must serve time in the penalty box. He must remain there until he is substituted for or informed by the timekeeper that he may reenter the game. The player is also released from the penalty box when the opposing team scores a goal or when the penalized team gains possession of the ball in its attack-goal area. Expulsion fouls and unsportsmanlike-conduct fouls, however, are such serious violations that they require that the full time always be served.

If a defending player commits a foul against an attacking player who has possession of the ball in the attack half of the field, a slow-whistle technique, similar to that used in ice hockey, is enacted. The official drops a signal flag and withholds his whistle until the scoring play is completed. The scoring play is considered to have been completed when the attacking team loses control of the ball, fails to move toward the goal, or takes a shot. Only one shot is allowed on the slow-whistle play.

Every player and coach should have a complete understanding of every rule in the game. The Official NCAA Lacrosse Guide gives a detailed explanation of the lacrosse rules and should be consulted.

what makes a player

After Johns Hopkins' domination of the collegiate lacrosse world in 1957, 1958, and 1959, the U.S. Naval Academy took over for an unprecedented stretch of eight consecutive national championships in the 1960s. Willis P. Bilderback developed a dynasty at Navy through his successful efforts in two primary areas. He recruited outstanding high-school lacrosse players and also did a superb job in working with the gifted athletes who had never even seen a game of lacrosse before arriving at the academy. Both Army and Navy have always been successful in turning out homemade lacrosse players, but the emphasis that Bildy placed on picking many of the best plebe athletes and teaching them the game paid off with royal dividends.

During the decade of the sixties, twenty-two Navy lacrosse players who had not picked up a stick before their arrival at the academy were honored as All-Americans for a total of thirty times. Quite an accomplishment, and it makes the point that in a short time a good athlete can learn the game of lacrosse and even become an outstanding player. However, he must be dedicated to the game and work diligently at developing his skill in handling the stick.

Although there have been many great football players who have picked up the game of lacrosse in college, two players, coincidentally both from the service academies, stand out in this category. Pat Donnelly of Navy, Class of 1965, and Bill Carpenter, West Point, Class of 1960, were All-American football players, Donnelly as a fullback and Carpenter as the famous "lonesome end." After exposure to the game as a plebe, Donnelly became a regular on the Navy varsity team, which won three consecutive national championships. He was honored as a first-team All-American as a senior and received the Schmeisser Memorial Award, which is given annually to the best defenseman in the country. He is considered by many to be Navy's best all-time defenseman. Carpenter was even more exceptional because he did not start playing lacrosse until his third year at West Point. He nonetheless played on one national-championship team and was also a first-team All-American and Schmeisser Award winner in his senior year.

While the natural athlete skilled in other sports can learn the game quickly and achieve All-American status, an individual with less athletic ability—but he must have some—can also become a contributing member of a college varsity team in just several years. Although he may not be an All-American, he can still help his team in many ways if he has an enthusiastic, competitive spirit. Having a love of the game and a willingness to work at the skills required in handling the stick are essential to the beginner's progress, but the key to his success lies in his competitiveness.

There have been many cases of average athletes who have picked up the game of lacrosse when they arrived on the college campus and have made noteworthy contributions to their varsity teams. Harry Stringer, a key figure on the Hopkins 1974 NCAA championship team, epitomizes this type. Harry was a defensive back on his high-school football team and did a very capable job. Nonetheless, his natural abilities were only average, as evidenced by his being cut from his high-school baseball team and not even trying out for the basketball team. He never considered giving lacrosse a try while he was in high school. However, when he came to Hopkins, he played on the football team in the fall and decided to take a shot at lacrosse in the spring. It may seem unusual for an athlete who did not even play lacrosse in high school to come to Hopkins, where the sport is played on the national level, and expect to make the varsity team. But Harry did it, mainly because he was such a tough competitor. After playing on the freshman team and working religiously on his stick work throughout the year, he not only made Hopkins' varsity team as a sophomore in 1972 but ran on the second midfield unit, which saw considerable game action. As a junior he ran on the first midfield unit, moving ahead of at least six of his teammates who were outstanding high-school players. In his senior year Harry established himself as one of the best defensive midfielders and ground-ball men and was instrumental in the team's successful drive to win the national cham-

pionship in 1974. In fact, his all-round team play in the three NCAA playoff games was outstanding that year; even though he did not score a single goal, he was recognized as one of the most effective players on the team. For an athlete who played only on his high-school football team, he did a remarkable job in beginning his lacrosse career as a freshman at Hopkins and playing as a regular for three years on a team that won the national championship once and was runner-up twice. As a matter of fact, Harry Stringer probably would have been an All-American if he had started his lacrosse career at an earlier age, because he did make the Club All-Star team in his first year of club lacrosse.

If the average athlete who has a real competitiveness and dedication to the game can get three or four years' or more experience prior to college, he will have an excellent opportunity to do extremely well in collegiate play and may even be an All-American. The classic example of an average athlete developing into a great player is Bill Morrill, Jr. Maybe Bill should be classified as slightly above average, because he was a good all-round athlete playing football, basketball, and lacrosse. But he certainly did not have the natural athletic talents (speed, maneuverability, size, and strength) that were commonplace to the Navy football players. However, Bill was fortunate to have as his father W. Kelso Morrill, who was one of the deans of lacrosse at Hopkins for four decades. When Bill was four years old, Kelso placed a stick in his hands, played catch with him, and encouraged him to make use of his garage wall for practicing his stick work. Bill pounded that garage wall until his stick work became exceptional. In fact, when Bill was twelve years old and the mascot for the 1950 Hopkins national championship team, which his father coached, his stick work was superior to that of half the members of the best college team in the country. I can make that statement without any hesitation because I was a member of that team and I know that Billy's stick work made me feel like a real beginner, and I wasn't alone in feeling that way. His persistence at practicing his stick handling enabled him to become an outstanding high-school player and a first-team All-American attackman at Hopkins for three years. He also received the Jack Turnbull Memorial Award as the most outstanding attackman in the country in 1959. Although he did not have the size, strength, and speed of a great natural athlete, his superior stick work, his competitiveness, and his expert knowledge of the game made him one of the best players I have had the pleasure of coaching. I predict that one day Bill will join his father as a member of the Lacrosse Hall of Fame.

The cycle is starting all over again now as Bill Morrill is exposing his two sons to the game. It is very interesting for me to watch them perform on the little-league level and observe their skills in handling the stick. They are receiving the same encouragement from their father that Bill received from Kelso, and I am sure they will follow in his footsteps and one day become excellent players.

For two of the most popular sports in the United States, football and basketball, size is extremely important and almost a necessity, but this is not true of lacrosse. The "little man" has equal opportunity to make it. Quickness, both physical and mental, can make up for lack of size. Jerry Schnydman, Hopkins Class of 1967 and a three-time All-American, bears this out. At just a shade over 5'1" in height, Jerry was one of the best at scooping ground balls and in controlling face-offs. Being built so close to the ground gave him a decided advantage over his taller opponents, which included every player in every game in which he competed. Not only was he able to scoop the ground balls more efficiently; he was also able to avoid the crushing body checks of his opponents, who were out to level him on the faceoff play. He would merely drop to his knees, and this was not much of a drop, and the big guys would go sailing over him. He would then rise to his feet, scoop the ball, and be on his way, to the delight of the Hopkins fans.

The 1965 Hopkins team is one of my favorites because it performed up to the maximum potential of its ability and never quit hustling. Six players on our starting team were 5'8" or shorter. Although the '65 team did not win the national championship, it lost only one game and was the number-two team in the country. Not too bad for a bunch of little guys.

To be successful in lacrosse, as in every team sport, the individual must love the game and be dedicated to self-improvement. Winning is not the only thing that counts in athletics, but certainly wanting to win is. Therefore, I would emphasize that having a competitive spirit and working conscientiously to develop clever stick

handling are the two most important ingredients of a lacrosse player.

TALENTS FOR EACH POSITION

Each of the four positions on the field requires certain basic talents of the players. Let's take a look at each position and the talents needed for playing it.

Goal

The goalie must be the most courageous player on the field, or some might say the craziest, because he must have no fear of being hit anywhere on his body with a solid rubber ball traveling at speeds that may reach 90 miles per hour. One of my great Hopkins goalies was affectionately known as "Goofy," and this nickname was obviously given to him for his fearlessness. Goofy, by the way, has his doctorate in environmental engineering and is teaching at one of our nation's foremost universities. During the average college lacrosse game, each goalie will have between forty and sixty shots fired at him, many coming at a distance of less than 25 feet. He must have very quick reactions in order to stop the shot with his stick and/or body. Courage and quick reactions are the most important credentials for the goalie.

In addition, he will have to be a team leader and field general, because he must engineer and direct the position of each man on the defensive half of the field while keeping constant sight of the ball, often through a maze of sticks and bodies. He will organize and execute the clearing of the ball to the offensive half of the field as many as twenty-five to thirty times a game. Considerable pressure is placed on him in these situations, because a failure to clear may result in a point-blank shot by the opposition. Even more pressure is placed on him when the opponent is on the attack, because he is the last line of defense, and most of the goals scored will be attributed to his play. However, when a goal is scored on him, he must keep his composure and not be hypercritical of himself or his teammates.

Although size and speed are certainly desirable for the goalie, they are not essential. In fact, I would estimate that the majority of goalies who have played the game during my career have been either small—5'9" or shorter—or with average to below-average speed. It does help to have speed for clearing the ball, but the number-one responsibility of the goalie is to stop the ball, not to clear it. So if the choice is between a slow, small goalie who is adept at stopping the ball or the tall speedster who is only average in the goal, the answer for me has always been the stopper.

Defense

Considerable pressure is placed on the defenseman every time the opponent brings the ball over the center line to attack the goal. Most teams give the ball to their attackmen to initiate the play, because they normally are the most dangerous offensive threats on the team. It is the responsibility of the defenseman to neutralize the star attackman by staying with him and ultimately preventing him from taking a close-range shot at the goal. Frequently the offense will try to isolate the defender against an attackman who knows exactly where he wants to go and what he wants to do. To be able to stop him, the defenseman must have agility and quickness in both moving and reacting. The more speed the defenseman has, the easier it is for him to stay with his man. The days of the big, strong, and often slow defenseman are over. Size does help the defender, because it gives him the advantage of reach over most attackmen, but it is not as essential as agility, quickness to react, and speed. The defenseman's stick work does not have to be as advanced as the attackman's, but he does have to know how and when to use his stick to pressurize the attackman effectively and to limit his penetration toward the goal. Patience is important, because the overly anxious and aggressive defender is often susceptible to being dodged or to committing a foul.

Midfield

The midfielders are normally considered to be the runners, the hustlers, the scramblers on the team, because they have to cover the entire field, playing both offense and defense. If the ball is not settled, a midfielder may find himself sprinting at full speed up and down the field as many as five or six times in a row without stopping. Between those sprints he may have to battle all out for a loose ball. The action is not only strenuous

and completely demanding physically but also continuous. Lacrosse players do not have that twenty-five-second break between plays that football players have, and they have to cover more ground as well, because a lacrosse field is bigger than a football field. Therefore, stamina and endurance are the prime essentials for the midfielder. Hustle and anticipation can make up for lack of speed.

Since playing defense is one of the most important jobs of a midfielder, he must be able to react quickly and with agility when playing his man. All midfielders do not have to be scorers, and a team can be successful with only one or two scoring threats on each midfield unit. Although every midfielder must stress his defensive play, a team actually needs two types of players —those with excellent stick work and shooting ability and those who may have only limited offensive ability but are relentless in their pursuit of the ground ball and smart in playing their man on defense. The midfield units on our 1970 Hopkins team, which shared the national championship with Virginia and Navy, had each type almost exclusively. Four of our nine were the scorers, as they totaled fifty-five goals in our ten games. They were the offensive workhorses of our team. The other five midfielders were limited on offense and scored a combined total of only seven goals for the season. This means that over half of our regular midfielders averaged just a little over one goal per man for the entire season. They obviously shot very little, but they did carry out in excellent fashion the important responsibilities of getting the ground balls and playing strong defense.

Attack

Attackmen are normally looked to as the team's primary scorers. The pressure is on the attack to direct the offense and to put more points on the scoreboard than the opposition does. Their stick work should be the best on the entire team, because they must shoot and feed the ball with the accuracy of an expert marksman. They should be able to handle the stick both left- and right-handed in order to attack the goal effectively from both sides. The two attackmen who play behind the goal should be excellent dodgers and feeders, whereas the crease attackman is primarily a shooter. If a team has three attackmen who have the talents to play either on the crease or behind the goal, added pressure can be placed on the opposition by rotating them.

Along with clever stick work and equally important, the attackman must have a "hard nose" and go to the goal for the shot. He must be tough enough to take the punishment of both the stick and body checks that the defense will be dishing out. If an attackman allows himself to be forced to operate closer to the end line than to the goal, his effectiveness will be minimized considerably. In addition to his stick-handling ability and physical toughness, the attackman must be mentally sharp enough to direct the offense and to make the decisions about when to shoot and when to pass. Agility, maneuverability, and speed are other qualities that make the attackman more dangerous. When the offense loses the ball, the attackman must also be a real hustler as he tries to prevent the defense from clearing the ball.

GUIDELINES FOR BEGINNERS IN DETERMINING WHAT POSITION TO PLAY

In determining the position a person should play when he first starts lacrosse on a team basis, an assessment of his athletic ability is most helpful. This certainly applies to a parent whose ten-year-old son is about to try out for a little-league team as well as to the high-school or college coach who is working with someone who has never played the game. In order to set the guidelines for the beginner, three categories of athletes can be identified: below-average, average, and above-average. The parent or coach can determine in which category the beginner belongs by evaluating the degree to which he possesses the following qualities: agility, maneuverability, aggressiveness, quick reaction, speed, and mental alertness. The athlete who has these qualities in abundance can be placed in the above-average category; to a moderate degree, in the average category; and to a limited degree, in the below-average category.

It is obvious that the athlete with above-average ability can play any of the four positions in the game of lacrosse without any difficulty. However, the average or below-average athlete should consider playing the position that best

suits his talents. Let's take a look at the three categories and the related guidelines.

Below-Average Athlete

With speed, he can play midfield or defense and experience reasonable success on most levels of competition.

Without speed, he should probably play defense and work hard at trying to improve his maneuverability. Crease defense is the position that requires probably the least running, maneuvering, and stick work and is, therefore, a good spot for those with limited ability. He can possibly make it in the midfield if he makes up for his lack of speed by being a real hustler.

I doubt that the below-average athlete can make it as an attackman who plays behind the goal, because the skills are so specialized there. However, if he develops excellent stick handling, he may be able to play as a crease attackman, because his main responsibilities are limited to catching feeds and shooting point-blank shots at the goal.

Average Athlete

With speed, he can play any of the four positions. However, I suggest that he start as a midfielder, and if his stick work progresses rapidly, he can move to the attack. The average athlete with speed and a competitive nature can be an outstanding midfielder or defenseman.

Without speed, he can become a good midfielder if he is a strong competitor. He can also do a very fine job on the defense; or if he develops exceptional stick work, he can play on the attack.

The average athlete who has a "hard nose" can be an outstanding goalie, regardless of his speed.

Above-Average Athlete

The above-average athlete who has many natural talents can play any of the four positions. Frequently he will play on the attack, since all the scoring revolves around this position, and youngsters like to score. If he likes continuous action, he will play in the midfield. He can also be an outstanding defenseman or goalie if his interests are at that end of the field.

WHAT MAKES A PLAYER

However, the above-average athlete who doesn't start playing the game until he gets to college will probably play on the midfield or defense. The skills required there are probably not as specialized or as difficult to master as the ones on the attack and in the goal. Coach Bill Bilderback's Navy teams of the 1960s bear out this point. Every one of the homemade All-Americans that Bildy developed during that decade played either on the defense or on the midfield. There were some who played on the attack or in the goal, but they did not excel at their positions, as did the midfielders and defensemen.

The gifted athlete who starts playing lacrosse even as late as his senior year in high school has an excellent opportunity to be an All-American at any of the four positions before graduating from college if he is a tough competitor and has the proper mental attitude.

II
techniques and tactics

funda-
mentals

Learning the fundamentals of handling the stick is the first step in the development of a lacrosse player. Too much emphasis cannot be placed on the proper techniques of catching, throwing, cradling, and scooping the ball. Even the more advanced players on the college-varsity level need constant practice in the basic skills. The beginner should concentrate on learning to handle the stick the right way to avoid picking up bad habits, which are difficult to break.

HOLDING THE STICK

The player must hold the stick properly in order to control the ball effectively in the pocket. Figure 5–1 shows a right-handed player with the proper grip of the stick. His left (lower) hand, with his palm facing down, grasps the stick at the end of the handle for protection purposes. If he fails to do so and a portion of the stick, even just 1 or 2 inches, is exposed, the defender has a good chance of making a successful poke check on the end of the handle and dislodging the ball. The right (upper) hand, with the palm facing up, is placed on the handle about 12 inches from the left hand. Both hands are in front of the hips or slightly outside them. Beginners often feel more comfortable grasping the stick with the upper hand closer to the head of the stick, giving them more control in catching and cradling the ball. However, they lose a considerable amount of leverage and power when releasing the ball with their hands too far apart on the stick. It is not advisable to slide the upper hand down the handle to get more leverage, because this takes a split second longer and the control of the stick is not as complete when the hand is sliding. More advanced players like to throw or shoot the ball with their hands about 6 inches or less apart, giving them greater leverage but consequently

Figure 5–1 Proper grip of a lacrosse stick.

the exception of the goalie stick, which may be of any length. Most attack players on the college level, even those over 6 feet tall, use a stick of 40 to 42 inches in length. Since midfielders have to play defense about half the time they are in the game, they will play with a slightly longer stick—about 42 to 44 inches long. A short midfielder, however, may play with a 40- or 41-inch stick. Most defensemen will play with a stick between 5 and 6 feet in length. Even though the longer handle enables the defenseman to be more effective, those who use the 6-foot stick often have difficulty controlling it. A stick between 5 feet to 5 feet, 8 inches long is ideal for most defensemen. Most college goalies play with a stick in a range of 46 to 60 inches. The optimum size is 50 to 56 inches. Goalies need the length for making long clearing passes, intercepting feeds, and reaching for ground balls outside the crease.

Youngsters up to age twelve or thirteen should definitely play with sticks shorter than those used by high-school and college players. If they are playing attack, their stick should not be longer than 40 or 41 inches, and possibly shorter than 40 inches if they are eight or nine years old or younger. Midfielders can follow similar guidelines, possibly with their sticks an inch or two longer than the attackmen's. Defensemen should play with sticks in the 4- to 5-foot range and goalies in the 40- to 52-inch range. A surprising number of youngsters in summer camps use sticks much too long for them. It is rare to find a youngster whose stick is too short.

CRADLING

Cradling is probably the most difficult technique for the beginner to learn, and it is obviously the most important. Each player must be able to run at top speed, often surrounded by opponents, and still control the ball in the pocket of his stick. The key to cradling is the looseness of the upper hand and wrist. The loose wrist motion of the lacrosse player's upper hand while cradling can be compared to the symphony conductor's handling of his baton. When the maestro conducts, he moves his entire arm as well as his hand. And so does the lacrosse player when he cradles. Most youngsters have played around with either a table-tennis paddle or tennis racquet, trying to keep the ball on the flat surface of the paddle or

detracting from their control of the stick and accuracy. The hands are placed the basic hip-width distance apart when catching, throwing, cradling, shooting, and scooping the ball.

The fingers hold the stick with a firm but not a tight grip. Beginners often make the mistake of "squeezing the stick to death" with a viselike grip and consequently lose the feel for controlling the ball. The stick rests more in the fingers than the palm of the upper hand. The thumb is on top of the handle. The elbow of the upper arm is pointed toward the ground and not out to the side. These points allow for a free and easy motion to cradle the ball and keep it in the pocket.

Stick handling is affected considerably by the size of the stick. Obviously the smaller the stick, the easier it is to handle. The Rule Book states specific dimensions for the length of the stick (minimum 40 inches, maximum 72 inches), with

Figure 5–2 Two-hand front cradle.

Figure 5–3 Two-hand upright cradle.

racquet by moving their arms and turning their wrists in a swinging motion. This technique is similar to cradling a lacrosse ball, and it may be helpful for the beginner to hold the stick in front of his body with only one hand and cradle the ball this way. The ball is not shaken or jiggled around in the pocket of the stick by the wrist action alone; it is rocked back and forth with a smooth, rhythmic motion of the entire upper arm as well as the hand. If the wrists are not locked but are allowed to move with the swinging motion of the arms, which results normally from running, the ball will come to a more positive rest in the pocket. Both hands are involved with the cradling, although the upper hand carries the bulk of the load. The lower hand has to have a loose enough grip to allow the stick to be turned in it. Beginners can look at the ball when cradling just to make sure it is under control in the pocket. As the player gains

confidence in handling the ball, he does not need to look at it because he has a feel for its position in his stick.

There are different types of cradles, but each has the same basic motion. Figure 5–2 shows the two-hand front cradle, which can be used when carrying the ball down the field without immediate opposition. This cradle cannot be used when a defender approaches, because the ball carrier's stick is in front of his body and is an easy target for a check. Figure 5–3 shows the two-hand upright cradle, which is used when a defender is playing the man with the ball. This cradle gives good protection of the ball and has the stick in a position to release the ball quickly and accurately. The one-hand cradle (see Figure 5–4) gives excellent protection, since the lower hand is placed in front of the body to prevent the defender's checks from getting to his stick.

FUNDAMENTALS

Figure 5–4 One-hand cradle.

THROWING

The techniques used in throwing a football or baseball are the same ones used in throwing a lacrosse ball with the stick. Figure 5–5 shows a right-handed player in the three phases of the throwing motion. The body is turned to the side and the feet are staggered. The upper hand is even with the shoulders or slightly above and controls the stick throughout the throwing motion. When one throws a football or baseball, the upper hand is well above the shoulder. However, the lacrosse player uses his stick to place the ball in this position, and therefore his upper hand remains at shoulder level or slightly above. The upper hand is primarily responsible for accuracy but also shares in providing the power with the lower hand, which is about 6 to 8 inches from the body. The stick is held at about a 45-degree angle from the horizontal and with the head of the stick facing in the direction the ball is to be thrown. The ball rests in the pocket, and the thrower should have a feel for it.

In the actual throwing motion the following takes place:

1. The body weight is drawn back first to the rear leg and then transferred to the front leg.

2. The upper body is turned from a side position to one facing directly to the front. The whipping of the shoulders gives added power.

3. The upper hand is drawn back several inches and then follows through with a snapping motion. This wrist snap is the key to throwing with the lacrosse stick, just the same as it is in throwing the football or baseball, because it gives both accuracy and power.

4. The lower arm is bent at the elbow and places the lower hand in a position closer to the body than the upper hand.

5. The lower hand pulls down on the end of the handle, making a small arc toward the middle of the body.

6. The ball leaves the stick from the center of the pocket.

7. The ball is aimed for the head of the receiver's stick.

8. The stick ends up pointing directly at this target and in a near-horizontal position.

To emphasize the similarity between throwing a baseball or a football and a lacrosse ball with the stick, the beginner can throw with just one hand, his upper hand, on the stick. The wrist snap is of primary importance, and the throw can be made with the identical motion used by the pitcher or quarterback. The accuracy and power with one hand on the stick are obviously more limited, but it is easy to feel the similarity in the throwing techniques.

The most common error the beginner makes is pushing the ball out of the pocket rather than throwing it. This is caused either by his failure to draw the stick back several inches just prior to his forward motion or by his failure to snap his wrist when making the throw. When the ball is pushed out of the stick, it has limited power and control. The beginning thrower also tends to use primarily the pull-down move by the lower hand to release the ball instead of using the joint action of both the upper and lower hands.

Figure 5–5 Three phases of the throwing technique.

CATCHING

When a player catches the ball, the positions of both his body and his stick are important (see Figure 5–6). The upper body squarely faces the ball in its flight. The feet are about shoulder-width apart and on line rather than staggered. This position allows the receiver to move quickly to either his left or his right, depending on where the ball is thrown. The stick is placed slightly above the head as a target for the pass. The pocket of the stick is positioned so that it is completely facing the ball. The catch is made in front of the body with the head of the stick reaching out for the ball, much the same as a baseball player using his glove to catch the ball. The baseball player doesn't catch the ball in a position even with his body or a position with his arm completely straightened out in front of his body. Rather, he reaches out with his gloved hand as the ball approaches and then cushions the ball into his glove, actually making the catch about 6 inches in front of his body. The lacrosse player uses the same techniques in catching the ball with his stick. The idea of catching in lacrosse is also much the same as trying to catch a thrown tennis ball with a tightly strung racquet. The stick must be withdrawn or the ball will rebound. The receiver cushions the ball in his pocket by bringing the head of his stick back toward his body and making use of a quick but soft wrist action. This cradle motion controls the ball in the pocket and keeps it from bouncing out.

Catching the ball on the backhand side—that is, the side opposite the receiver's stick—requires a different maneuver. The receiver swings his stick across the front of his body into the backhand position (see Figure 5–7). The entire stick is

FUNDAMENTALS

Figure 5–6 Three phases of the catching technique.

moved to the backhand side, not just the head of the stick. Beginners will often move just the head of the stick and leave the butt end on the forehand side. This makes for a very awkward catch. The wrist or cradle action is the same, except that it is done in the backhand position. The receiver will either sidestep or cross over to get to a ball thrown to his backhand side. If the ball is close to his body, a right-hander will sidestep with his left foot. Figure 5–7 shows a right-hander who has pivoted on his left foot and made the crossover with his right foot because the ball was not near his body. The crossover step gives him extra reach.

There are several ways of playing a ball that is thrown directly at the receiver's head or body. The right-hander can either move his body to his left by sidestepping with his left foot and then catching the ball in the forehand position, or he can pivot on his right foot and step back with his left foot, catching the ball in the backhand position. The footwork is opposite for the left-hander.

Once the receiver catches the ball, he always turns into a position with his body between his stick and the nearest opponent. This gives him the best possible protection of the stick. Begin-

ners and even some advanced players often make the mistake of turning the wrong way and bringing the stick in front of their body where the opponent can check it. Failure to turn or circle properly with the ball was one of the pet peeves of one of the great Hopkins coaches, Dr. W. Kelso Morrill. Many a time his voice was heard shouting across the practice field, "Judas Priest, you turned the wrong way!"

SCOOPING

Control of the ball is a significant factor in a team's success. Since the ball is on the ground for a portion of every game, it is vital for a team to try to gain possession of it more than 50 percent of the time. Scooping a ground ball that is being contested by as many as four or five players requires not only mastering the basic skills of actually scooping the ball but also a determination and fierce competitiveness. A team's mental attitude is usually reflected in its play of the ground ball, and in most cases the team controlling the ground ball wins the game.

Maintaining the proper body and stick position

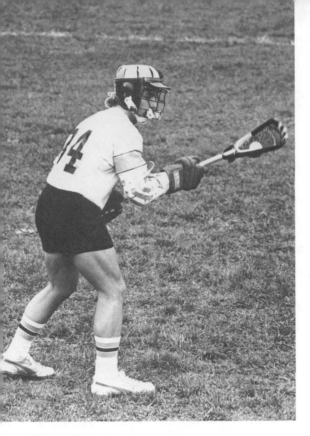

Figure 5–7 Backhand catch.

Figure 5–8 Scooping the ball.

is essential for the scooper. When he gets within several yards of a ground ball, he bends his knees and upper body in a semicrouch position. If he is holding his stick right-handed, then his right foot is forward on the scoop to give a free-flowing scooping motion with his arms (see Figure 5–8). The left (lower) arm determines the angle that the stick makes with the ground in the scoop. The angle will vary according to the size of the player, but a general guideline of approximately 30 degrees can be established. Normally the lower arm will be close to a straightened position in the scoop rather than with a sizable bend at the elbow. If the angle approaches 60 degrees, it is going to place the stick at too steep an angle, and this minimizes the effectiveness of controlling the ball in a fast-moving, pressure situation. Instead of getting their nose down near the ground to play the ball, players will often take the lazy man's approach—scooping the ball with their body in an upright position and with their stick at a sharp angle. This technique is referred to as "spiking" the ball and definitely should be avoided.

The end of the handle is held to the side of the body rather than in front, where the stick could dig into the ground and force the butt end of the handle into the scooper's groin or midsection. The head of the stick hits the ground 1 to 2 inches from the ball. A common mistake is for the scooper to try to place the head of his stick right next to the ball, which may cause it to hit or go over it. He must keep his eyes on the ball until he has scooped it into his stick with a shovellike motion, and he should keep moving. He should not flip the ball into the air as he scoops it. If a player is completely ambidextrous, he may scoop the ball either left- or right-handed. However, if one hand is obviously stronger than the other, he should scoop the ball only with that hand and not try to scoop with the weaker hand in a pressure situation.

Stress should be placed on the importance of scooping the grounder with both hands on the stick. It may seem easier to scoop with just the lower hand gripping the stick at the butt end of the handle, but the percentages are not with the one-handed scoop. The one-handed scoop with just the upper hand should also be avoided, because the end of the handle is exposed to the opponent's check. The chance for error is far less in the two-handed scoop, because the scooper

Figure 5–9 Upper arm protecting the stick after scooping the ball.

gets his body closer to the ground. He can also control the stick better with two hands on the stick. The two-handed scoop is a must for even the most experienced college varsity player, although a few of the superstars have been given the green light on the one-handed scoop. However, these were exceptional lacrosse players who could handle the stick well enough to perfect the one-handed scoop.

Once the ball is in his stick, the scooper's primary concern is protecting it. He has several courses of action, depending on the circumstances. As soon as he scoops the ball, he determines the location of the opposition. If he is surrounded, he tucks the stick close to his body and tries to dodge out of trouble. This maneuver is referred to as the "scoop and tuck." If after the scoop he sees an open area, regardless of whether it's toward the offensive or defensive half of the field, he bursts full speed for daylight. If he receives pressure from the side once he is on the run, he can hold the stick with one hand and protect it with the other.

Figure 5–9 shows a right-hander being played by an opponent on his right side. If he were to keep both hands on the stick and start cradling right-handed, his stick would be an easy target for his opponent. However, by removing his right (upper) hand from the stick and holding his forearm in front of his body and parallel to the ground, he gives his stick excellent protection. The left

(lower) hand remains in the same position at the butt end of the handle and cradles the ball with a minimum of motion. The stick is held to the scooper's left front and in a position close to the horizontal. Younger players have difficulty holding the stick with only one hand at the end of the handle, but as they get older and their wrists strengthen, they will have no problem. Since the scooper is able to wriggle out of trouble with this maneuver, it is identified as a "snakeout." It is one of the most effective ways of avoiding the opponent's check.

If the pressure comes from his left, the right-handed scooper can hold the stick with just his right hand in its normal position, about 12 inches up the handle. In this case, the left arm is held out in front of the body to protect the stick (see Figure 5–10).

Communication between players is essential in every phase of team play, including the scooping of ground balls. Instead of two teammates battling for the ball against one opponent, it is much more effective for one to play the ball and one to play the man. This 2-on-1 situation or even the 3-on-2 situation is not an uncommon occurrence. There are several different calls that can be used. A number of teams simply have their players call out "Ball, ball" every time they scoop a loose ball. At Hopkins we have always used the command, "Take the man." Any other player near the scooper will then block out an opponent who

Figure 5–10 Lower arm protecting the stick after scooping the ball.

is also contesting for the ball. When the scooper has the ball in his stick, he must call out "Drop off," or "Release," to tell his teammate to stop his body contact with the opponent. It is a technical foul to make physical contact with the opposition when a teammate has the ball. If a player hears his name being called when he is fighting for a ground ball, he should use his stick to try to flick the ball in the direction of the teammate who is calling.

A final point to be made on the control of ground balls is making use of the feet. Whenever three or more players are contending for the ball, there is continual checking with sticks, and the ball will often remain in the middle of the crowd. A player who kicks the ball with his foot gains an advantage over his opponents because he knows exactly when and where he is kicking the ball and can move quickly to it. The ball should be kicked to an unoccupied area on the field. Defensive players should not kick the ball toward their own goal, because this will put added pressure on the goalie if the opposition gains control of the ball near the goal. The one exception to this occurs when a loose ball is behind the goal and within several yards of the crease. In this situation a defensive player can kick the ball to the goalie if he is in the crease and calling for it. Defensive players normally kick the ball toward the side-line, back line, or midfield line. Offensive players can kick the ball in any direction, toward any open area.

Practice, and more practice, of the fundamentals used in handling the stick is essential, no matter how talented the player may be. Lacrosse fundamentals can easily be practiced alone or with only one partner. When a player is working alone, the only prop needed is a wall. All the skills of catching, throwing, and cradling can be practiced by banging the ball against a wall. Scooping can also be practiced alone on any lawn or playing field.

FUNDAMENTALS

individual offense 6

There are four basic skills that all offensive players should continually practice in order to achieve maximum effectiveness in attacking the goal. The proper techniques for dodging, shooting, cutting toward the goal, and feeding (passing the ball to an open teammate in the crease area) are essential for every midfielder and attackman. Goalies and defensemen must also be able to execute the basic dodges, because they frequently receive considerable pressure from riding opponents, whom they must dodge. Defensemen must also know how to shoot properly for those occasions when they clear the ball to the offensive half of the field and go right in toward the goal for the shot. (Clearing is the movement of the ball from the defensive to the offensive half of the field; riding is the counter-move to prevent a clear.)

DODGING

Every player on the team must strive to master the face, roll, and bull dodges. These three dodges give the man with the ball the capability of going by his opponent and advancing the ball toward the goal. Most dodges occur as a result of an opponent's mistake or overcommitment. Incorrect body or stick position by the defender can also encourage the dodge. The ball carrier can initiate the dodge himself by baiting his opponent into making a mistake and then taking advantage of it.

Protection of the stick by the dodger is probably the most important factor in completing a successful dodge. A simple rule to achieve this protection is: keep your head between and in direct alignment with the head of your stick and the opponent. If you maintain this "head-on-head" position, the defender cannot check the ball carrier's stick without hitting him on the helmet and committing a foul.

Figure 6–1 Two phases of the face dodge with a sidestep.

There are several other points to be made about dodging. The attacker should avoid forcing his dodge into a defense that has backup men on either side of the dodger and also between the dodger and the goal. When the defense is stacked and waiting for the dodger, he should be ready to pass off to a teammate rather than trying to barrel through. If an attacker is successful in dodging his opponent, he should not try to dodge one or two more defenders on the same play. The odds normally catch up with him, and he will lose the ball. The ball carrier should vary his dodges and not use the same one again and again.

Let's take a look at the three basic dodges. For simplicity's sake, the explanation and the illustrations are for a right-handed ball carrier. The moves for the left-hander are the same but to the opposite side.

Face Dodge

The face dodge is best used when an opponent delivers a slap check at the ball carrier. As soon as he sees the stick coming, the ball carrier pulls his own stick across the front of his body. Actually

the stick goes in front of his face, hence the name "face dodge." It is more difficult to execute the face dodge against the opponent's poke check because it is aimed generally in the path of the dodger's stick, whereas the slap check somewhat facilitates the dodge. The ball carrier can help set up the face dodge by faking a pass to a teammate. He can use a head-and-eye fake, looking in the direction of the anticipated pass and even calling a player in that area by name. He should have two hands on the stick when faking the pass to make it more realistic. If the opponent raises his stick in the air to block the faked pass, this will open up the opportunity for the face dodge just as well as the opponent's using an aggressive slap check.

Figure 6–1 shows a right-handed player executing the face dodge. In one simultaneous motion he pushes off with his right foot, sidesteps to the left with his left foot, and pulls the stick across his face. When the face dodge is done with quickness and agility, the dodger gains at least a step on his opponent in the new direction. Once driving to his left, the driver should stay with a right-handed grip on the stick for at least the first two or three steps. If he changes to a left-handed grip immediately after making the face dodge, his opponent may be able to reach around him from the rear and check his stick. He should also avoid bringing his stick back into the normal right-handed position, to the right front of his body, immediately after the sidestep. He should stay with the right-handed grip, but the head of his stick should be more in a position to the left front of his body and in a direct line with his own head and his opponent. When he is certain his opponent cannot make a successful check, he can either bring the stick back for a right-handed shot or change to a left-handed grip on the stick.

The face dodge can also be done with a crossover step as opposed to the sidestep. Figure 6–2 shows a right-hander who has pivoted on his left foot while crossing over with his right foot and pulling the stick across his face. The crossover technique is difficult to use in a running situation but can be very effective from the stationary position. The best example is for an offensive player with the ball in his possession to take a step or two toward the goal, faking the crankup for an outside shot at about the 16-to-18-yard mark. The defender will normally make a slap check to break up the attempted shot. This gives the attacker the opportunity to make the crossover step, which carries him at least two feet past his opponent, whereas the sidestep gains only about one foot on the defender in the new direction.

Roll Dodge

Of all the dodges the roll dodge is probably used most frequently. It is effective when the opponent is very aggressive with stick checks, especially the slap check when it is delivered with a horizontal thrust and almost turns or pushes the driver in the opposite direction. The check actually helps him to roll away from the pressure. The roll dodge can be done in either a slow-moving or a fast-moving situation. It is not necessary to keep two hands on the stick because the success of the dodge is dependent more on the footwork than on the handling of the stick. Figure 6–3 shows a right-handed attacker who, while driving toward the goal, has reacted to the check of the defender with a roll dodge. He pivots on his left foot, which is his lead foot, then pushes off his left leg and takes a step with his right foot in the

Figure 6–2 Face dodge with a crossover step.

direction opposite his original path. This step is a sizable one of 2 or 3 feet and is the key to the roll dodge. It should be as close to the defender as possible to facilitate his rolling by him in the new direction. If he rounds out on the first step, moving away from his defender, he will not gain an advantage, because the defender will have the chance to recover his positioning on him.

When he takes the first step on the roll dodge, the ball carrier faces away from his opponent and throws his hips into him. The head of his stick stays even with his own head as he makes the pivot. If he keeps the head of his stick well above his head, the defender may be able to check it. If he trails the head of his stick, the defender can reach around him and also make the check. However, if it is even with his own head, the stick is well protected and the defender will either jeopardize his positioning by making a reckless swing with his stick or foul him.

It is important for the attacker to grip the stick with his hands in the same position throughout the pivot and even after the first two or three steps in the new direction. The reason is the same for the roll dodge as for the face dodge. If the attacker roll-dodges right-handed and immediately changes to a left-handed grip of the stick, he exposes himself to being checked by the defender on a reach-around move. He should be completely confident that the stick is well protected before he changes his hand grip on the stick.

When the roll dodge is used in the midfield area, the driver must be cautious about taking too deep a step after his pivot if it occurs at a distance of about 14 yards or closer to the goal. The crease defenseman will have a good chance of making an effective backup on him at this location on the field. This is the one time when the roll dodger moves more laterally on his first step after the pivot to give himself enough cushion from a sliding defender, while at the same time giving himself a good shot at the goal from 14 yards or less. When out near the restraining line, the dodger can take his regular pivot and step to gain distance from his man and go for the goal.

The time he wants to be the tightest to his man on his pivot and roll is when the attacker drives from behind the goal and is in the area 5 to 6 yards in front of the goal and 5 to 6 yards from the center of the field (see Figure 6–4). The roll dodge, when executed properly at this location, gives the dodger a point-blank shot at the goal. If he doesn't drive to at least the 5-yard mark, he will be vulnerable to the defender pushing him into the crease after he has made his pivot and roll. He also will decrease the effectiveness of his shooting angle if he drives less than 5 yards in front of the goal. He can put the greatest pressure on the defender by getting to his point with a hard drive as opposed to a stop-and-start, back-and-forth motion. When he arrives at this particular spot, he must give a strong threat of the forehand shot. He may move to this point with one hand on the stick, but he should then put on his other hand to fake the shot. In most cases the defender will respond with a hard check, and when it is delivered, the attacker will pivot and roll tight to his man. He does not want to make contact with the defender because he could be knocked off stride. He goes right for the goal and does not change hands but keeps his stick directly in front of his head in the complete pivot and when taking the shot itself. If he were to change hands, the left-handed shot would give him a poorer angle, along with exposing him to a

Figure 6–3   Three phases of the roll dodge.

reach-around move by the defender. This dodge is referred to as the "inside roll dodge" because the attacker is actually rolling inside the defender and climaxing the move with a point-blank shot. It is, without a doubt, one of the best offensive maneuvers in the game.

Bull Dodge

Whereas both the face dodge and roll dodge have the dodger changing his direction and going in a direction opposite to his original path, the bull dodge starts one way and climaxes in the same direction. The name of the dodge indicates brute strength overpowering the defender, and when a Jimmy Brown type, 6′2″, 230 pounds, matches up against a Jerry Schnydman, 5′1¾″ and 145 pounds, the name is accurate. Although the Brown-Schnydman matchup is the extreme, there are many instances when a bigger, stronger, and faster offensive player will drive by the defender for a good shot in the "hole" area, which is the prime shooting area directly in front of the goal. When executing the bull dodge, the attacker normally holds the stick with only the upper hand. He protects the head of his stick by keeping it even with his own head. The lower

hand is held to the front of his body to guard against poke or slap checks directed at the handle of his stick. (See Figure 6–5.)

The bull dodge is most effective when sheer speed is used to beat the defender. When the attacker has the ball in a midfield wing area at the restraining line or a yard or two inside it, he can make use of a burst of speed for approximately 10 yards to gain a step on his man and consequently get a good shot in the hole area. Since the attacker has the advantage of knowing when he is going to start his burst, he will be able to beat even a defender who is as fast as he. If the defender is slower, the attacker should have no trouble gaining the advantage if he runs at full speed throughout the dodge.

If the defender has similar to or greater speed and size than the attacker, the attacker can make use of change-of-pace maneuvers, head fakes, and stick fakes to throw the defender off balance. By driving hard and using one of these techniques, then bursting full speed in the original direction, he can gain a jump on his man.

The path that the attacker takes to get into prime shooting area is very important. Figure 6–6 shows three routes to the goal:

Route A. Too wide a path with much wasted motion. It is a roundhouse path that does not place pressure on the defender through most of the route.

Route B. The most effective path because the angle toward the goal keeps the defender on his toes throughout the dodge.

Route C. Just a bit too direct toward the goal and would necessitate complete overpowering of the defender. It also can make the attacker more susceptible to being double-teamed (played by two defenders), or in the case of the drive from behind the goal, the attacker can be shoved into the crease.

There are other dodges, which for the most part are combinations of the basic three—face, roll, and bull. Mastery of these three, however, will give a player all the weapons he needs to dodge his opponent. This applies to players on all levels, from "little league" to college varsity. The dodges can be used by players in all positions—goalies and defensemen as well as midfielders and attackmen. Defensemen, since their sticks are much longer than other players' sticks, are not able to bring the head of their sticks even with their own head for protection purposes. They should anticipate their opponents' trying to go over their head with a stick check.

INDIVIDUAL OFFENSE

SHOOTING

Since games are won by the goals scored, shooting plays a vital role in a team's success. Although being able to shoot the ball with power is important, the crucial factor in effective shooting is accuracy. One of the shocking statistics in lacrosse is the high percentage of shots that miss the goal completely. This statistic can be determined by adding the number of goals scored by a team and the number of saves by its opponent's goalie to give the total number of shots on the goal or "on target." The remainder of a team's total shots obviously have missed the goal. During my last three years of coaching at Hopkins, in 1972, '73, and '74, the team was NCAA runnerup twice and national champion in my final year, 1974. These were three excellent lacrosse teams, but the following statistics on shooting are surprising:

	Shots	Goals	Saves by opponents	On target	Missed goal
1972 Season (13 games)	630	159	187	54%	46%
1973 Season (14 games)	659	173	218	59	41
1974 Season (14 games)	771	228	239	61	39

The alarming fact is the large number of shots, a range of 39 to 46 percent, that did not hit the goal. The goal is certainly big enough, 6 feet by 6 feet, for much better accuracy on the part of the shooters. And what is more amazing, we really stressed accuracy in shooting in all of our practices, but nonetheless the results were not too promising. Our 1974 championship team did shoot 7 percent more accurately than the 1972 runnerup team, and in the three playoff games during each of those two years the '74 team was on target 61 percent of the time, compared with 50 percent for the '72 team. This improvement of 11 percent helped to make the difference between a championship team and a runnerup team.

When a shot ends up on target, inside the 6-by-6-foot area, three things can happen, and two of those are to the advantage of the offense.

1. The goalie makes a "clean" save and catches the ball in his stick.

2. The goalie makes a save with his body or stick but is unable to gain control of the ball.

3. The goalie misses the ball and a score results.

Obviously the first event is to the advantage of the defense and the other two favor the offense. When the goalie fails to make a clean save and get the ball in his stick, he is still in a vulnerable position because the ball often rebounds directly in front of the goal, where an offensive man can hit, kick, scoop, or catch it and shoot it into the goal. This type of score can be considered as a "cheap," or "garbage," goal, but it still puts one point on the scoreboard, the same as a spectacular dodging or passing play that brings the crowd to its feet.

One of the problems that plague all coaches is the desire of most players to take fancy but wild shots at the goal. These shots are fun to practice and bring loud acclaim from everyone watching when they go into the goal. However, the percentages of scoring are so poor that these shots often do more harm than good. When a cannonball shot rockets near the goal, all the "ohs and ahs" of the spectators do not add up to a single point on the scoreboard, and that is what counts.

In team practice sessions, the offensive players should take only the shots they will use in the game. They should not practice the fancy shots at all during this time. Emphasis must be placed on taking only the good shots and keeping them "on target" or on the "6-by-6." Shots can be classified in two general categories: outside shots and close-range shots.

Outside Shots

Outside shots are those normally taken between the restraining line and approximately the 12-yard mark and in a lateral area about 10 yards on either side of the center of the field. A shot taken past the 20-yard mark is considered to be too long and not very effective unless the shot is exceptionally hard and well screened. The man on the crease is responsible for screening, or interfering with, the goalie's vision when the driver has the ball in the area between the 20-yard and 12-yard marks. It is the responsibility of

Figure 6–4 Three phases of the inside roll ► dodge.

Figure 6–5 Two phases of the bull dodge.

the shooter to make sure he has a screen on the crease before taking the outside shot, especially those near the 20-yard mark. The closer he gets to the 12-yard mark, the less he has to check for a screen. Most outside shots should be bounced at the goal because they are harder for the goalie to follow than are the shots that are thrown into the air. If the shot is thrown at the feet of the screener, who is about 2 or 3 feet from the crease, the ball will normally bounce into the goal at a height between 2 and 6 feet. A bounce shot at this level is more difficult for the goalie to handle than one that stays fairly close to the ground. The one exception is a bounce shot on a wet field or on a thick, grassy field which, instead of rising, just skims the ground and catches the goalie off guard.

There is a simple key to aiming the long outside shot taken near the 20-yard mark—just shoot the ball at the center of the goal. More than likely it will go a foot or so to either side of center. But it will end up inside the 6-by-6. When a shooter starts aiming for a spot just inside the pipes, he is asking for trouble, because the margin of error will cause the ball to go outside the pipes too many times. When approaching the 12-yard

mark, the shooter is actually close enough to consider placing the ball on either side of the goalie with a high or low bounce shot. But he still should not get too fancy and try to place it just inside the pipes.

Close-Range Shots

Any shot taken between the 12-yard mark and the crease can be considered a close-range shot. These shots are high percentage scorers because of the proximity to the goal. The shooter keys on the body and stick position of the goalie and tries to place the ball where the goalie is most vulnerable. If the goalie's stick is high, the shooter can direct the ball low and vice versa. He also has the option of bouncing the ball or firing it in the air. But most important, he should shoot the ball hard and for an open area. At times a cutter or crease attackman who receives a feed from behind the goal makes the mistake of shooting the ball too fast and with little power, giving the goalie a better chance of making the save.

When an attacker who is behind the goal drives to the front, he should be mindful of going far enough to get a good angle for his shot. A shot taken from an angle of 15 degrees or less from

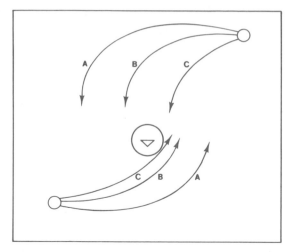

Figure 6–6 Attacker's path to get to the goal for a shot. Route **A** is too much of a roundhouse. Route **B** is most effective. Route **C** is too direct and unrealistic.

the plane of the goal is a poor risk, simply because the goalie's position will prevent it from scoring. Frequently the driver comes from behind the goal and just fires the ball at the goal without looking at the goalie's position. He makes the goalie look like an All-American by hitting him with the ball. Instead, he must try to place the ball. If the goalie fails to cover the near pipe properly and leaves too large a gap between his body and the pipe, the shooter aims for this area. It is easier to score this way than by going for the far side of the goal, because the ball travels a shorter distance and the goalie has less of a chance of stopping it with his body. If the goalie protects the near pipe well, then the shooter must go for the far side, either in the air or with a bounce shot.

If the shooter has the time, he can use a head-and-eye fake and/or a stick fake to make the goalie react. He then counters by shooting the ball to the area opposite the goalie's movement. The shooter must be careful not to overdo the fakes and thus delay his shot long enough for a defender to check his stick.

Close-range shooters often make the mistake of revealing where they are going to shoot the ball. A good example of this is when the shooter decides he is going to fire a low shot and moves his stick from the regular upright cradling position to a point below his knees. This maneuver

tips off the goalie, who then anticipates the low shot and makes the save. If the shooter decides he wants a low shot, he has a much better chance of scoring by shooting low from the three-quarter-arm position rather than from the underhand position with the head of the stick at the knees or lower.

It is amazing just how many times the shooter will miss the goal completely when the goalie is out of the goal. Instead of just shooting the ball at dead center of a wide-open goal, the shooter often goes for a spot just inside the pipes and misses. There is nothing quite so frustrating to a team than for one of its players to miss a wide-open goal. A classic example of this occurred on Homewood Field in the 1968 Army-Hopkins game. Geoff Berlin, our All-American goalie, made a save and ran behind the goal with the ball. He was a little slow in finding an open man and was double-teamed by the Army crease attackman and another attackman, who scooped up the ball and headed for the goal. He was a full 3 yards ahead of Berlin and there were no Hopkins players near the goal. It was a sure goal, at least to everyone in the stadium. However, instead of firing the ball directly into the middle of the wide-open goal, the Army attackman shot the ball about 6 inches from the ground. Instead of conceding the goal, Berlin, still trailing the Army man, took a head-first dive from behind the goal and landed with his shoulders next to the near pipe. He stretched his arms out with his stick on the ground in front of the goal, and sure enough, the only possible spot on the 6-by-6 where the attackman's shot could be stopped was exactly where he put it. It was an unbelievable effort on Berlin's part, and the crowd went wild. But then again, all the Army man had had to do was to shoot for dead center and he would have scored.

There are a variety of shots that offensive players can use in trying to score. Let's take a look at them.

Three-Quarter-Arm, or Over-the-Shoulder, Shot

The three-quarter-arm shot is the most effective of all the shots because it gives the greatest accuracy, and this is the most important factor in shooting. It also has as much power behind it as the other shots. The upper hand of the shooter is in a position over his shoulder, in much the same way that most pitchers and quarterbacks hold their arms when throwing. The same basic techniques that apply to throwing the ball also apply to shooting it, except it is done with as much power as possible. (See Figure 5–5 in Chapter 5.) The upper hand follows through in a vigorous throwing motion with a snap of the wrist as the lower hand pulls down hard on the butt end of the handle. The body weight transfers from the rear to the front leg in much the same fashion as an outfielder in baseball who catches a fly ball and fires to home plate to get a runner tagging up and trying to score from third base. The head of the stick actually ends up pointing to the ground because the body follow-through is so complete.

Sidearm Shot

The sidearm shot is popular among the players because considerable power can be generated with it, as much as if not more than with the three-quarter-arm shot. Its main shortcoming is that its accuracy is not consistent. However, if the head of the stick goes no lower than the shooter's belt, the sidearm shot can be developed to a point where it is effective from a stationary or slow-moving position. When the player is driving at full speed for a shot in the midfield area, the sidearm shot should be avoided, because it is difficult to control while on the run. The techniques in firing the sidearm shot are identical with those used in the three-quarter-arm shot with one exception: the path of the head of the stick. In the three-quarter-arm shot it is above the shoulder; in the sidearm shot, below the shoulder. Figure 6–7 shows a shooter with the sidearm motion.

Beginning players can be steered away from using the sidearm shot until they have mastered the basic techniques in handling the stick and shooting three-quarter-arm. An easy way to sell youngsters on this is to point out how few professional pitchers and quarterbacks use the sidearm throwing motion.

Underhand Shot

The underhand shot is very hard to control and should be eliminated from a shooter's repertoire unless he is able to keep it on target at least 75 percent of the time in a pressure situation. The

Figure 6–7 Three phases of the sidearm shooting motion.

techniques are the same in the underhand shot as the three-quarter-arm and sidearm shots, except that the head of the stick takes a path at or below the knees. If the control is limited from a sidearm position, it is obviously more so from the underhand position. In my twenty years of coaching only three or four players have been given the green light to shoot the underhand shot.

One-Hand Shot

The one-hand shot is not a routine shot because the shooter can get only a limited control of the stick with a one-hand grip compared with two. The shot became popularized with the advent of the plastic-head stick, which enables better ball handling. It is used primarily by attackmen who have maneuvered to a position no farther than 3 or 4 yards from the crease. Since defensemen are usually looking for the standard shots with two hands on the stick, they can be caught off guard and somewhat helpless in stopping the one-hand shot. The shooter gets power, although somewhat limited, by snapping his wrist and following through with either a sidearm or an underhand motion. Two of Hopkins' great attackmen, Jack Thomas, class of '74, and Franz Wittelsberger, class of '76, used this shot effectively. To get enough power and accuracy to take the one-hand shot from the midfield area, 15 yards

or more from the goal, requires an athlete with exceptional ability. The only one I have ever seen who used this shot at that distance from the goal was Jim Brown of Syracuse University, and he did it with a wooden stick, too. Brown put on a one-man show in the 1957 North-South College All-Star game at Homewood Field. In the first thirty-five minutes of the game he scored five goals for the North, the most spectacular being a 16-yard one-hander, which took his defender, the South goalie, and everyone else in the stadium completely by surprise.

The one-hand shot should not be taught to all offensive players but only to the most skillful attackmen, who will be operating close to the goal. A Jimmy Brown comes along only once or twice in every ten years, so midfielders in general should not be concerned with practicing this shot.

Backhand Shot

The backhand shot can be useful but only on a limited basis and at close range to the goal. Backhand shots are more difficult to control than forehand shots. The three-quarter-arm backhand shot is the most accurate and therefore the most effective. Both the defender and the goalie can be surprised with the shot, because the attacker can release the shot quickly from a position be-

hind his back and without giving any warning. Since the defender must place his stick in front of the attacker to prevent him from taking the forehand shot, the attacker can release the ball backhanded without interference from the defenseman's stick.

The sidearm shot taken on the run, as well as the underhand, one-hand, and backhand shots are very difficult to control and definitely should not be used by 95 percent of even first-line college players.

FEEDING

Passing the ball to an offensive man breaking toward the goal is referred to as "feeding." Most feeds come from attackmen operating behind the goal or on the side of it. They are made either to midfielders cutting for the goal, the crease attackman, or the attackman who operates behind the goal on the side opposite the feeder and breaks for the crease. This attackman is referred to as the "offside attackman." Some feeds are made by midfielders who pass the ball to attackmen in the crease area.

One of the most important factors in feeding the ball is proper positioning on the field. Proximity to the goal is essential in aiding the feeder to

INDIVIDUAL OFFENSE

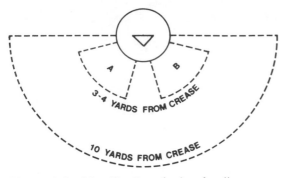

Figure 6–8 Identification of prime feeding areas behind goal. Areas **A** and **B** are the best.

determine the open man in the crease area. He must be able to get the ball to him quickly and with a limited chance for it to be intercepted or blocked. The farther the distance from the goal, the greater the opportunity for the feed to miss connection. Figure 6–8 shows the prime feeding area for an attackman operating behind the goal. The distance from the crease should not be greater than 9 or 10 yards at any point. If the defender is able to keep the feeder outside this area and near the back boundary line, the effectiveness of his feeding is curtailed considerably. The best feeding positions are identified as A and B in Figure 6–8, and they are at a distance of no farther than 3 or 4 yards from the crease. These positions are more desirable than the one directly behind the goal, because the feeder is closer to the man breaking to the onside of the field and his passing angle makes it easier for the cutter to catch the ball than to catch a feed from directly behind the goal. The feed to the offside cutter also has a good chance of being completed without the goalie's interference, because the goalie must be primarily concerned with the onside feed. This really opens up the back-side, or "back-door," feed. When the ball is fed from the point, a position directly behind the goal, the goalie's position will be in direct alignment with the feeder and the cutter about 50 percent of the time. This certainly gives him opportunity for more interceptions than the feeds from areas A and B.

A number of other considerations go into the development of a skillful feeder. He must keep his defender active and moving. When he is in the stationary position, the defender can put more pressure on him. By being moved toward the

goal, the defender has to be concerned with the possibility of his man trying to get to the front of the goal for a shot and therefore must play him as much as a dodger as a feeder. The attackman who doesn't drive for the goal but is content to play just as a feeder is going to take considerable punishment from his defender and be less successful as a feeder. Anticipation of a teammate's being open is a key factor in feeding, because if the feeder waits until he is open, it may be too late to get the ball to him. The feeder must keep his eyes glued on the hole. Teammates are working to get open to receive the pass, and the feeder must be looking for them. A common mistake for the beginner is either to look at the ground or to be so completely engrossed with his defender that he fails to see the open man. He should be aware of his defender's position and stick checks, but not oblivious to the crease area. A helpful hint for the feeder is to keep his "big eye" on the crease area and his "little eye" on his defender.

In actually making the pass the feeder can help himself by using both stick and head fakes just before releasing the ball. A quick fake in one direction and then a pass in another will take the pressure off the feeder. The defender's job is made much easier by the attackman whose eyes light up when he spots an open man. He tips off his feed and gives the defender an opportunity to block it. The pass itself should be thrown sharply, but its speed should be geared to the distance between feeder and cutter. The feeder does not want to knock his man over with a bulletlike feed when at close range. The feeder should give the cutter a lead pass to his stick side and slightly above his head. When receiving the ball in this position, the cutter can shoot the ball quickly and accurately.

CUTTING

The cutting game can give the offense its best scoring opportunities, because the cutter normally receives the feed right in front of the goal and is shooting at point-blank range. The goalie is in a disadvantageous position, looking at the ball when it is behind the goal with the feeder, and then with the pass he has little time to react to the cutter's shot. Since the pass by the feeder and the catch and shot by the cutter all take no longer than about two seconds, the goalie and his defensive teammates are placed in a precarious position.

Definite controls must be placed on the midfielders to keep them from cutting at inopportune times. It is the responsibility of the cutter to wait for the attackman to move into proper feeding position. It is senseless for the midfielder to cut when the feeder is too far from the goal to have a reasonable chance of getting the ball to him. Only one midfielder at a time should be allowed to cut. If two break for the goal at the same time, the crease area will be jammed with too many people, because the crease attackman is normally there also. Six bodies, including the three defenders, make for a lot of confusion and limit the chance for a completed pass and shot.

A number of techniques must be utilized by the midfielder in making his cut for the goal. Various fakes can throw his defender off stride. By looking one way and holding his stick on that particular side as he cuts, he can cause the defender to anticipate the feed there. Consequently the cutter will gain a step or two on his defender when he breaks to the side opposite his fakes. He can also cause the defender a problem by using a stutter-step maneuver running directly at the goal, giving several short steps to get the defender to lean in one direction and then breaking in the opposite direction for the feed. It is done most effectively down the middle of the field and by running right at the defender. The cutter should hold his stick close to the front of his body at the outset of his cut. When he is about 4 or 5 yards from the crease and a step or two ahead of his defender, he then gives the feeder a target with the head of his stick slightly above his head and on the side to which he is breaking.

Since the cutter receives the feed in prime shooting area, he can expect the defender's check to come fast and with power. He must therefore be ready to take his shot quickly. In the "quick-stick" technique the cutter draws back with the head of his stick a split second before the ball hits into his pocket, then in one motion he catches and shoots the ball. He does not bat the ball. The shot is released quickly, but often the cutter has difficulty in getting his shot to go on target. The better technique is the "quick-wrist." In catching the ball, the cutter gives one quick cradling action with his hand and wrist and then shoots the ball. The control of the ball is much better and so is the accuracy in shooting, because the cutter has a split second longer to look at the goal and determine the goalie's location. It is important in both the quick-stick and the quick-wrist techniques for the cutter to look at the goal before shooting. At times cutters release their shot so fast they really don't see the goal but are just throwing the ball blindly in the right general direction.

If the cutter does not receive the ball after making his cut to the crease, he has several options. He can break to the other side of the crease for a possible feed. He can set a pick for the crease attackman in an effort to free him for a feed. (A pick is the positioning of an attacker's body in the way of a defensive player, thus causing the defender to have difficulty in staying with his man.) He can return to the midfield area, near the restraining line, to open up the crease area for another midfielder to make a cut. The one thing the cutter does not want to do is to stay in the crease area for more than five or six seconds and jam up the area. The opportunity to feed the crease is better when the action is continuous, with different players making cuts.

INDIVIDUAL OFFENSE

7

team
offense

The structuring of a team's offense is vital to its success. Games are won by scoring goals, and a team must utilize the talents of its ballplayers to give them the opportunity to score. This requires detailed organization by the coach and a thorough understanding of the offensive strategy by each attackman and midfielder. A disorganized offense can completely demoralize a team. Confusion will reign when there is little coordination between attack and midfield units and players are allowed to free-lance and "do their own thing" without their teammates' awareness and cooperation.

Normally a team will score close to half its goals on the unsettled play—intercepting a clearing pass, taking the ball away from the goalie or a defenseman, dodging an overaggressive defender who forces the attacker to dodge, gaining possession of a ground ball after a big scramble and pressing for the goal, and fast breaks that initiate at the defensive end of the field. The goals scored in these situations are the easy ones, because the defense is not settled and ready to meet the attack. The more goals a team can score this way, the better its chances of winning.

The other half of a team's goals come from the settled, all-even play. A team has to work with persistence and patience in trying to score in this situation. Some offenses are attack-oriented, some midfield-oriented. The capabilities of the players determine the emphasis. In any offensive play, all six players are involved if it is to be successful. Some may have to be good "actors" while others are carrying out the primary effort to score. However, no player can just "stand around" and watch the play and consequently allow his defender to help stop the play.

Down through the years the great national collegiate championship teams have been well balanced in scoring ability from both the attack and midfield positions. However, there have been many other championship teams that have geared their offense primarily to the attack. In 1957–59 Hopkins had the Gold-Dust twins, Billy Morrill and Mickey Webster. In 1964–66 Navy had Jimmy Lewis, and many of us can still hear Bildy (Coach Willis P. Bilderback) shouting to his team, "Get the ball to Jimmy." Joe Cowan led Hopkins in 1967–69 and Jack Thomas in 1972–74. Each of these players was a first-team All-American attackman for three years, so obviously the offense of their teams was geared to the attack.

Although definitely in the minority, there have been championship teams with midfield-directed offenses. The 1975 Maryland team was led by one of the all-time great midfielders, Frank Urso, and his faceoff specialist partner, Doug Radebaugh. These two were first-team All-Americans and the backbone of the Maryland team, which finished the '75 season like gang busters. This Maryland team and the 1970 Hopkins team were the only two national champions in the past twenty-five years that did not have an attackman on either the first or second All-American team. Midfield offense was predominant with both these teams.

This was especially so with the 1970 Hopkins team, which only lost one game and shared the national championship with Navy and Virginia. Joe Cowan had graduated in 1969, and our attack group had limited varsity experience. We therefore set up an offense that centered on midfield plays, midfield dodges, midfield flipoffs (midfielders making short passes to open teammates), and midfield invert action (midfielders operating behind the goal instead of in their regular midfield position). Four midfielders—Charlie Coker, Doug Honig, Bill Donovan, and Gary Handleman—carried the scoring load for the entire team. In a ten-game schedule these four scored fifty-five goals and the other five players who ran regularly on our three midfield units scored a total of seven goals for the season. Although the three starting attackmen scored only thirty-two goals for the season, they carried out their responsibilities extremely well in other areas—setting up the midfielders, hustling for ground balls, and riding with determination. None of our attackmen made any of the All-American teams, not even Honorable Mention. This was the only time in the fifty-four years since the All-American team was first selected in 1922 that the national-championship team did not have

an attackman on one of the All-American teams. In forty-two of those years the champion has had either two or three of its attackmen on one of the All-American teams and only in eleven years has it had just one. We were very proud of the 1970 team and its unheralded attack but felt the key to our success was our midfield-oriented offense.

BASIC STYLES OF OFFENSE

There are different styles of offense, and most teams make use of a combination of them. Dodging and flipoffs, the cutting game, set plays, inverts, and a fast-break, move-the-ball offense are the basic ways to score in the settled situation. Regardless of the style, discipline is a key factor. Each player must know his responsibilities within the system and carry them out to the letter.

Dodging and Flipoffs

One of the easiest ways to get a goal is to give the ball to a talented dodger, clear out the area, and unleash him for the goal. The clearout, or isolation, maneuver gives the dodger an entire section of the field in which to beat his man. As soon as the defender commits himself, the driver gains at least a half step and moves in for a medium- to close-range shot. If a team has talented dodgers, it should make maximum use of their skills.

A numbering system can be used to simplify the organization of the offense. Figure 7–1 identifies the positions with the odd numbers 1 and 5 on the left side and the even numbers 2 and 4 on the right side. Numbers 3 and 6 are in the middle and have no significance in the signal system. By using a two-digit system an offensive player can make a call that will tell all five of his teammates what he is planning to do. An odd number call indicates he is going to the left side of the field and an even number to the right.

If an attackman wants to drive for the goal through the 1 position, trying to dodge his man in the 1-to-5 area, he calls out any two-digit odd number. For example, in Figure 7–2 player O2 calls out, "37," and then times his drive to give O1 a chance to move inside him to the even side of the field. Also O3 and O5 can cut to that side. However, O1 actually maintains a position on the crease that mirrors, or is directly opposite, the

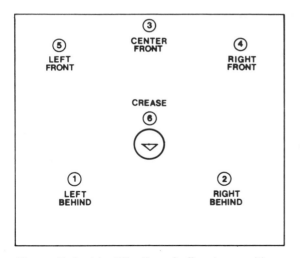

Figure 7–1 Identification of offensive positions around the goal.

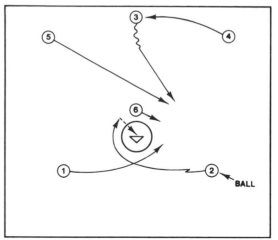

Figure 7–2 Clearout maneuver for O2, who drives for the goal in the 1–5 area and takes a shot.

dodger. This clearly removes his defender from helping out. The call lets every offensive player know exactly where the dodger wants to go and consequently clears out the entire side for his attempt. Then O4 moves toward the middle of the field to act as an outlet, just in case O2 does not complete the dodge.

Clearouts can be set up for midfielders in a similar manner. If O4 wants a right-handed drive, he calls out an odd number. This causes O1, O3, and O5 to respond by breaking to the even side of the field to get their men out of the backup position. They should be good actors when they make their move, because it is important for their defenders to go with them. They can fake their man by calling for the ball, putting their sticks up as if they want a pass, or setting a pick for a teammate on the side of the field to which they are going. It is not advisable to set a pick for the dodger, because it enables the defense to switch or double-team him.

Dodges can also be disguised by faking a set three-man play. The man who is normally the feeder in the play turns out to be the dodger. This maneuver can be planned when a midfield unit is on the sidelines or during a time-out. If the unit has already used the three-man play in the game with its special call, it makes the same call but then fakes the play with the feeder going for the goal. If the feeder gives a realistic fake of a feeding attempt, he will often draw overaggressive

checks by his defender and gain an advantage for his dodge. Figure 7–3 shows O4 faking the feed to either O3 or O5 and then going for the goal. Players O3 and O5 fake their three-man play with both breaking to the even side of the field as if they are going to receive the pass, but in reality they are just clearing out the area for O4's dodge. Also O1 makes a clearout break. The same kind of action can take place with the close attackmen faking a three-man play and opening up an area for a dodge.

The flipoff game is a natural complement to the dodging game. When the defense gets burned by dodgers, it becomes very anxious to back up on them. This is the time for the offense to make use of flipoffs. By giving the ball to the dodger and making a call similar to the one used in a clearout, the offense can capitalize on the defense's anxiety to stop the dodger. In 1965 the primary scoring threat of our Hopkins team was Jerry Pfeifer, an All-American attackman. In preparing for our game with the University of Virginia at Homewood Field, we emphasized the flipoff game in our practices that week, because we anticipated Virginia's double-teaming Pfeifer every time he drove for the goal. Sure enough, Virginia's defensemen did just that, and although they held him to just one goal in the game, they were completely vulnerable to his flipoffs to open teammates, and he registered eight assists in a

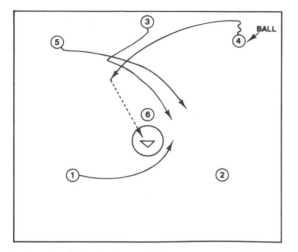

Figure 7–3 The fake of the three-man midfield play and the clearout for O4, who takes the shot.

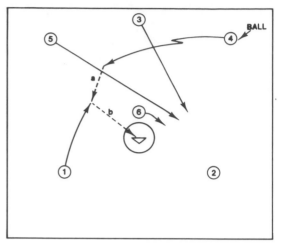

Figure 7–4 The fake of a clearout for O4 and the flipoff (**a**) to O1, who takes the shot (**b**).

17–6 Hopkins victory. Although not normally a feeder, as indicated by a total of only sixteen assists for the rest of the season, he found an open man time and again for flipoffs and excellent shots that day.

In the flipoff game one man is placed in the area to which the driver is going, and he anticipates his defender's move toward the dodger. This leaves him open for a flipoff from the dodger. In Figure 7–4 the flipoff man is O1. When his defender moves, he follows him, trying to get into position for a good shot. He keeps his stick to the outside, away from possible defensive stick checks on the inside, and gives the dodger a target with his stick. When he catches the ball, his feet should be positioned to allow his body to turn immediately toward the goal. He is primed to shooting the ball quickly, because he will undoubtedly draw a hard charge from the nearest defender. In making use of the flipoff game, the best left-handed shooters should be placed in the flipoff position for a midfield dodger going to the left (odd) side or an attack dodger going to the right (even) side, and vice versa for the best right-handed shooters.

When the defense is very slide-conscious to both the dodger and the flipoff man, the offense can counter with another maneuver. It can fake the dodge and the flipoff and make use of a cut by an offside midfielder into the hole area. Since

the defense becomes especially ball-conscious when an attackman forces into good shooting position near the goal, it is vulnerable to the cut. Figure 7–5 shows O1 driving for the goal, faking the flipoff to O5, and passing the ball to O3, who makes his cut when his defender either turns his head to look at the dodger or starts to slide toward the ball. Actually any of the offside attackers (O2, O3, or O4) can make the cut, but it is advisable to designate one. Otherwise two or even all three may cut at the same time and jam up the area.

Two-Man Plays

In addition to the set plays, which are used for dodging and flipoff purposes, there are several effective maneuvers for just two players. The two-man plays involve mostly the setting of the pick or faking the pick. They are used both behind the goal and in the midfield. Proper use of the pick depends on both the man setting the pick as well as the man with the ball. The pick man tries to set the pick no farther than 3 to 4 feet from the defender playing the ball. He actually tries to get as close to the defender as possible without moving into him and committing a technical foul. He faces the defender squarely and places his feet a little wider than shoulder-width, splitting the heels of the defender. This position places the middle of his body directly in the defender's

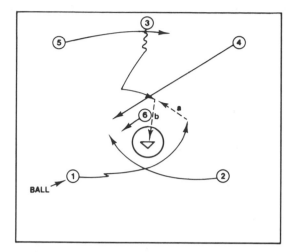

Figure 7–5 The fake of a clearout for O1, who fakes the flipoff to O5 and passes the ball (**a**) to O3, making a cut from the off side.

path and forces the defender either to hit him or to maneuver around him. If contact is made, the pick man should be ready to move back rather than to give any impetus into the defender that could be interpreted by the official as a moving pick. This is the most common error in using the pick. Another routine mistake is to set the pick in front of the defender, where the pick will serve no purpose because the defender will run by it. The pick man wants to pick the defender, not thin air. After a successful pick, which necessitates a switch of men by the two defenders, the pick man breaks for the goal, looking for a short lead pass from the driver. This pick-and-roll maneuver is identical with the one basketball players use as one of their key offensive weapons.

The fake of a pick can upset the defender playing the ball. The offensive man runs right at the defender, then breaks behind him, making sure he does not hit him. This momentary distraction is often enough to give the driver a half-step advantage, which is all he needs to open up the opportunity for a good shot. Another fake-pick maneuver that is troublesome for the defender is accomplished by the attacker driving toward the defender playing the ball as if to set a pick on him. When 2 or 3 yards from him, he breaks for the goal and looks for an over-the-shoulder pass. He frequently is open in this situation because

his defender is anticipating the pick and the possibility of his having to call for a switch so he can play the driver. This play is more effective when run by the midfield in front of the goal rather than the attack behind the goal, because there is more room for the break to the goal. It is advisable to use the play only after several picks have been executed successfully.

The stackup maneuver is another offensive weapon that stems from the pick play and is used primarily behind the goal by attackmen. Figure 7–6 shows the entire play. Once the ball carrier moves into the stackup position, which is directly behind the pick man, he has the opportunity to feed the ball without pressure from his defender. If the pick is set close to the goal, he is in ideal feeding position. When the two defenders try to dismantle the stackup, they subject themselves to a difficult situation that frequently results in both playing the same man, allowing the other to break open for the goal. When the ball carrier moves into the stackup position, he is facing the goal in order to see both defenders and to react to their movement. The pick man also faces toward the goal for the same purpose. If the defender makes his move from the left side, the ball carrier counters by going to the right and vice versa. The pick man waits for an opening to be created by both defenders becoming involved with the ball carrier and disregarding him. He then breaks for the goal, calls to the ball carrier to alert him, and looks over his shoulder for the pass. When the ball carrier gets double-teamed, he backs away from the defenders rather than trying to force through them and looks to pass off to the pick man.

Three-Man Midfield Plays

The three-man plays involve basically a pass in one direction and a pick in the opposite direction. Figure 7–7 shows the three-man play that starts with O3 in the midfield. He passes the ball to O5 and then runs to set a pick at the heels of the defender playing O4. When O4 sees his teammate running his way, he takes several steps toward the goal to force his defender to move in. When O3 is about 2 to 3 yards away, O4 breaks behind him and tries to direct his defender into the pick. If the pick is successful, O4 is open to receive a pass from O5. It is important for O5 to make an accurate pass, because O4 will more

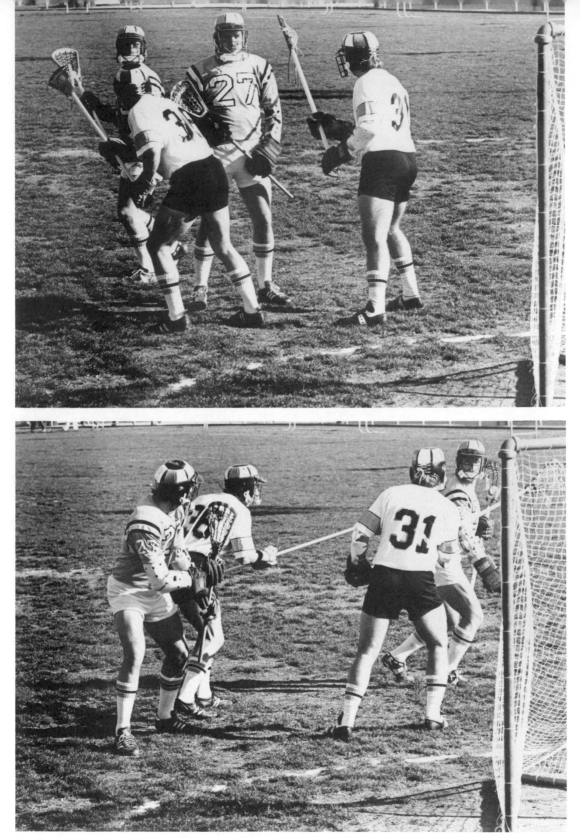

Figure 7-6 Two phases of the stackup maneuver.

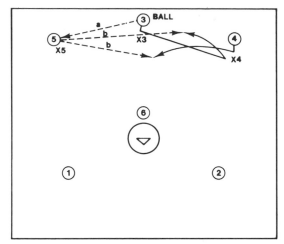

Figure 7–7 Three-man midfield play with O3 passing to O5 (**a**) and setting the pick for O4. After O4 drives off the pick, O3 rolls back, looking for the pass. Player O5 has the option of passing to either O4 or O3 (**b**).

than likely have some sort of defensive pressure, even though he has gained a step or two on his man. Player O5 must occupy his defender by first driving a few steps for the goal in the right-handed bull-dodge position, then roll back toward his original position to make a left-handed pass to O4. A common mistake is O5's failure to move and thus to disguise the fact that he is really a feeder in this play. With his movement, however, he doesn't want to get too far away from O4 and make a pass that is any longer than 10 to 12 yards. When O4 receives the pass, he makes a decision to shoot the ball, to keep driving for the goal to get a closer shot, or just to keep control of the ball because the defense has reacted well and not given him an opening.

If the two defenders make a switch in this situation, O4's effectiveness is minimized, but his teammate O3 should be open on the pick-and-rollback maneuver. Player O4 drives toward the goal as soon as the switch is made, trying to make it difficult for X4 to cover O3. On his roll back O3 moves toward O5 and away from the goal, creating a gap of about 3 yards or more between X4 and himself. This puts O3 in an advantageous position, because he has time to crank up and take the outside shot at about the 15-yard mark. If X4 rushes at him to stop the

shot, he is in an ideal position either to face- or to roll-dodge and go for the goal.

Another offensive wrinkle from the pass-and-pick series is the stepout move for O4. It is similar to the rollback maneuver used by O3. When O3 sets the pick, O4 does not drive off it but instead steps back to open up a distance of about 3 yards from his defender (X4) (see Figure 7–8). This gap gives him the opportunity to take the outside screen shot or, better yet, the fake of the shot and the crossover-step face dodge. When making his pass O5 wants to be closer to the middle of the field rather than in his wing position. After setting his pick, O3 breaks for the goal to clear out his defender and give O4 a 1-on-1 situation.

The three-man midfield plays just explained can be run on the opposite side of the field. In addition, the same three-man plays can be effective by combining an attackman with two midfielders. Player O4 becomes the middle man, who starts the play by passing the ball to O3 and then moving to O2 for the pick action. The various maneuvers (drives off the pick, rollbacks, and stepouts) can place even more pressure on the defense, because the attackers are operating closer to the goal and a completed pass can result in a close-range shot. The relative distances between players should be the same for the combination midfield-attack three-man plays

Figure 7–8 The stepout move for O4, who steps back from O3's pick rather than breaking off it. Player O4 receives the pass (**b**) from O5 and can either shoot or dodge.

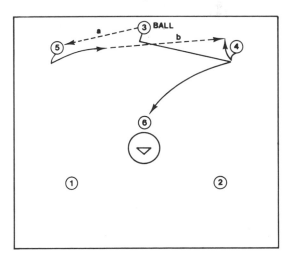

as for the all-midfield plays. Figure 7–9 shows the three players executing a pick-and-rollback play from a balanced alignment. This maneuver, plus the other two, can also be worked from the other side of the field.

Additional pressure can be placed on the defenseman (X2) by involving the crease attackman (O6) and having him set a double pick with O4. A double pick is the positioning of two attackers side by side in an attempt to prevent a defender from staying with his man. Proper timing in setting the pick and breaking the attackman off the pick is an important factor. A complementary play using the crease attackman in a double pick is shown in Figure 7–10. Player O2 breaks off the double pick and goes to the opposite side of the crease; O4 remains in a stationary pick position. As soon as O2 runs by the double pick, O6 breaks off O4's pick toward O3, who is the feeder. When he catches the ball, O6 is ready to shoot immediately.

The fishhook move is similar to the rollback. Any of the three midfielders can initiate it by passing the ball to another middie and then driving for the crease attackman. Figure 7–11 shows O4 faking the pick for O6 and hooking back toward O3 for the feed. Player O3 should fire the ball directly at his head or slightly to the outside.

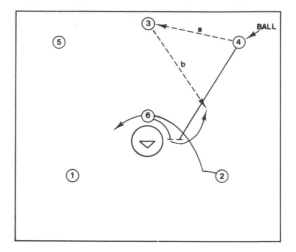

Figure 7–10 Three-man play with O6 setting a double pick with O4. After O2 drives off the pick, O6 breaks off both O4 and O2, looking for the pass (**b**) from O3.

As soon as he receives it, O4 can take a right-handed jump shot or else be ready to make a quick roll dodge and shoot left-handed.

Figure 7–9 Three-man play with midfield and attack working together. Player O4 passes (**a**) to O3 and sets pick for O2. After O2 breaks off the pick, O4 rolls back looking for the pass (**b**).

Figure 7–11 The fishhook move by O4, who passes to O3 and breaks for O6. After O6 cuts off his moving pick, O4 hooks back toward O3 and looks for the pass (**b**).

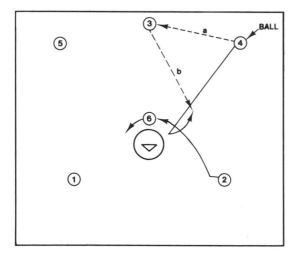

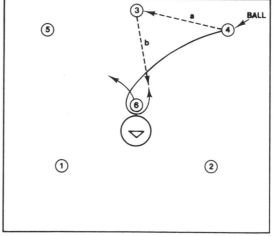

Three-Man Attack Plays

An unlimited number of workable plays can be designed for the three attackmen. However, a series of four that complement each other will be explained. The man with the ball initiates each of these plays by making a predetermined call or signal and then passing the ball to his teammate behind the goal.

The first play involves the basic pass-and-pick maneuver (see Figure 7–12). Player O1 passes the ball to O2 and breaks hard for the crease area to set a pick for O6, the crease attackman; O6 positions himself 3 or 4 yards from the crease and in line with the offside pipe of the goal. This gives him enough room to break off the pick and receive the feed in a position with a good shooting angle. If he starts from the middle of the field, his angle will be less effective because he will be 4 to 5 feet closer to the plane of the goal. Then O6 tries to drive his defender into the pick, and as soon as he does, he gives the feeder a target with his stick in front of his body and on the right side. After setting the pick, O1 breaks for his left-handed shot.

If the defenders switch on the pick play, O6 realizes he probably will not be open and he runs a wider path to his right. He does this in an effort to get his defender away from the crease, because O1 actually reverses his path, breaking for his right-handed shot on the crease. There is a good chance O1 will be open when the defenders switch. Since the primary action is geared to the left side of the crease, O2 should time his maneuvering behind the goal to be in the best feeding position to deliver the ball to the right-handed cut of O6. This position is in the left behind and no farther than 5 yards from the crease.

The second play follows the same pattern as the first up to the point of O6's cut. Instead of breaking off O1's pick to free himself, he breaks directly toward the goal and right next to O1, giving a target with his stick as if he were trying to get open for a feed. Actually, he is just acting as a moving screen for O1, who breaks off him as soon as he goes by (see Figure 7–13). The defender playing O1 normally has difficulty in covering him, especially if O1 makes his break parallel to the plane of the goal or even slightly away from the goal to gain distance from him. It is especially important on this play for the wing midfielder (O5) to cut to the opposite side of the field to prevent his man from interfering with O1's

Figure 7–12 Three-man-attack play with O1 passing to O2 (**a**) and setting the pick for O6. After O6 drives off the pick, O1 breaks for the goal. Player O2 has the option of passing to O6 or O1 (**b**).

Figure 7–13 Three-man-attack play with O1 passing to O2 and setting pick for O6. Player O6 does not use the pick himself but breaks directly for the goal, acting as a moving screen for O1, who steps out for the feed (**b**) from O2.

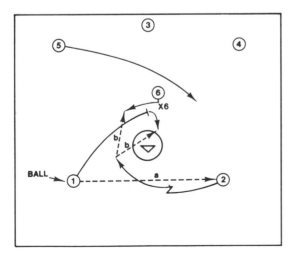

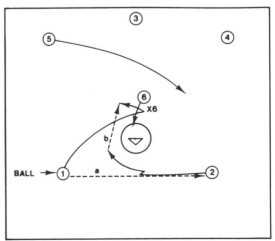

stepout play; O2 makes his feed from the left behind position.

The third play is identical with the first play in its entirety but adds another pick, which often catches the defense by surprise. Since this play complements the first play, it should be used only after the first one has been run. See Figure 7–14. Players O1 and O6 overact on their first cuts, trying to get the defense to relax after stopping them. Then O6 pivots and quickly sets a pick for O1, who has cut left-handed and is trying to occupy his defender on his left side. As soon as the pick is about to be set, O1 makes his break close to it and in a path parallel to the plane of the goal or slightly away from the goal. This gives him a cushion from O6's defender, who may make the switch; O2 maintains the same feeding position as on the first two plays. He anticipates O1's move off the pick and fires the ball slightly to his right, giving him a point-blank right-handed shot. Since this play makes use of two picks, it is known as the "double play."

The fourth play is merely an alternative move for the other three plays. Figure 7–15 shows O1 driving for the crease as if to set a pick for O6. However, when he is about one yard from his normal pick position, he breaks back toward the sideline and slightly away from the crease. This

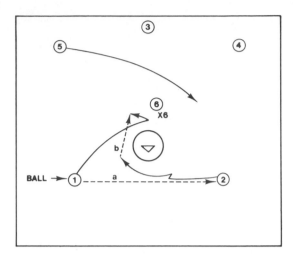

Figure 7–15 Three-man-attack play with O1 passing to O2 and driving for the crease as if to set pick for O6. When a yard or two from O6, he breaks back for the feed (**b**) from O2.

gives him the same gap he tries to get on his stepout move. Often the defender is so engrossed with the possibility of a switch developing when O1 moves toward the crease that he is caught unaware of O1's comeback maneuver. Player O2's feed must be even more accurate on this play than on the others because the shooter normally has less time to take the shot. It also must not be late, because O1 will then have a poor shooting angle.

All four of these plays can be run on the right side of the field as well as the left. Regardless of which side is being used, the same key points must be emphasized. The midfielder on the side of the ball, known as the "onside midfielder," cuts to the opposite side of the field to clear out his defender and keep him from jamming up the critical area and possibly double-teaming the shooter. The feeder makes his passes from the best feeding position. Too many times he fails to do so and makes a feed that is blocked or intercepted by a defenseman or goalie. Since the plays complement one another, they should be run with a definite pattern or sequence. Finally, all six players on the offense should know exactly what play is being run so they can get in the proper positions to carry out their responsibilities.

Figure 7–14 Three-man-attack play identical in its first phase with Figure 7–12. It adds the second phase with O6 setting a second pick for O1, hence the name "double play."

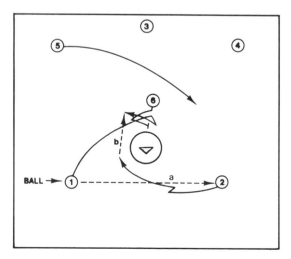

The Cutting Game

Scoring opportunities that result from successful cuts and feeds to the crease area are the most productive, because the cutter ends up taking either a close-range or point-blank shot. However, coordination between the feeder and cutter is not easy to achieve, because it requires discipline and control as well as excellent stick work. The individual techniques of feeding and cutting are explained in Chapter 6.

A team can employ two types of cutting systems. One is a free-lance system with cutters making their moves on their own although within certain general guidelines. Proper timing, allowing only one cutter at a time, and backing up the feeds are the most important considerations. The crease attackman can position himself in either a high post (6 to 7 yards from the crease) or a low post (3 to 4 yards from the crease). After the midfielder makes a cut and doesn't get the feed, he can double back and set a pick for the creaseman. If the creaseman makes a cut to the side opposite the middie's initial cut, he can wait on the crease for the middie to execute the same double move that is used in one of the three-man attack plays.

The other system employs a series of predetermined cut-and-pick plays, which are executed on a specific call or signal. These plays can be run from any of the basic offensive alignments, but one of the most successful is the 2–1–1–2 alignment or, as it is sometimes called, "the I," because of its shape. Figure 7–16 shows the alignment of personnel. Players O1 and O2 are in their normal attack positions behind the goal; O4 and O5 line up at the restraining line or a yard inside it and about 10 yards apart. The crease attackman (O6) assumes a high-post position, 6 to 7 yards from the crease; O3 moves directly behind O6 and about 2 feet from him, both facing the goal. This position almost forces O3's defender to play next to or in front of O6. If he decides to play in the gap between O3 and O6, he is vulnerable to being picked off. The two defenders playing O3 and O6 are placed in a pressure situation where complete coordination is essential. If there is a breakdown in their communication and teamwork, one of the cutting attackers will be wide open for a point-blank shot on the crease.

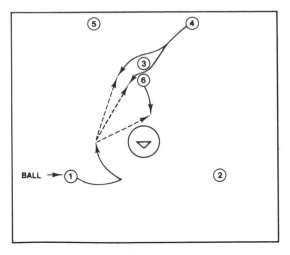

Figure 7–16 The I-formation with O4 cutting behind or in front of O3. Player O6 reads the defense's reaction and cuts for the goal. Player O1 has the option to feed either cutter.

Any number of plays from both sides of the field can be worked from this alignment. One of the basic ones is a cut off the double pick by the offside midfielder, who is on the side away from the ball, as shown in Figure 7–16. The call or signal that identifies the play is given to alert all six offensive men. It is important for O4 to wait for O1 to get into prime feeding territory before making his cut; O4 has the option of making his cut either behind O3 or between O3 and O6. Either route can place pressure on his defender, because he must move through an area that is fairly congested with four bodies. Once he drives off the post, he goes directly for the goal, giving a right-handed target with his stick. Player O6 watches his defender's reaction to the cut, and if he either switches to play O4 or just gets confused with the action, then O6 makes his cut for the goal. He can cut left-handed for the back-side feed from O1, or he can cut right-handed for the onside feed. After the action off the double pick, O3 looks to back up the feed just in case the pass is not completed. Player O1 has the option of feeding O4 or O6, or, if neither is open, he can pass the ball to O5. Often O5's defender will drop in close to the double post to help jam up O4's cut, but by so doing he opens up too much distance from O5. When O5 receives the pass from

O1 in this situation, he is in a favorable position to dodge. It obviously makes sense to place the best midfield dodger in this spot. Since O3's responsibility is limited to setting a post and backing up the feed, the midfielder with the least offensive ability can be assigned to this position.

An effective followup play is the double pick for the offside attackman (see Figure 7–17). After O4 makes his right-handed cut to the goal, he then cuts across the crease with his stick in his left hand as if anticipating a feed from O1. He continues to a point about 1 to 2 feet from the crease and sets a pick near the plane of the goal. Player O6 times his left-handed cut, about a second or two after O4 has passed him, to assure his arrival at the right side of the crease at just about the same time as O4. He stations himself next to O4, forming a double pick. Player O2 must also time his break for the goal to enable him to use the double pick no more than a second or two after it is established. He anticipates a pass from O1 immediately after he comes off the pick and is ready for the point-blank, right-handed shot. On this play O3 moves back to the restraining line after O4's initial cut, because he wants to move his defender from a position where he might possibly interfere with O2's shot. If O1 decides not to feed the ball to O2, he then has the option of

Figure 7–17 The I-formation double-pick play with O4 and O6 setting the pick after their cut. Player O2 makes his break off the pick and looks for the feed from O1.

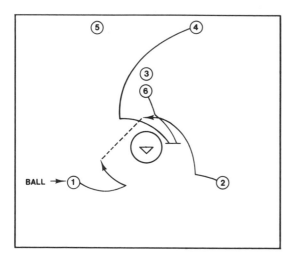

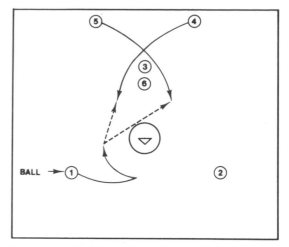

Figure 7–18 The I-formation double cross cut by O4 and O5. Player O1 has the option to feed either cutter.

dodging himself on the left side of the goal, since the area is cleared out, or he can pass the ball out to O5 for a possible midfield dodge.

Another play is shown in Figure 7–18. It involves a double cross cut by the two outside midfielders. Player O3 moves to the restraining line immediately after the second cutter goes by, because he must be in position to back up O1's feed; O6 remains in his high post to open the crease area for O4 and O5. However, if there is a foulup by the defenders and he sees an opening, he makes a break for the goal.

There are many other plays that can be run from the I formation. However, it is important for a team to select only the ones that make the best use of its personnel, to practice these plays every day, and to strive for perfection. Timing is the key. Too many plays, none of which are run with precision, can result in a disorganized, ineffective team offense.

Inverts

By inverting the offensive personnel—midfielders operating behind the goal and attackmen in the midfield area—the defense is given another headache. Its defenders are not comfortable playing their men in unfamiliar areas. Defensemen are normally not as confident playing attackmen in the midfield as behind the goal for several reasons. The attackmen have more operating room in the midfield; they are facing the goal, and a quick move in either direction can gain an advantage that results in a good shot. Midfield defenders are even more unsure of themselves playing a man behind the goal. They normally get very little practice in the techniques of guarding a man in this area and stopping his penetration to the goal. They also do not have the advantage of the longer defense stick to put pressure on their man and keep him from getting close to the crease for the point-blank shot. Since most teams have at least one midfielder who is not a strong defensive player, it is advisable to try to take advantage of his weakness by dodging him behind the goal, where he will be even more vulnerable than in the midfield. In addition to dodging from the invert position, many two- and three-man plays can be run.

Fast-Break, Move-the-Ball Offense

With the advent of the plastic stick and the growth of little-league lacrosse, many more high-school and college players than ever before have superior stick work. Consequently teams in the seventies have stressed continuous movement of the ball with both short and long passes. The NCAA national championship teams of Virginia 1972, Maryland 1973, and Hopkins 1974 displayed superior stick work and moved the ball with real authority.

The fast break is a basic offensive weapon, giving many excellent scoring opportunities with an extra-man advantage. Even if the extra-man advantage is not achieved, the quick movement of the ball to the offensive half of the field puts more pressure on the defense than the deliberate, slow-moving advance. Following the pattern of the fast-break game used in basketball, lacrosse teams clear the ball by sending their midfielders into specific lanes and their attackmen into specific locations to facilitate the movement of the ball to the goal. When the ball advances to an attackman behind the goal, he has the choice of feeding an open cutter, dodging his defender, or passing the ball to a teammate just to keep the ball moving and the defense adjusting. The dodge from this wide-open situation is often more effective because the defense is not in position

to back up on the dodger and jam the crease area. The offense tries to take advantage of this free-wheeling opportunity, but if nothing develops as all six players move inside the perimeter, the regular offense with dodges, flipoffs, set plays, cuts, or inverts is employed.

SCREENING

The attack tries to make it difficult for the goalie to see the ball clearly when it is near or inside the perimeter in the midfield area and up to a point about 12 yards from the goal. This interference with the goalie's vision is known as "screening." Screen shots, especially those taken near the 20-yard mark, can be very demoralizing to a team when they go into the goal. Since the shot is such a long one, the defenders often feel the goalie should have made the save and consequently they lose a little confidence in him. They don't realize that the screen made it difficult for him to follow the flight of the ball. This type of a score is frustrating to the goalie, because he knows it makes him look bad in the eyes of the fans, his coach, and, most important, his teammates.

The crease attackman is responsible for doing most of the screening and assumes his position when the ball is several yards from the restraining line. The optimum spot is about one yard from the crease. Much less than that makes him vulnerable to being pushed into the crease on a loose ball within 5 yards; much farther makes it difficult for him to interfere with the goalie's vision. He places himself in a direct line with the goalie and the man with the ball. Since the ball leaves the shooter's stick about 2 to 3 feet to the shooter's side rather than directly in front of his body, the screener actually lines up with the goalie and a point several feet on the ball carrier's stick side. This is a vital point in screening, because too often the screener does not take this position but, rather, lines up with the shooter's body and the goalie and consequently does not give an effective screen. As the ball is moved within the midfield area, he moves with it in order to maintain his screening position. When the shooter fires the ball, he tries to stay in front of it as long as possible. He jumps in the air if it is shot at his feet or quickly moves to the side if it is in the air. He keeps his eye on the ball at all times, and as soon as the ball passes, he immediately turns to face the goal and looks for a rebound off the goalie's stick or body. The screener's stick is kept close to his body until the ball is loose in the crease area. Then he strikes with cobralike quickness to avoid the defender's check and to direct the ball into the goal.

Since the defender will be trying to shove him either into or away from the crease to keep him from playing the loose ball, the screener must be ready to use his body to counteract the pressure from the defender. When the ball carrier approaches the 12-yard mark, the screener no longer maintains the screen, because it is too difficult for him to avoid being hit with the ball at such close range. He moves to the side of the pipes to open up the entire goal for the shooter. Once the ball is shot, however, he moves in front of the goal to play the rebound if the goalie does not make a clean save.

BACKING UP THE GOAL

Although the term "backup" is used by the defense for a maneuver to give assistance to the man playing the ball carrier, the offense uses the same term but with a different meaning. An attackman backs up the goal whenever a shot is taken. He lines up about a yard or two from the back edge of the crease and tries to catch any shots that miss the goal. Once he makes the backup, he looks immediately to the crease area for a possible feed to an open man. If he misses the ball and it starts to go out of bounds, he runs at top speed for the point where the ball will go out of play. If he is closest to the ball when it goes out, the referee will give him possession. Although one attackman can accomplish the job, normally two, one on each side of the goal, will back up shots by the midfielders. When an attackman dodges from behind the goal and shoots, only one attackman makes the backup by moving to a position on the crease that is opposite to the shooter.

Midfielders are also involved in backups when an attackman feeds the ball into the crease area. They back up the feed to try to keep the ball from going to their defensive half of the field. It takes two midfielders to effectively back up a feed. They should position themselves about a yard inside the restraining line and stay about 8 to 10 yards apart to prevent the ball from getting between them and going to the midfield line. Once a midfielder makes a backup, he has several options. He can pass the ball into the crease area if a man is open, shoot the ball, or fake the shot and dodge a charging defender.

ZONE OFFENSE

A team cannot play its regular offense against an opponent using a zone defense. The zone defense stresses the defenders covering specific areas of the field and any attacker who happens to be in the area. The man-for-man defense calls for each defender to guard a specific attacker, regardless of where he goes on the field. Therefore the regular offense, which is geared to a man-for-man defense, must be adjusted or a new offensive alignment must be installed. Excellent stick work, which enables quick movement of the ball, is of primary importance in attacking a zone. The defense must be forced into adjusting to the ball as it is passed around the perimeter. The zone must be attacked by movement of men as well as of the ball. This is accomplished by giving certain attackers the responsibility of either cutting or sneaking into specific areas. Since the zone places emphasis on following the ball, the offense can often gain a 2-on-1 advantage by an effective cut or sneak. The zone defense also has trouble handling an offense that places its men in an unusual alignment or one that overloads a specific area.

Only a handful of my Hopkins teams played against teams that used a zone defense. Fortunately for us, we had some of our best stick handlers on those teams and we were able to practice our zone offense for each of those games. In 1958, Gene Corrigan's Washington and Lee team gave us a fit with his zone defense, and so did Howdy Myers' Hofstra team in 1974. Gene put in the zone defense that season especially for the Maryland and Hopkins games. W & L was successful in holding a high-scoring Maryland team to nine goals and in battling our undefeated Hopkins team right down to the wire. Billy Morrill and Mickey Webster, our two high-scoring All-American attackmen, led us to a hard-fought 14–11 victory. Howdy Myers' zone defense completely frustrated our 1974 NCAA championship team for three-quarters of play in the quarter-finals of the playoffs. Near the middle of the third quarter we had outshot Hofstra by 44 to 23, but we were losing on the scoreboard by a 7–6 count. Hofstra's All-American goalie, Joe Zaffuto, stopped just about everything we threw at him, and he even received help from his crease defenseman, who also made a number of saves. It wasn't until early in the fourth quarter that the shots finally started to drop for us, and we went on to win the game by an 18–10 score. Although we were favored to win by at least ten goals, Howdy really had us sweating it out for most of the game.

The offense that we used in those two games, as well as the three or four other times we faced a zone defense during my career, was similar to our basic man-for-man alignment, a 2–1–1–2 set-up (see Figure 7–19). Since most zones play their two defensemen on the attackmen (O1 and O2) when the ball is behind the goal, we prefer to have these two men quarterback the offense. As good attackmen, they should be able to dodge and to feed effectively. However, since the zone normally has a backer waiting to pick up the dodger, the attackmen will minimize their dodging. When they do try to force in toward the goal,

it will be primarily with the idea of passing off to an open teammate rather than trying to climax the dodge with a shot. The main responsibility of O1 and O2 is to look for opportunities to feed the ball to open men who are in a position to shoot. If no one is open for a shot, they must keep the ball moving between themselves and the two front midfielders, O4 and O5. This makes the defense react and adjust.

The midfielders, O4 and O5, should be able to shoot effectively from the outside with hard, accurate shots. They also should be clever cutters, moving into open area near the crease. Ideally they should be able to handle the stick both left- and right-handed. Player O4 will execute most of his cuts right-handed, and his sneaks down the back side will be for left-handed shots; O5's moves will be just the opposite.

The two men who operate in the crease area, O3 and O6, should not only be able to shoot well but also be able to take considerable punishment, because they will be operating in an area with heavy defensive traffic. The crease attackman fills one of the positions, along with a midfielder who has the proper credentials. One will operate a yard or two from the crease and the other about 5 yards from the crease. As the ball moves around the perimeter, the deep creaseman (O3) looks for the feed at any time, because he can be fed by an outside midfielder as well as an attackman, especially if the attackman moves with the ball several yards in front of the goal. The inside creaseman (O6) plays the normal crease attack position and looks for feeds primarily from O1 and O2. The two creasemen can work as a unit, picking for each other, or independently, just trying to get open. If O3 and O6 make intelligent moves in the crease area, the defenders must give considerable attention to them, almost to the point of covering them man for man. This can create an opening for an outside midfielder to cut into open area on the crease.

On a prearranged signal the two creasemen can break to their left and call for the ball. This maneuver gives O4 the opportunity to break right-handed into the open area created for him. Player O5 reads the defense's reaction and is ready to back up O1's feed to O4, or if there is an opening, he can sneak in toward the goal to about the 13-yard mark for a shot from that position (see Figure 7–20). This move must be coordinated so that all

Figure 7–19 Basic alignment of personnel (2–1–1–2) to attack a zone defense.

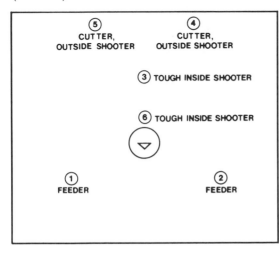

TEAM OFFENSE

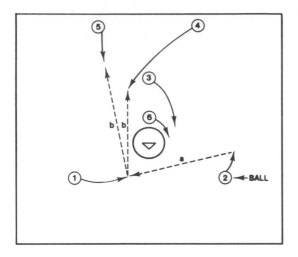

Figure 7–20 Set play to attack a zone defense. On a signal O3 and O6 cut toward O2, who fakes a pass to them and throws to O1. Player O1 feeds (**b**) either O4, who cuts for a right-handed shot, or O5, who sneaks down the back side.

Figure 7–21 Overload offense to attack a zone defense. Players O3 and O6 cut when O2 receives the ball. Player O5 cuts down back side, and O4 swings to the middle of the field when O1 receives the ball. Player O1 has the option either to feed O5 or loop-pass to O4 (**c**).

six attackers know what is happening. Communication is just as important, if not more so, in attacking the zone defense as it is in the man-to-man defense. Set plays, similar to those used by the two outside midfielders and the two creasemen against the man-to-man defense, can be used effectively against the zone.

Moving into an overload alignment (with more players on one side of the field than the other) can cause a zone defense some problems. If the offense is subtle in its movement to one side of the field, the defense may get caught overbalanced and therefore vulnerable to back-side cuts or sneaks (see Figure 7–21). On the overload to the right side of the field, the ball is passed between O1, O2, O4, and O5. The offensive pressure appears to be on the right side of the field. Player O2 initiates the play by giving O3 a signal to cut. Then O2 fakes the feed to O3 if he is covered and passes the ball to O1. With this pass O6 breaks left-handed toward O1, but more than likely he, too, will be covered, and O1 will then look for O5 either cutting or sneaking down the back side. Player O5 will take the right-handed shot if he is open, or, if he is covered when he catches the ball, he looks to pass it to O4, who is rotating to the middle of the field for a shot at about the 14-yard mark. If a shot is not taken, the offense can keep the ball moving and try the

Figure 7–22 Overload offense to attack a zone defense. With O2's pass to O1, O3 and O6 cut right-handed and O5 cuts left-handed, looking for the feed (**c**) from O1.

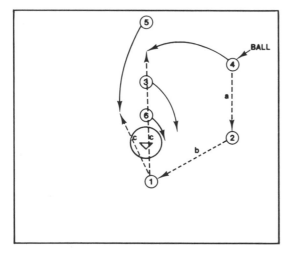

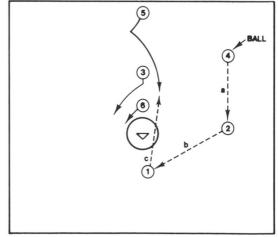

same play over again, with the cutters taking a slightly different route in trying to get open. The quarterback can also call for the overload to shift to the left side, where the same maneuvers can be tried. However, on that side of the field O4 will be making his cut or sneaking down the back side for a left-handed shot.

Another maneuver, the onside cut through the zone by O5, shown in Figure 7–22, complements the back-side play in Figure 7–21. When O2 gets the ball, O3 cuts to the opposite side of the goal. So does O6 when the pass is made to O1. This opens up the left-handed cut by O5, who first fakes several steps down the back side and then breaks into the area vacated by O3 and O6. He should time his cut so that he will be in position to receive the feed no longer than a second or two after O1 has gotten the ball in his stick. There are a number of other offensive wrinkles that can be worked from the overload.

8

extra-man offense

When an opponent commits a foul and has to serve time in the penalty box, the unpenalized team is given a golden opportunity to score. To make the most of having an extra man, the offensive unit must be highly organized and well drilled and able to move the ball with precision around the goal. It waits for the defense to make a mistake or to fail to cover the extra man, and then it takes a high-percentage shot with a good angle and from close range. Since most college teams will average between six and ten fouls per game, the team that is more successful in handling extra-man situations will be the winner most of the time.

This point is borne out by the record of my recent Hopkins teams. Let me cite just three of the many possible examples. The 1969 championship team, led by Joe Cowan, scored goals on 53 percent of the extra-man opportunities in the nine games that we won but on merely 17 percent in our only loss of the season (to Navy). The 1970 championship team also lost only one game—to the University of Virginia. We were successful in two of eleven extra-man attempts against the Cavaliers for a measly 18 percent. The 1973 NCAA runnerup team lost just one game during the regular season. In that game, against the University of Maryland, we scored one goal in fifteen extra-man plays—less than 7 percent, as compared with 41 percent in the nine other games.

The best offensive players are selected to play on the extra-man offensive unit. Their ability to handle the ball is of primary importance. In addition they must exercise good judgment in determining the open man. At least ten players should be taught extra-man offense; six will be the starters, and the four next-best offensive players will be the substitutes. Every starter and substitute learns two positions on each extra-man play. Normally the three starting attackmen and the three best midfielders will constitute the extra-man unit. It makes no difference whether the midfielders play on the same midfield unit or not. If a team has an excellent fourth attackman, he will often be on the unit along with the three starting attackmen and two midfielders. Even five attackmen can be used in extra-man play, provided that all of them are drilled in playing defensively as midfielders whenever the man-down defense gains possession of the ball and clears it to the attack-goal area. This does happen occasionally, and all the extra-man players must be geared to playing defense. But the most important thing is that the six best offensive players be in the game.

In order to get the most effective extra-man offense, a team must make maximum use of the talents of its players. If a team has superior stick handling, it can employ a considerable number of passes and a more intricate play. If its stick work is limited, it should have a simple play with a minimum of passes. If a team has an excellent feeder, it should gear its offense to a variety of cuts and maneuvers on the crease to give him the opportunity to pick out the open man for close-range shots. If there are several outstanding midfield shooters, the play should revolve around action that gives them shots at the 12-yard mark or closer to the goal. If the crease attackman is a potent scorer, he should be set up for shots in the crease area. Contrary to the popular belief that a player should not dodge when his team has an extra man, it is a wise move to devise one play that uses the dodger's skills. Since the man-down defense does not normally expect a dodge, it can get caught flatfooted against such a play. The play is most effective when the ball is passed around the perimeter at least one time and there is diversionary action on the crease prior to the ball being thrown to the dodger in the midfield area. As soon as he receives the ball, he fakes a shot at about the 16-yard mark and then drives toward the goal into an area that has been cleared out for him. It is difficult for the defense to back up on the dodger because it is already one man short.

For organizational purposes, extra-man plays are identified according to the number of players in the midfield, on the crease, and behind the goal. For example, the 3–1–2 play shown in Figure 8–1 has three players in the midfield, one on the crease, and two behind the goal. Figure 8–2 shows a 2–3–1 play, with two players in the midfield, three across the crease, and one be-

hind the goal. Some teams reverse the order and count first the players behind the goal, then on the crease, and finally in the midfield.

There are two basic styles of extra-man offense. One style makes use of set plays, and the other uses free-lance moves from various offensive alignments. Most teams favor the set-play style, because it gives specific assignments to each player, and, if carried out properly, a close-range shot should result. The set play is designed with a series of passes and one or two cuts to cause the defenders to make adjustments. Each player knows every step of the play and is ready to capitalize on a defensive mistake at any time. The free-lance style gives the players the freedom to move the ball in any manner from a basic alignment. There is no special sequence of passes. Since the offense has an extra man, it should be able to get a good shot by just moving the ball sharply and looking for a defensive lapse. A free-lance play is usually more effective than a set play when less than ten seconds remain in a penalty and the ball goes out of bounds. A complicated set play is very difficult to work in such a short time, whereas several quick, free-lance passes from one of the basic alignments may provide an opening for a shot in the hole area.

A college team normally prepares at least three or four extra-man plays for each game. This sounds like an excessive number, but it really is not. The extra-man offense must practice at least two plays for the basic defense that the opponent uses. However, if the opponent changes its man-down defense for that particular game, the offense will be in trouble if it does not have at least one play for the alternate defense. A team must also be ready to attack a man-down defense that is shutting off its best offensive player. If it is unable to get the ball to him, it must have a play that bypasses him and attacks the goal with 5-on-4 rather than the normal 6-on-5 alignment. In addition, the offense must be ready to operate with a two- or three-man advantage if a second or third defender fouls. Since the man-down defense will not go behind the goal in these situations, the extra-man offense does not want to have more than one man positioned behind the goal. It is surprising how many times a team that uses two players behind the goal on a regular one-down situation does not change its alignment when an opponent has two men in the penalty box.

After the team practices three or four extra-man

plays for the opening game of the season, it is advisable to install a new play at various times during the season. If a team does not vary its extra-man plays, its opponents will be able to prepare their man-down units for those specific plays. Seeing familiar plays on game day boosts the opposing defense's confidence more than anything else. It is sound strategy to prepare a new play, similar to one of the offense's regular plays but with several subtle changes in it. It takes a clever man-down unit to make the proper adjustments and avoid the trap. A team may have as many as seven or eight extra-man plays by the end of a season, but it normally practices just the three or four it plans to use for a specific game.

When a foul occurs, it is the responsibility of the coach to determine which play to use. He informs his offensive leader, who in turn tells the other members of the extra-man offensive unit. It is imperative that all six players know which play has been called. Usually there is no problem in doing this at the outset of an extra-man play. However, confusion often reigns in the latter part of a play when a shot is taken and the offense regains possession of the ball either in bounds or out of bounds. At this time, in particular, the attack leader must sound off which play is to be used. The offense should identify its plays without tipping off the type of play to the defense. If a 1–4–1 play is to be used, the players are not being deceptive if they call out either "1–4–1" or "1–4." We have identified our extra-man plays at Hopkins by giving each play a name associated with our opponents—for example, Tiger, Billy Goat, Mule, Wahoo, or Turtle.

After a play has been called and the whistle blows, there is a need for a signal to initiate the action. While the ball is being passed around the horn (around the perimeter) to get the defense moving, a designated player can call out, "Let's go," and this puts the play in motion. Another way is to start the play when a certain player catches the ball either the first or second time after the whistle blows. This is a more subtle way and does not sound the alarm to the defense as the call does.

Most of our extra-man offense at Hopkins revolves around the set play rather than the free-lance play. However, we do use the free-lance action at the conclusion of a set play with less than ten seconds remaining in the penalty. Our basic strategy is to start our set plays with one

alignment and then, by cutting or just adjusting our personnel, to move into another alignment. For example, Figure 8–1 shows a play that, for illustration purposes, can be called "Tiger." It starts with a 3–1–2 alignment and changes to a 2–3–1. If a shot is taken from any one of the first three parts of the play, the offense has the option of starting the play all over again, assuming there is enough time left in the penalty, or, if not, going directly into the second phase of the play, which is the 2–3–1. The attack leader calls out either "Tiger 1" or "Tiger 2," depending on which play he wants.

My Hopkins teams have used a variety of extra-man plays. Some have been consistently successful; others have looked potent on the drawing board but have failed miserably on the field. Often the simple plays are more effective than the complicated ones. Let's take a look at five plays that have been old reliables for us. These same plays can be mirrored and run on the opposite side of the field.

3–1–2

Figure 8–1 shows the 3–1–2 play with the ball being moved around the horn in a clockwise direction. The play actually begins the second time O2 catches the ball.

Part 1. As O3 is about to make his second pass to O2, O5 starts a cut for a left-handed shot at the goal. He times it to arrive at a point about 5 yards from the crease as soon as O2 catches the ball. The crease attackman (O6) makes a break for a right-handed shot, and O2 has the option of feeding either O5 or O6. If neither is open, he passes the ball to O1.

Part 2. As O2 starts to pass to O1, both O3 and O4 begin their moves. When O1 catches the ball, O3 is in the middle of the field at about the 16-yard mark, and O4 is about 5 yards from the crease. Player O5 remains on the opposite side of the crease, and O6 moves there, too, trying to clear the area for O4's cut. Player O1 feeds O4 if the latter is open; if he is not, he passes the ball to O3.

Part 3. Player O2 makes his move to a point about 5 yards from the crease just as O1 is about to pass the ball to O3. Player O5 breaks to the opposite side of the crease to clear out the area for O2's rotation; O6 stays on the crease to screen the goalie. When O3 receives the pass, he has

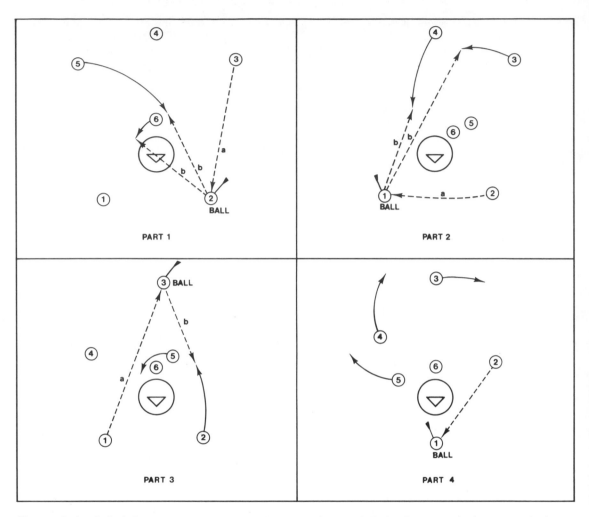

Figure 8-1 A 3-1-2 extra-man play, which moves into a 2-3-1 alignment in its second phase (Part 4).

the option of feeding O2 for a point-blank shot or, if O2 is covered, taking the shot himself inside the 14-yard mark.

Part 4. If the offense is unable to get a good shot, it moves into a 2-3-1 alignment with O3 and O4 in the midfield area; O2, O6, and O5 across the crease; and O1 behind the goal. This is the second phase of the 3-1-2 play.

2-3-1

In the 2-3-1 play shown in Figure 8-2 the ball moves around the horn in a clockwise direction.

The play starts when O2 touches the ball the second time.

Part 1. When O2 receives his second pass, O4 starts his cut for a left-handed shot at the goal. He wants to be 5 yards from the crease when O2 passes to O1. The crease attackman (O6) makes a break for a right-handed shot, and O1 has the option of feeding either O4 or O6. If neither is open, he passes the ball back to O2.

Part 2. When O2 receives the ball, he has the option of passing the ball either to O3 for the midfield shot or to O5 for the left-handed shot on the opposite side of the crease at a point about 5 yards from it.

TECHNIQUES AND TACTICS

80

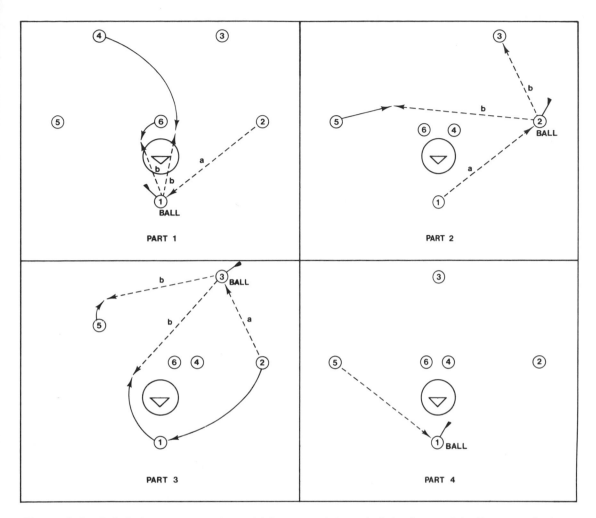

Figure 8–2 A 2–3–1 extra-man play, which moves into a 1–4–1 alignment in its second phase (Part 4).

Part 3. If O3, after receiving the pass from O2, decides not to shoot, he can choose between passing to O5 for the left-handed shot or to O1 for the left-handed rotation. Player O1 times his break to arrive in front of the goal about 3 yards from the crease when O3 is looking for the open man. Player O6 breaks to the opposite side of the crease to clear out for O1's rotation; O2 moves behind the goal to back up the shot.

Part 4. If the offense is unable to get a good shot, it moves into a 1–4–1 alignment with O3 in the midfield; O2, O4, O6, and O5 across the crease; and O1 behind the goal. This is the second phase of the 2–3–1 play.

2–2–2

Figure 8–3 shows the 2–2–2 play with the ball moving around the horn in a clockwise direction. Play starts when O1 gets the ball for the second time. Player O5 is in a high-post position about 5 yards from the crease, and O6 is in a low-post position about 1 yard from the crease.

Part 1. When O2 is getting ready to pass the ball to O1, player O3 starts his cut for a right-handed shot at the goal. He times his cut to arrive just a yard past the high post when O1 catches the ball. Player O1 has the option of feeding either O3 or O6, who breaks for a left-

EXTRA-MAN OFFENSE

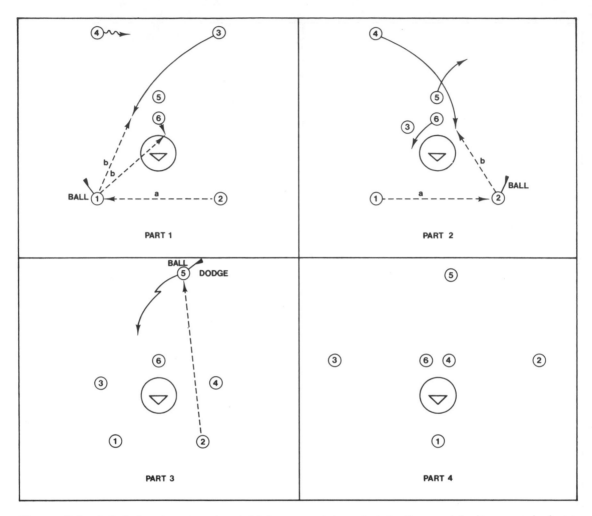

Figure 8–3 A 2–2–2 extra-man play, which moves into a 1–4–1 alignment in its second phase (Part 4).

handed shot when O1 receives the ball. Player O4 moves several yards toward the middle of the field to back up the pass.

Part 2. If neither O3 nor O6 is open, O1 passes the ball back to O2. With this pass, O4 starts his break to the opposite side of the high post, looking for a left-handed shot. He wants to be a yard past the post when O2 is ready to feed. Player O5 moves from his high-post position toward the restraining line in order to back up the feed; O6 moves to the opposite side of the crease to clear out the area for O4's cut.

Part 3. If O4 is not open, O2 passes the ball to O5, who is at about the 18-yard mark. This part of

the play is designed to give O5 the opportunity to fake the outside shot and dodge the defender who is guarding him. Players O3 and O4 stay on the side of the crease about even with the plane of the goal to give O5 plenty of room for the dodge; O6 maintains a normal screening position. Players O1 and O2 stay behind the goal to back up the shot.

Part 4. If the offense is unable to get a good shot, it moves into a 1–4–1 alignment with O5 in the midfield; O2, O4, O6, and O3 across the crease; and O1 behind the goal. This is the second phase of the 2–2–2 play.

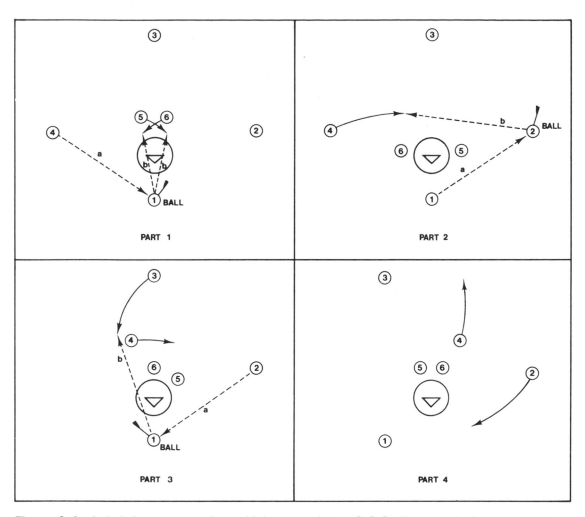

Figure 8–4 A 1–4–1 extra-man play, which moves into a 2–2–2 alignment in its second phase (Part 4).

1–4–1

In the 1–4–1 play shown in Figure 8–4 the ball moves around the horn in a counterclockwise direction. The play starts when O4 gets the ball for the second time. Players O5 and O6 line up about 5 yards from the crease and about 2 yards apart.

Part 1. When O4 passes to O1, players O5 and O6 cut for the goal posts diagonally opposite, looking for the feed and a point-blank shot on the crease.

Part 2. If neither is open, O1 passes the ball to O2. With this pass, O4 starts his cut across the front of the crease. He wants to be about 4 yards from the crease and directly in front of the goal when O2 is ready to feed him for a left-handed shot. Both O5 and O6 move to positions on each side of the goal and even with the plane of the goal. This clears out the crease area for O4's cut.

Part 3. If O4 is not open, O2 passes the ball back to O1, who looks for O3 sneaking down the back side for a right-handed shot at about the 10-yard mark. Player O6 moves to the front of the goal and out of the path of O1's feed; O4, O5, and O2 stay on the opposite side of the field to clear out the area for O3.

Part 4. If the offense is unable to get a good

EXTRA-MAN OFFENSE

shot, it moves into a 2–2–2 alignment with O3 and O4 in the midfield, O5 and O6 on the crease, and O1 and O2 behind the goal. This is the second phase of the 1–4–1 play.

3–3

Figure 8–5 shows the 3–3 play with the ball moving around the horn in a clockwise direction. The play starts when O2 gets the ball for the second time.

Part 1. When the second pass is on the way to O2 from O3, both O5 and O1 start to move toward the middle of the field. When O2 receives the

ball, O1 is directly behind the goal, waiting for O2's pass.

Part 2. When O1 catches the ball, he is ready to feed either O5, cutting for the left-handed shot on the crease, O6 for the right-handed shot on the crease, or O4, cutting for a right-handed shot about 6 yards from the crease. Player O3 moves toward the middle of the field to back up O1's feed.

Part 3. If O4 receives the pass from O1 but decides not to shoot, he has the option of passing the ball to either O3 or O2. Players O5 and O6 move to the opposite side from O2 to clear out the area for his cut.

Part 4. If the offense is unable to get a good

Figure 8–5 A 3–3 extra-man play, which moves into a 1–3–2 alignment in its second phase (Part 4).

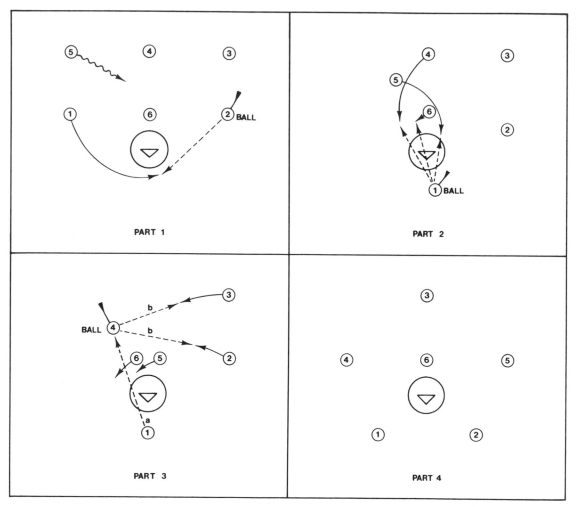

shot, it moves into a 1–3–2 alignment with O3 in the midfield, O5, O6, and O4 across the crease, and O1 and O2 behind the goal. This is the second phase of the 3–3 play.

ADDITIONAL GUIDELINES

1. Do not rush the play and try to score in ten seconds or less when operating with a one-minute penalty.

2. As the ball is moved around the horn, make sharp and accurate passes to the outside of each player. If the pass is thrown to the inside, a sliding defender has an opportunity to intercept it or check the attacker's stick as he is catching it.

3. Keep the offensive players spread far enough apart so that one defender cannot guard two attackers. This does not apply to the players in the crease area, because their positions, even though just 3 or 4 yards apart, are dangerous enough to warrant being covered by two defenders.

4. The ball carrier should force a defender to guard him by moving toward the goal.

5. Back up every shot with at least one man behind the goal.

6. Back up every feed to the crease with at least one man in the midfield area.

7. Never use two players behind the goal if the man-down defense is in a five-man zone that keeps all defenders in front of the goal. Against this type of defense only one attacker goes behind the goal. He can be given the ball and allowed to quarterback the play by driving toward the goal, looking for a prearranged cut and forcing a defender to play him when he is even with the goal pipes. He can then move the ball because there are only four defenders to cover five attackers in front of the goal.

8. Never use two players behind the goal when the opponents have two or more men in the penalty box. Since they will not play the ball carrier behind the goal in these situations, it is senseless for the extra-man offense to use more than one player there.

9. If the man-down defense uses a shutoff maneuver (guarding a player so closely that he is unable to get the ball) on the offense's best shooter or feeder, the extra-man unit must have a specific plan to counter this move. One way is to move the player who is being shut off to the side

of the field about 15 yards from the goal. The defensive player will go with him in most cases, because he has been instructed to stay with the key attacker as if he were his shadow. By getting him out of the play, the offense can attack the goal with 5 on 4, using either a 2–1–2, 3–1–1, or 1–3–1 offense. The offense can use a set play or just free-lance to get a close-range shot.

10. Use at least two extra-man plays against the opponent's basic defense during the course of a game. This keeps the defense "honest" by making it adjust to different plays, instead of allowing it to get a comfortable feeling in seeing the same play again and again.

11. When only ten seconds or less remain in a penalty, be ready to use a set play or free-lance maneuver that may provide a quick opening and a close-range shot after just several passes and a cut or back-side sneak.

12. Don't be discouraged if unable to score on extra-man plays in the early stages of a game. As long as close-range shots are being taken, the percentages will work in favor of the offense eventually scoring goals.

13. When the man-down defense gains possession of the ball with the play being stopped by the official's whistle, the extra-man unit must ride all five defenders and the goalie with a tight man-for-man coverage. The best rider on the team plays the opponent who is bringing the ball into play. The other five attackers try to shut off their men and keep them from receiving a pass. If they are successful, the ball carrier has no one to whom to pass the ball and frequently will have difficulty protecting it from the hard-riding attacker. In this situation, the three defenders on the opposite half of the field must also guard their men closely to prevent the completion of a long clearing pass. If the extra-man offense regains possession of the ball, it presses for the goal for a quick score.

Extra-man offense is such an important part of team play that it is normally practiced for twenty to thirty minutes per day for three days prior to every game. When inclement weather forces a team to practice indoors, extra-man offense can receive an intensive workout, even in a gymnasium. A team with a well-organized, well-prepared, and confident extra-man unit will capitalize on an average of 30 to 40 percent of its opportunities, and this often will be a decisive factor in the outcome of the game.

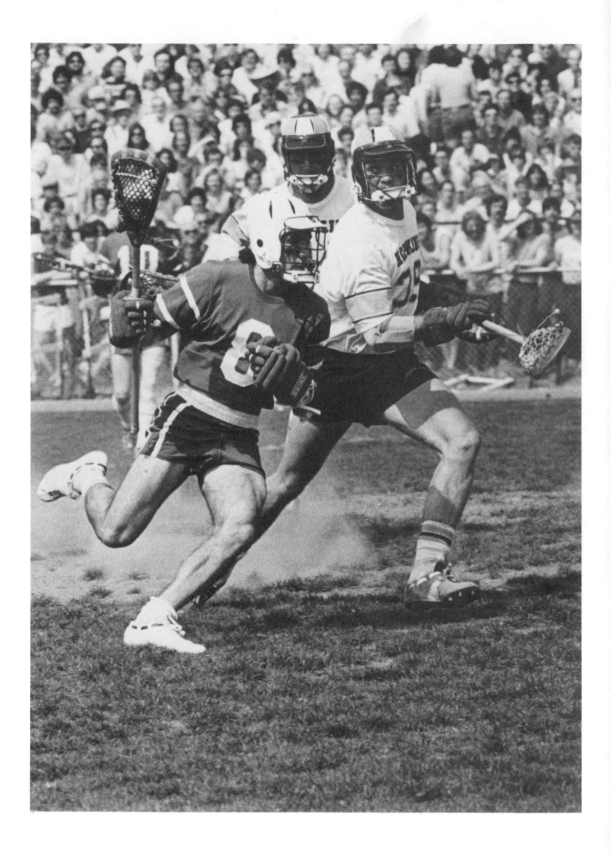

9
individual defense

A complete understanding of the basic skills of defending against an opponent with the ball is essential to every player on the field. Each defenseman and midfielder obviously becomes involved with the primary responsibility of neutralizing his man when he has possession of the ball. Attackmen also make use of the same principles when they play an opponent who is attempting to clear the ball. The goalie must know the defensive techniques in order to assist his defensive teammates with positive verbal instructions.

The techniques for playing 1-on-1 defense in lacrosse are identical with those used in basketball, although the lacrosse player does have the advantage of using a stick. However, it is imperative that he handle the stick more like a foil than a bludgeon. Too many defensive players feel they must be extremely aggressive with the stick and show their superiority over their opponent by pounding him with the "wood" and trying to gain possession of the ball. They feel this style is more challenging to them personally and gives them more notoriety than the patient, position-conscious defensive game. Although a defender may have an easy time handling a weak attackman, he may run into trouble when playing against one who is his equal or better. The take-the-ball-away approach will often lead the defender to committing a foul or being dodged.

The Hopkins philosophy of individual defense has been a more conservative one than that of most schools, mainly because the percentages favor this style. Even if the defender actually takes the ball away from his opponent 75 percent of the time, the odds are still in favor of the attacking team because of the excellent scoring opportunities that result in the remaining 25 percent. When a defender tries to take the ball away from his opponent, the following things can happen, most of which are on the negative side:

1. He may knock the ball out of his opponent's

stick but foul him in the process. This will place his team at a definite disadvantage, since he will have to spend time in the penalty box.

2. He may fail in his attempt to knock the ball out of his opponent's stick when he commits the foul, thus allowing the attacker to continue to the goal for a scoring attempt. If the goal is scored after the defender has committed a personal foul, he must still serve time in the penalty box, and this penalizes his team twice.

3. He may be dodged by his opponent and create an easy opportunity for a point-blank shot.

4. He may be successful in knocking the ball out of his opponent's stick but without necessarily getting the ball. A scrap for the ball will ensue, and the percentages are about 50–50 as to who the winner will be. If the defender does get the ball, he must still clear it to the offensive end of the field before completing his assigned responsibility.

It is not an easy job to sell an aggressive defenseman on the more conservative style of defensive play. However, we feel it is essential in our concept of team defense and have used the following illustration every year to help ram home the position-patience philosophy. If a defenseman tries to take the ball away from his man ten times during a game and is successful in knocking the ball out of his stick in eight of those attempts, he nonetheless has not made a significant contribution to his team. He still has to fight for possession of the loose ball, and if he does get it, he must then clear it from the defensive to the offensive half of the field before his team has a chance to put a point on the scoreboard. But in the two times that he fails to get the ball from his opponent, the defender subjects himself to either a dodge and a point-blank shot or a foul that results in an extra-man opportunity. In both of these cases he has given his opponent the high-percentage shot and a good chance to score, and this far outweighs the positive benefits of knocking the ball out of his opponent's stick. In our way of thinking, the point is clearly made to our defensemen: don't try to be the hero and continually take the ball away from your man but, rather, play position, apply pressure, and be patient.

I have been fortunate to have coached some excellent defensemen during my career. Four of the best (Walt Mitchell, Mike Byrne, Hank Kaestner, and Mike Clark) received the Schmeisser Award, which is given annually to the outstanding defenseman in the country. Hank Kaestner won the award in both his junior and senior years, and our coaches referred to him as having a "magic" stick, because he was always able to get his stick on his opponent's. Hank was in a class by himself in taking the ball away from his man, and since he was so skillful at it, he had the green light to make the aggressive move on his man at any time. In our style of defensive play, Hank was the exception rather than the rule. His adeptness came naturally because his father, Bud Kaestner, was a three-time All-American defenseman at Hopkins in the early forties and taught Hank all the tricks of the trade at an early age. His knowledge of the game, his extremely quick hands, and his ability to check his opponent's stick without overcommitting himself made Hank extremely effective.

Mike Clark was also very successful at taking the initiative in playing his man. Nevertheless, as great a player as he was, Mike did meet his match in a big game his senior year. Hopkins traveled to West Point to play Jim Adams' fine Army team on April 26, 1969, in a classic battle of two undefeated teams. Mike was ready for the assignment of stopping Pete Cramblet, Army's All-American attackman. In fact, in the preceding year at Homewood Field, Mike handled Cramblet with little difficulty, and Hopkins won 15–8 on the way to an undefeated collegiate season and a national championship. But in the next meeting of the two at Michie Stadium, Cramblet was ready for Mike's over-the-head maneuvers and aggressive take-the-ball-away play. He did burn Mike with two point-blank goals and several other excellent shots. Cramblet had a great day with six goals, although only two were against Mike. Fortunately for us, Charlie Coker countered with six goals for Hopkins, and we won the game by a 14–11 score.

I don't like to single out Mike Clark for losing the individual battle with Pete Cramblet that particular day, because Mike won most of the encounters during his brilliant collegiate career. However, it does help to make my point that a great defensive player can be beaten by a great offensive player if the defenseman commits himself too aggressively when initiating a maneuver to take the ball away. The percentages are with the offense in this situation.

Therefore, the primary responsibility of a defensive player is to maintain proper positioning on his man and to be patient in waiting for him to make a mistake. I stress the following defensive responsibilities in order of priority:

1. Play position on your man to prevent him from getting into prime shooting area.
2. Hinder his shooting. Don't give him a good-angle shot.
3. Keep pressure on him when he is trying to feed.
4. Gain possession of the ball and clear it to the attack.

STANCE

The stance of the defensive player is vital to his effectiveness in playing the man with the ball. He must have control of his body and be ready to move in any direction. His feet should be spread a little wider than shoulder-width and staggered in a heel-to-toe alignment. The defender must maintain his balance by keeping most of his weight on the balls of his feet. His heels should make contact with the ground to give him stability. Knees should be flexed and upper body bent slightly forward. This semicrouch position resembles that of a boxer (see Figure 9–1, top).

EYES

The defender's eyes do not center on any one thing but, rather, look through the attacker's hands, stick (pocket), and eyes, as each of these can give a tipoff. If the attacker has only one hand on the stick, he normally will not be able to shoot or feed effectively from this position. Therefore, the defender can concentrate primarily on maintaining proper position and getting primed to execute his poke or slap check when the attacker puts his other hand on the stick. However, he can use the poke check to annoy the attacker when he is carrying the stick in one hand. When two hands are on the stick, the defender should be ready to apply pressure. The attacker's eyes will often betray when and where he is going to throw the ball. Only the best attackmen will look one way and then throw the other way. Most ball players look exactly where they are going to throw the ball, and their faces will almost light up when they spot the open man and are ready to release the ball. The defender must be ready for the clever at-tacker who will fake with his eyes and then make a countermove.

POSITIONING

Being in the proper position when the offensive player gets the ball is extremely important for the defender, because he does not know where his man is going, when, or at what speed. He assumes a squared-up position with his body in a direct line with the ball carrier's stick side and the center of the goal. The alignment of his feet is also determined by the attacker's stick position. If the attacker has his stick in a right-hand position, the defender should have his left foot back and right foot forward in a staggered alignment, as shown in Figure 9–1, top. (His feet would be reversed if the attacker has his stick in his left hand, as shown in Figure 9–2, top.) This will allow the defender to move off more quickly in the direction his opponent is facing. If the attacker bursts at full speed for the goal, the defender can either take a lead step with his left foot first, or he can pivot on his left foot and take a crossover step with his right foot first.

Often a defender will pick up the man with the ball in the more comfortable position, but this can only cause him trouble if he happens to have the wrong foot forward. If he has his left foot forward when the attacker bursts for the goal right-handed, he will have to take a step back before he can pivot and run, or else take the awkward and dangerous crossover step with his trailing right foot. He may also turn his back to his man in an effort to maintain the proper position, but this can be dangerous, because he loses sight of his man for a split second. When the defender does this, the attacker can change his direction and gain a decided advantage. These maneuvers place the defender in a precarious position because he will lose at least a half step on his man. And this certainly can make the difference in giving the attacker a point-blank shot.

FOOTWORK

The speed at which the offensive man moves will determine the footwork of the defender. He uses a "shuffle" with short, choppy steps and no crossover steps when his opponent moves at a slow to

Figure 9–1 Two phases of the backhand position used by a defender in guarding the ball carrier.

half-speed pace. When shuffling, the feet should remain spread about shoulder-width to provide a solid base. They should never come closer than about 8 to 10 inches apart. This footwork is similar to a boxer's maneuvering in the ring. His body is squared off and facing his opponent when

Figure 9–2 Two phases of the forehand position used by a defender in guarding the ball carrier.

using the shuffle. When the attacker increases his speed to the point where the defender would trail him with the shuffle, he then changes to a "hip-to-hip" running position (see bottom illustrations in Figures 9–1 and 9–2). The defender's body is turned in the same direction as his opponent's body, and his hips are even with him. This allows him to maintain the proper defensive position between his man and the goal. If the attacker slows up, the defender will resume his shuffling.

HANDLING THE STICK

Proper handling of the stick by the defender when playing the ball is almost as important as his footwork. If he uses a stick of attack or midfield length, his hands should be about body-width distance apart. If he uses the long-handled stick, his hands should be farther apart to control the bigger and heavier stick better. With either stick, the lower hand should be at the butt end of the handle and the upper hand the proper distance up the handle and never at the throat of the stick. Placing the stick across the chest or on the numbers of the opponent's jersey can be most disconcerting to him. From this position the defender can execute any of his checks or holds.

A player who is basically a right-hander should play right-handed when on defense and vice versa for the left-hander. He should not change hands when on defense, because the switching of the hands will not give him complete control of his stick. If he tries to change hands every time his attacker changes direction, shifting the stick back and forth will place him at a decided disadvantage. Another reason for not changing hands is to have the defender holding the stick with his stronger hand when the ball is on the ground. This will allow him to scoop the ball more easily if he does check it out of his opponent's stick. If he has to change hands for the scoop in this situation, the extra second or two of delay could cause him to lose the ball.

It is debatable whether the forehand or backhand stick position is stronger on defense. The forehand position can be defined as that used by a right-handed defender who is guarding a left-handed driver (see Figure 9–2). The backhand position, as shown in Figure 9–1, is used when a right-hander plays against a right-handed driver. Some players definitely prefer the forehand position, but I feel there are two important advantages to the backhand position:

1. The stick rests across the chest of the opponent and acts as a natural deterrent to his taking a shot at the goal. If the attacker is forcing his way into good shooting area, the defender can use the

backhand hold to stop his penetration and turn him back. The arms of the defender and his stick act as a natural "hook" on the attacker.

2. When the attacker runs toward the goal at full speed, the defender can run with him and still keep his stick resting across the attacker's body and deliver checks that will interfere with his shooting. It is extremely difficult, if not impossible, for the defender to do this when he is holding the stick in a forehand position and moving at full speed.

BASIC CHECKS

Poke Check

The poke check is one of the most effective checks, because the opportunity to dislodge the ball from the opponent's stick without overcommitting is greater than in the other checks. The poke check, shown in Figure 9–3, consists of a thrust of the stick, propelled through the upper hand by the lower hand. This technique is similar to the billiard player's handling of his cue stick. The lower hand draws the stick back slightly just prior to his stroke to give him more power with it. It is important for the upper hand to remain in contact with the handle as it slides through the fingers to give better control. If the upper hand loses its grasp, the lower hand will not be able to control the stick, thereby giving an advantage to the attacker. If the attacker is holding his stick with one hand, the thrust can be directed at any part of the handle that is showing. If he has two hands on the stick, it can be aimed at the cuff of the glove holding the butt end of the stick. The defender must guard against an overaggressive poke that will cause him to step into his opponent and give him an opening to roll by on the side opposite his check.

Slap Check

The slap check, as the term implies, is merely a short, slapping blow directed at the attacker's lower gloved hand or the handle of the stick just above it (see Figure 9–4). It·is used mainly when the attacker either has both hands on the stick or is about to put his lower hand on it. The slap check will not be effective if the attacker is holding the stick in one hand and protecting it well with the other. The wrist action of the upper hand

Figure 9–3 Two phases of the poke check.

INDIVIDUAL DEFENSE

Figure 9–4 Two phases of the slap check.

TECHNIQUES AND TACTICS

on the stick delivers the check, and it should be as quick as possible. The head of the stick will be directed at the target anywhere from a horizontal position up to an angle of approximately 45 degrees above the horizontal. The check should not cover a distance any greater than approximately 18 inches. In fact, the shorter the check, the less it is telegraphed. When the defender hauls back with his stick as if to bludgeon his opponent, he not only tips off his maneuver but also begins a check that generates so much power it gets out of control and exposes him to a face or roll dodge. The head of the defender's stick should not go beyond a position horizontal to the ground when it is in the downward motion. If it does, it can cause a foul by hitting the attacker on the lower part of his body or even trip him. When making the slap check with the stick moving in a horizontal path, the defender must guard against using too vigorous a check, which will give the attacker an easy roll dodge.

Figure 9–5 Over-the-head check with the defender taking his upper hand off the stick.

Over-the-Head Check

I hesitate mentioning the over-the-head check because it is dangerous and requires extreme caution. If the defender does not knock the ball out of his opponent's stick, he is in a vulnerable position and will probably be dodged. There is a variety of techniques in executing the over-the-head check.

1. The defender takes his upper hand off the stick and raises his lower hand over his opponent's head. His arm will be straightened out, and with a quick flick of his wrist the stick will then swing like a pendulum, checking the throat of the opponent's stick and not the end of it. Figure 9–5 shows a right-handed defender directing his stick over the head of a right-handed attacker. The technique is probably even more effective when a right-handed defender makes the move against a left-handed attacker. The opposite applies when a left-hander is playing a right-hander.

2. The defender takes his lower hand off the stick and raises his upper hand over his opponent's head, as shown in Figure 9–6. The arm is straightened out, and with a quick snap of the wrist the butt end of the stick will make the pendulum swing and check the opponent's stick. This technique is best used when the attacker is forcing in to the defender.

3. The defender can make the over-the-head

check with both hands on his stick and directing them over his opponent's head. His arms will almost straighten out completely, and by snapping both wrists he can check the stick. This check is not as popular as the one-hand checks.

Wraparound Check

The wraparound check is almost as dangerous as the over-the-head check, because it is a one-hand maneuver and the defender consequently does not have complete control of his stick. However, it can be effective if the attacker has worked his way into a good shooting position close to the goal. The defender takes his lower hand off the stick, straightens the other arm, and directs his stick in a horizontal position toward his opponent's stick. By snapping his wrist he can wrap his stick around his opponent and check his stick. This check is more effective when a right-handed defender is playing against a left-handed attacker who is going to his left, as shown in Figure 9–7, and vice versa, when a left-handed defender is playing against a right-hander going to his right. It is difficult to execute when a right-hander is playing a right-hander and a left-hander playing a left-hander.

Figure 9–7 Wraparound check.

Figure 9–6 Over-the-head check with the defender taking his lower hand off the stick.

HOLDS

The Lacrosse Rule Book states that a player shall not hold an opponent or his stick in any manner. It also states that this does not prohibit holding off a player in possession of the ball with his closed, gloved hand on the handle of the stick or with either forearm. For simplicity in defining the technique used by the defender in stopping the attacker's penetration toward the goal, I will use the term "hold." The hold should be used only when the offensive player is bearing in toward the goal and is in prime shooting area: for midfielders, in front of the goal about 10 yards or less from the crease, and for attackmen, in front of the goal but off to the side, about 5 yards or less from the crease. Holds should not be used in areas beyond these distances, because the defender will not be able to get as much backup help from his teammates when he is farther away from the goal. When closer to the goal, the defender can receive effective support when he stops the driver with a hold and forces him to change direction. There

are two basic holds—the forehand and the backhand.

Forehand Hold

It is used when a right-handed defender is playing a left-handed driver, as shown in Figure 9–8, and vice versa. To stop the offensive man from bearing in to the goal, the defender places the heel of his lower hand into the upper arm of the attacker. Depending on the size of the attacker and the way in which he forces in, the defender can dig in with his fist either just below the armpit and next to the shoulder blade or slightly in front of the upper arm, allowing his wrist and lower part of his forearm to equalize the attacker's pressure. The defender's stick should be in a high-port position (about 45 degrees above the horizontal), ready to check the attacker's stick. Too often the defender will hold the stick in a horizontal position when using the forehand hold, causing the stick to travel in too big an arc before it makes contact with the opponent's stick. The shorter the distance the stick travels in a check, the better the control and the less chance of a foul.

Backhand Hold

It is used when a right-handed defender is playing a right-handed driver as shown in Figure 9–9,

Figure 9–8 Forehand hold.

Figure 9–9 Backhand hold.

and vice versa. The holding technique is done with the forearm of the upper hand on the stick. It will be in a horizontal position and placed on the opponent's upper arm. The stick will remain in its position across the front of the attacker's body and can be used to check his stick when he tries to shoot or pass off.

When using both of these holds, the defender should spread his legs a little wider than his normal defensive stance to give a strong base of support. The defender is allowed to hold the attacker from the rear but only by exerting equal pressure. He is allowed to push the attacker with either hand and either forearm as long as the push is done from the front or side of the attacker and his hand is on the stick.

HIGHLIGHTS OF INDIVIDUAL DEFENSIVE PLAY

1. Be patient and play position first—the percentages favor this style of play over the aggressive, take-the-ball-away approach.
2. Pressurize the feeder and don't give the dodger a good-angle shot.
3. When you pick up your man with the ball, keep the foot back on the side to which he is going.

4. Run hip to hip with your man when he has the ball and is going at top speed; shuffle when he slows down.
5. Keep your stick in the same hand when playing your man.
6. Place your stick in a position in front of the number on your opponent's jersey and be ready to check his stick.
7. The right-handed defender is more effective playing an opponent who is primarily a right-handed driver, and a left-hander versus a left-hander, because he has the advantage of a better running and checking position and the stronger backhand hold.
8. Don't step into your man when using poke and slap checks.
9. Be very cautious with the use of over-the-head and wraparound checks. They are most effective when a right-handed defender is playing a left-handed attacker and a left-hander against a right-hander.
10. A check that travels a short distance is the most effective.
11. The defender must keep his legs spread to provide a strong base when using a hold.
12. Holds should be used only when the attacker is in front of the goal—10 yards or less from the crease for a midfielder and 5 yards or less from the crease for an attackman.

10

team defense

Defense is the most important phase of team play in lacrosse. The goalie, three defensemen, and three midfielders must blend together into a well-coordinated group that presents a solid, unified front to the opposition. The defensive players must be concerned not only with guarding their own men but also with assisting each other. If the game were strictly a series of 1-on-1 confrontations, the defense would lose out most of the time, because the offensive man would find it easy to get a close-range shot at the goal if he had the liberty to maneuver the defender over the entire field without interference from any other defensive players. It is reassuring for each member of the defense to know that he is not alone and operating by himself but definitely has the support of his teammates.

The mission of the defense is obviously to prevent the opponent from scoring. The philosophy for team defense follows the pattern established for individual defense. Position and patience are the watchwords as opposed to an aggressive, take-the-ball-away approach.

DEFENSIVE AREAS

Before we get to the specifics of team defense, it will be helpful to first identify certain areas on the defensive half of the field. These areas are crease, hole, perimeter, and press. Each area has definite rules governing the playing of offensive personnel. (See Figure 10–1.)

Crease

The crease has relevance in the defensive plan only according to the liberties and limitations imposed by the Rule Book. The goal crease is a circle around each goal with a 9-foot radius. The crease area is defined as the circular ground ter-

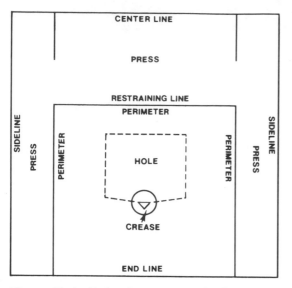

Figure 10–1 Defensive areas on the field.

ritory about each goal, within and including the goal crease. An attacking player may not be in the opponent's goal crease at any time. A defending player may run through the crease when he does not have possession of the ball, but he cannot enter the crease with the ball in his stick. Once the goalie gains possession of the ball in the crease, he must leave the area within four seconds.

In addition to the Rule Book definition of the crease as the area inside the circle, the area immediately in front of the goal outside the circle is also referred to as the "crease area."

Hole, or Critical Area

The boundaries for the hole area are as follows:

Directly in front of the goal, 10 yards from the crease (13 yards from the face of the goal). This is the area where midfielders normally operate.

To the side of the goal, 1 yard in front of the face of the goal and 5 yards from the crease. This is the area where attackmen normally operate. (See Figure 10–1.)

The hole area is the most critical territory on the defensive half of the field, because any offensive player, with or without the ball, is a potential scorer with a high-percentage shot. The defense must regard this area as the last line of defense. It is an area of tight playing of men, double-team-

ing, hard checking, and, when necessary, rugged body contact. The following rules are essential:

1. The man with the ball who is driving toward the goal should not be allowed to take his forehand, strong-side shot. He must be turned back by the defender.

2. All defensive players should be alerted to the driver's penetration into the hole area, because they become very conscious of double-teaming and backing up.

3. Cutters must be played closely.

4. Feeds into the hole must be followed by hard checking of the attackers' sticks in this area.

Perimeter

The boundaries for the perimeter are the goal area lines which form a rectangular box around the goal, 35 yards by 40 yards. It is at the outer limits of this area that the defender plays the man with the ball. The defender guards him deliberately and with enough pressure to keep him from shooting the outside screen shot or feeding leisurely into the crease area. The area between the outer edge of the perimeter and the outer edge of the hole can be used as a cushion against the hard-driving attacker. The defender uses this cushion area to maintain position on his man and to keep pressure on him, too. The closer the attacker moves to the goal, the more dangerous he becomes as a shooter and feeder.

Press Area

The territory outside the perimeter is known as the "press area." Offensive players are not normally played in this area because they are too far from the goal to be effective. If they are played, they have so much running room that the defender will have difficulty maintaining his position. Also, the defender may get overanxious and try to take the ball from his man, get dodged, and create a 6-on-5 scoring opportunity for the offense. There are several occasions when a team may want to play men in the press area.

1. When a team has an extra man and loses the ball. At this point it plays the opposition all over the field in an effort to regain possession of the ball.

2. When a team is behind in the latter stages of the game and must gamble to get the ball.

3. When an offensive player is considered to be such a potent scoring threat that the strategy

calls for him to be shut off from receiving the ball. The defender plays him man for man over the entire defensive half of the field.

COORDINATION OF TEAM DEFENSE

Each player on the team must have a complete understanding of the interworkings of team defense. The goalie is the backbone of the team defense and directs all the action. The defensemen and midfielders have definite responsibilities concerning the men they are playing as well as their defensive teammates. Even attackmen must know defensive strategy, because they may find themselves at the defensive end of the field when they are forced to go over the center line in a riding situation.

There are two types of team defense: man-for-man and zone. The more popular one is the man-for-man defense. The Hopkins philosophy of team defense stresses a combination of the two defenses. Our defense is basically man-for-man but with an emphasis on zone principles in certain situations.

When the opponent clears the ball into the offensive half of the field, the three midfielders and three defensemen drop back inside the perimeter and pick up their men. The defender playing the man with the ball meets him at the perimeter. The other five defenders will "sag off" their men at varying distances, which are determined by the location of the offensive players. The defender can sag only to the point where he can effectively guard his man if he were to receive the ball. The farther the offensive men are from the ball, the greater the distance in the defenders' "sagoff." The sag principle is a vital part of team defense, because it places the five defenders in a position to help out the teammate who is playing the ball.

To simplify the identification of men on the field, an imaginary line can be drawn down the middle of the field from one end line to the other and through the center of each goal. The half of the field where the ball is located is known as the on side and the side away from the ball, the off side.

In Figure 10–2, X1, X2, X5, and X6 are on the on side of the field. Players X3 and X4 are on the off side. The offside men are sagged the farthest from their opponents, because they are the least dangerous when they are so far from the ball. The

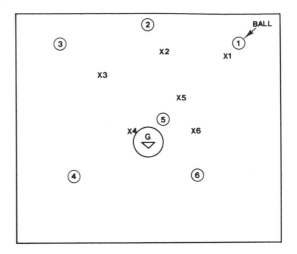

Figure 10–2 Positioning of defensive personnel when the ball is inside the perimeter.

onside defenders are sagged off their men but not quite as far as their offside teammates.

The five defenders who are playing men without the ball must make use of their peripheral vision to locate both the ball and their man. They cannot afford to take a long look at the ball and let their man cut by them toward the goal. Then again, if they play their man eye to eye, they will not be in a position to assist the teammate who is playing the ball and in need of help. Therefore, quick turns of the head as well as use of peripheral vision will assist the defenders in locating both their man and the ball.

A basic rule for the defenders who are playing men without the ball: Play your man but also locate the ball. Your man is more important when the attacker with the ball is moving on the perimeter and not driving toward the goal. The ball is more important when the attacker starts to force in toward the hole area. When he is in the hole, the defender concentrates more on the ball and is ready to back up his teammate if he needs help.

When the ball is in the midfield, the defenders who are guarding men behind the goal must play a yard or two in front of the goal to enable them to back up their teammate and to slide to pick up the midfield dodger. However, if a dodge is not imminent, and their attackmen exchange positions behind the goal, they must stay with them and move from one side of the goal to the other. They must avoid interference with the goalie as they make their move across the crease. As illustrated in Figure 10–3, the defender on the side of the ball (X6) moves in front of the goalie, near the front edge of the crease. The offside defender (X4) takes the route between the goalie and the goal. He can take this path without interfering with the goalie because the goalie should be located approximately 3 feet from the goal when the ball is in the midfield. This distance gives him enough room to slide through. However, he should tell the goalie when he is about to make this move. If the offside defender feels there isn't enough room to take that route, he can go behind the goal.

If the two attackmen change positions frequently in an effort to cause increased movement —which annoys the goalie and impairs his ability to follow the ball—the two defenders can make a switch call and exchange men. This cuts down on the confusion in front of the goal.

Playing the Man with the Ball

The man with the ball is the most dangerous on the field, and the defender playing him must be alerted to his offensive capabilities and his location on the field. A scouting report can be of tremendous help, but if one is not available, the de-

Figure 10–3 Paths taken by the defensemen when the ball is in the midfield and their men exchange positions behind the goal. Player X4 goes either behind the goalie or behind the goal, and X6 goes in front of the goalie.

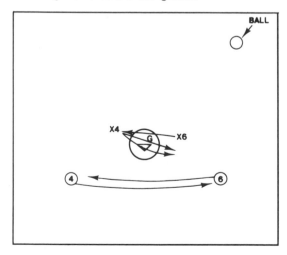

fender will just have to size up his opponent during the course of play. If the opponent is ambidextrous, the defender's job is much more difficult, since he must be ready to stop the driver both right-handed and left-handed. There is an obvious difference between a driver bearing in toward the hole area and going for the goal and one who is moving at half to three-quarter speed on the perimeter. The defender should treat them differently, too. If the driver is ambidextrous and is bearing in, he should be stopped on that particular side. If he is moving casually, the defender should be with him but anticipate his sudden change of direction and burst for the goal. The majority of midfielders cannot go to the goal effectively both ways and therefore their stronger side should be favored. If the opponent is a right-hander and in the right front position, the defender must be geared to stopping his right-hand drive to the goal and not be deceived by his fakes to the left. And even if he does go to his left, the angle of his shot is not nearly as good as the angle he gets when he drives toward the center of the field for his right-handed shot. So often the defender knows his opponent's strength but will allow himself to go for the fake and then get beaten by the driver going to his strong side. Know your opponent's strength and stop it.

Since most attackmen are capable of going to the goal both right-handed and left-handed, the most important factor for the defender is his awareness of his position on the field. When he is located behind the goal anywhere in Area C, as shown in Figure 10–4, he must be concerned primarily with the attacker driving to the front of the goal and getting a right-handed shot, because it is the better-angle shot on that side of the goal. Another reason for being primed to stop the right-handed shot in Area C is that the route to the goal is shorter: If the attacker goes from Area C to Area A, the defender can take the shortcut through the crease to get to the front of the goal, allowing him to maintain his position, since his opponent must stay outside the crease. Area C will be identified by the goalie as the "right behind," and this call will help to condition the defender to think, "I'm on the right-hander's side—stop the right-handed shot."

The same reasoning applies when in Area A; the only difference is that this side gives the advantage to the left-hander, and so the defender must concentrate on stopping the left-handed

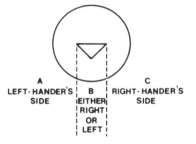

Figure 10–4 Identification of the areas behind the goal that alert the defender to the attackman's most effective route to the goal.

shot. The goalie will also help the defender when he makes his call, "Ball left behind."

When the ball is in Area B, the goalie will call, "Center behind." This is the most difficult area for the defender, because the attacker can make his move to the front of the goal by going either right- or left-handed. The attacker's route to the goal is almost a straight line, compared to his following the arc of the circle when moving from Area A to Area C and vice versa. The defender may still cut through the crease to get to the front of the goal, but he doesn't have as much advantage as when the attacker is in Area A or C. Area B is the toughest spot to defend behind the goal, and therefore the defenseman must be extremely alert and geared to go either way to the front of the goal.

The approach the defender makes to his opponent when he receives the ball must be controlled and timely. As the pass becomes more imminent, the defender must close the distance to his man to force him to receive the ball at the edge of or outside the perimeter. When the ball arrives, he should be about one stick's length away from his man and ready to deliver a check. He should be in a squared-up and well-balanced position, with his stick no higher than the numbers on his opponent's jersey and in front of his body. He should sound off, "I've got the ball." A late approach does not put pressure on the attacker, but it is much safer than the overaggressive approach, which may disrupt the opponent if successful but open up a dodge if unsuccessful.

When the attacker passes the ball to a teammate, the defender should deliver a poke or slap check to interfere with the accuracy of the pass. However, as the ball leaves the opponent's stick, the defender should back off his man several steps and then locate the ball. He does this to protect himself from his opponent using a "pass-and-cut-for-the-goal" maneuver.

Backing Up

The backup principle is the basis for establishing the necessary teamwork in team defense. Each member of the defensive unit is ready to help out, or back up, a teammate who is in trouble. The defensive players who are adjacent to the man playing the ball will let him know they have him backed on either side. Player X2 (see Figure 10–2) will call out, "I've got you backed on the left," and X6, "I've got you backed on the right." If the attacker with the ball dodges his defender, the zone principles of defense are in effect as each defender moves to play a different offensive man. If the dodge occurs on the left side of the defender (X1) who is playing the ball, X2 becomes the backup man who plays the dodger. Player X3 is ready to shift, or "slide," to X2's man. If the ball is passed counterclockwise, X4 is ready to slide to X3's man, X6 to X4's man, and X1 to X6's man, and now all five defenders have new men. However, the scoring attempt by the offense has been stopped by a coordinated defensive effort.

There are occasions when X5, the crease defenseman, will be the backup man. This normally occurs on a dodge that takes place in the midfield area, with the dodger driving directly down the middle or near the middle of the field. The crease defenseman is often the closest man to the dodger, and he should make the slide. When he does, either X4 or X6 is ready to play X5's man, the crease attackman.

When an attackman dodges from behind the goal, it is much safer to have the onside midfielder make the slide to back up, rather than the crease defenseman. The midfielder's slide does not give the offense as good a scoring opportunity as the defenseman's leaving the crease area where a passoff can result in a point-blank shot directly in front of the goal. If the attackman dodges X6 on the right side behind the goal, X1 becomes the backup man who picks up the dodger. If the ball is passed counterclockwise, X2 is ready to slide to X1's man, X3 to X2's man, X4 to X3's man, and X6 to X4's man. When the complete slide is made, all defenders except the crease defenseman have new men.

There is a definite technique in making an effective backup. The defender uses his body, not his stick, driving his shoulder into the numbers on his opponent's jersey. The body check is more effective when the contact is made high on the opponent's body, because it will then be virtually impossible for him to shoot or pass off. However, when the attacker is hit low, on the hips or legs, he still has control of the stick and can take a shot or pass the ball to a teammate. Too often defenders make the mistake of backing up with their sticks, and this makes it easy for the attacker to face-dodge or roll-dodge. The defender is more likely to miss the opponent's stick than his body. Therefore he should avoid the temptation of going for the stick and hit him with his body.

Playing the Cutter

Any time an offensive player cuts for the goal, he becomes a dangerous threat. If the cutter receives a pass in the hole or crease area, in most cases he is looking down the goalie's throat with a point-blank shot. Therefore the proper techniques to defend against the cutter are of primary importance. As soon as his man makes a cut for the goal, the defender calls out, "Man cutting." The goalie always faces the ball, and since he will not normally see the cutter, he relies on this call to alert him to a possible feed being directed to the crease area. The defender gives ground toward the goal when his man starts his cut. He is not concerned with locating the ball at this time but, rather, plays his man eye to eye, but he will notice if another offensive man is trying to set up a pick to free the cutter.

The defender holds his stick in a vertical position with the head of the stick well above the helmet and ready to come down when the goalie calls, "Check." When the cutter is moving to the hole area, the defender keeps his stick In this "high-port" position and on the same side the cutter is carrying his stick. The defender's check should hit squarely on the head of his opponent's stick or just on the inside wall and continue down on the upper arm of the cutter. If the upper arm is neutralized, the cutter cannot shoot the ball, whereas if the check is delivered to the lower gloved hand, the shot can still be taken with the follow-through of the upper arm. When the goalie makes the call for a check, there occurs one of the few times a defender should step into his opponent and fully commit himself in an effort to break up the reception of the pass or to dislodge the ball from the cutter if he has already caught it. The closer the cutter gets to the crease, the tighter he is played by the defender.

Playing a Man on the Crease

Since the offensive player on the crease has such an excellent position from which to score, he must be played extremely well by the defender. When the ball is behind the goal, the defender will cover the man on the crease much the same as a defender playing a cutter. Emphasis will be on maintaining a body-on-body and eye-to-eye position as opposed to one that allows locating the ball as well as the man. During my early years in coaching we used the split-vision approach on the crease, and it does have some advantages. However, the main problem of looking too long at the ball and permitting the attacker to break for an opening places too much pressure on the defense. On crease defense play we have stressed "follow the man and forget the ball."

The goalie who is always watching the ball acts as the eyes for the defender on the crease. The defender's ears help to compensate for not being able to see the ball as he listens intently for the goalie's call giving the location of the ball behind the goal—"Right behind," "Center behind," or "Left behind"—and also his check call. When he hears, "Check," he steps in to his opponent, follows through with an aggressive stick check, and drives his shoulder into his upper body in an attempt to completely neutralize him.

A basic rule for the defender on the crease is always to play between his man and the ball to keep the attacker from having a clear path to the ball. When the ball is behind the goal, the defender positions himself between his man and the goal. If the attacker is 1 to 3 yards from the crease, he plays between 1 and 2 feet from his man in order to enable his defensive teammate to slide through an offensive pick. If his man is more than 3 yards from the crease, the defender will loosen up more than 2 feet from his man. The farther the attacker moves away from the crease, the more the defender will sag off. If the opponent is 10 yards or more from the crease, the defender will treat him the same as an offensive midfielder, and the sag will be a minimum of 2 or 3 yards.

When the ball is in the midfield, the defender

will play between his man and the ball, about 1 to 2 yards from his man. He can afford to use his split vision to locate the ball more than when the ball is behind the goal, because the feeds to the crease are not as frequent. The crease defender uses his stick as a "feeler" to maintain contact with his man. Dodges from the midfield need backup help, and the defender on the crease is often in the best position to make the slide. The two defensemen whose men are behind the goal can cover for the crease defenseman in this situation.

Often the offensive team will operate with two men on the crease. This presents a problem for the defenders playing these men. If the defenders play too close to their men, they are vulnerable to a pickoff play, which will free an attacker for a point-blank shot. Each must therefore play about 1 to 2 feet from his man, allowing for enough room for the teammate to slide through. They must talk continuously to help each other. Their sticks must be in a vertical position to prevent any hindrance to their maneuvering.

When the ball is loose on the ground in the area in front of the crease, the defender continues to play his man and forgets the ball, unless he is certain he can gain control of the ball and get it out of the crease area. If he can kick the ball with his foot or flip it out of the crease area with his stick while driving into his man, this is a good play. If, on the contrary, he plays the ball and misses it, the attacker is free to take his chance to gain control of it and get off a shot. If the defender can drive his man into the crease by hitting him with a shoulder block from the side or the front, a technical foul will be called against the offensive team. The defender must be alert to the goalie's call of "Drop off" when he gains possession of the ball, because the defender will be guilty of a technical foul if he continues to block his man after the goalie has the ball in his stick.

Playing the Pick

The pick is an offensive technique that is used in lacrosse in just about the same manner as in basketball and several other team sports. An attacker positions himself in such a way as to impede the movement of his teammate's defender and to cause a breakdown in defensive coordination. There are two philosophies of defending against the pick: one favors switching men auto-

matically every time, and the other favors sliding the defender past the pick whenever possible and switching only when the defender actually is picked off. The Hopkins approach has been to avoid the automatic switch and to emphasize trying to have each player stay with his own man. As a basic rule, the switch is used only when the man playing the ball gets blocked or bumped by the pick.

Communication between the two defenders involved in handling the pick play is essential and involves a preparatory warning and a command. Since the defender who is playing the ball doesn't normally see the attacker who is setting the pick, he must receive help from his teammate who is playing the pick man. The defender playing the pick man does most of the talking, because he doesn't have as difficult a job as the man playing the ball. He sees the pick being set up, and he therefore makes the call. Player X1 (Figure 10–5) will call to X2, "Doug, watch the pick on your left"; X2 is alerted to the pick and is ready to maneuver through it. If the pick is too far from X2 or if O2 does not drive close enough to the pick, then X2 can go "over the top" of the pick. This route is between the two offensive men and can be taken only in the event of a poor pick. If the pick is set properly, X1 will call, "Pick on your left, slide through," and X2 will move between O1 and X1.

Proper positioning for the defender (X1) who is playing the pick man is very important in the defensive coordination. Once he is aware of his opponent's setting a pick, he calls to alert the teammate (X2) who is playing the ball and immediately concerns himself with proper positioning.

Figure 10–5 The defender playing the ball behind the goal moves to either the front or the rear of the pick.

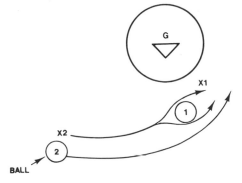

TEAM DEFENSE

He then lines up about 2 feet to the side of the pick man (O1), on the side to which the driver is going if he uses the pick. If his teammate (X2) gets bumped off by the pick and the switch is necessary, the defender is able to make the switch and to be in a good position to play the driver (O2). If, on the other hand, the defender plays directly behind the pick man and doesn't make use of the 2-foot offset position, he will end up trailing the driver to the front of the goal when the switch is made. Since it does take a second to determine whether the switch is necessary and then to react accordingly if it is, the offset position is mandatory. In addition to being 2 feet to the side of his opponent, the defender should be backed away from the pick man about 3 to 4 feet to allow his teammate plenty of room to slide through.

As soon as the defender playing the pick man decides the switch is necessary, he must shout the command "Switch" loud and clear to his teammate, to leave no doubt that they are to exchange men. The switch call definitely comes from the defender playing the pick man, because he can see the entire play. The call should not be made by the man playing the ball. The switch move should be made aggressively by the defender (X1), who should try to turn back the driver. If he is able to do so, X2 has a golden opportunity to double-team the driver and to take the ball away from him. However, if on the switch the pick man cuts for the goal, X2 must react quickly and take the shortest route to the front of the goal. He holds his stick in the high-port position, listens for the goalie's check call, and is ready to break up a return pass from the driver (O2) to the pick man (O1). This maneuver is the same as that used by basketball players defending against the pick-and-roll play.

Playing the Stackup

The stackup is an offensive maneuver by two attackmen who are operating behind the goal. It can cause the defense a great deal of difficulty if it is not defended properly. The ball carrier moves close to the pick set by his teammate, and instead of continuing through the pick he merely stops and steps back about one yard from the pick. If his defender moves behind the pick and the other defender does not make the switch, he

is unmolested and in an excellent feeding position.

Consequently the defense must break up the stackup maneuver and must understand completely how to do so. The two defenders must talk to each other as soon as the attackmen move into the stackup. One will call, "I've got him on the left," and the other, "I've got him on the right." Then they move into a position on either side of the pick man (O1), as shown in Figure 10–6. If the man with the ball is right-handed, X1 calls, "I've got the ball, and moves into him with either a poke check or a slap check to interfere with his feeding. (If the man with the ball is left-handed, then X2 plays him.) If O2 moves away from X1's advance by pulling his stick across his face or roll-dodging, X1 will try to stay with him by going between him and the pick man (O1). If X1 can't make it through and gets rubbed off by the pick, X2 will call, "Switch," and then play the ball. All the techniques for playing the switch are then used.

The defense must be trained to handle the stackup on a step-by-step basis, making use of continual talking by the two defenders involved. The defenders must be cautioned against overreacting and making their moves too hastily.

ZONE DEFENSE

Although most teams play man-to-man defense or a combination of man-to-man and zone defense, some teams play zone defense exclusively. The zone principles used in basketball have been adapted to lacrosse. Several coaches, in particular, have been involved with the development of

Figure 10–6 Positioning of the defenders playing the stackup behind the goal.

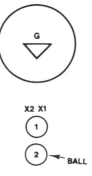

zone defense. Avery Blake was the first to popularize the zone defense and used it for many years during his illustrious career at Swarthmore College and the University of Pennsylvania. George Chandlee gave his Baltimore high-school opponents many problems with it during his outstanding tenure at the Gilman School. However, Howdy Myers of Hofstra University was the one who brought national attention to his zone defense during his twenty-six years at the Long Island school. After ten straight championships in the Baltimore area in the forties (seven at St. Paul's School and three national championships at Hopkins), Howdy moved to Long Island and promoted lacrosse at Hofstra. Since most of his lacrosse players had no previous experience, he felt he could teach them to play zone defense more easily than man-to-man. As one of the great innovators and teachers in the game's history, Howdy developed a very effective zone defense, which incorporated many man-to-man defensive principles. The success of his Hofstra teams with the zone defense caused other schools to try it as their basic defense.

The zone defense stresses the following points:

1. Place considerable pressure on the offensive man with the ball. The defender can do so without concern about being dodged, because there will be backup assistance from a teammate.

2. Designate a backup man who will be located near the crease and in a position to play the dodger.

3. Determine the zones (areas of responsibility) for each defender.

4. Jam the crease to prevent a successful feed or dodge in this area. This will take away the point-blank shots.

5. Encourage the opposition to take outside shots from about 18 to 20 yards. With the crease defenseman as well as the goalie trying to make the save, the chance of the outside shot scoring is limited.

Some teams have used a zone defense as a changeup defense for just a portion of a game. If a team has always played man-to-man defense, it can often disguise a zone defense well enough to prevent the opposition from knowing it and consequently completely disrupt the opponent's offense. Wilson Fewster, who coached at Hopkins for thirteen years and who was certainly one of the greats as both a player and coach, made use of his "mule" defense as a changeup at varying

times in the fifties and sixties. In the seventies the highly successful teams of Jerry Schmidt at Hobart College and Buddy Beardmore at the University of Maryland emphasized zone principles with aggressive play by the defender playing the ball carrier and with the other five defenders anxious to double-team and back up. In the 1975 NCAA championship game, Maryland employed a pure zone defense at varying times against Navy, and it was very effective.

The big advantage to using the zone defense is that it forces the opposition to make special preparations for it, since most teams use man-to-man defense. When a team has to deviate from its normal pattern, it is at a disadvantage. And if a team can disguise a changeup zone defense for a portion of a game, it can just about destroy the opponent's offense.

HIGHLIGHTS OF TEAM DEFENSE

1. Defense is teamwork; it is not a case of a series of 1-on-1 matchups.

2. Know the guidelines for defense in each of the four defensive areas on the field.

3. The entire defensive unit must be geared to back up a teammate who needs help. The backup should be executed with the body and not the stick.

4. The defender playing the driver in the hole area must not give him a forehand, strong-side shot. The driver must be turned back, and the entire defense must be ready to back up.

5. The defense makes use of the sag principle to help out the man playing the ball. The farther the offensive men are located from the ball, the greater the distance in the sagoff by their defenders.

6. When playing the men without the ball, the defenders should use peripheral vision and quick turns of the head to cover their men and watch the ball. The man is more important when the ball is being moved on the perimeter; the ball is more important when the ball is in the hole area.

7. Know the opponent's strength and his location on the field. Don't give him a good-angle, forehand shot.

8. When the attackman is in the right-behind area, the defender can concentrate on stopping the right-handed drive. When in the left-behind

area, the defender concentrates primarily on the left-handed drive.

9. The defender has his toughest job when the attackman is in the center-behind area, because he can get to a scoring position in front of the goal either right- or left-handed.

10. When his man receives the ball on the perimeter, the defender should be under control and in a position where he can put pressure on him. When his man passes the ball, he should try to check his stick but then immediately drop off several steps from him.

11. When a cutter moves into the hole, the defender must give him his undivided attention. His stick is raised in the high-port position, ready to check the cutter's stick. When the goalie calls, "Check," he actually steps into his man in order to make solid contact and deprive the cutter of a point-blank shot.

12. The crease defenseman plays his man eye to eye rather than using split vision when the ball is behind the goal. When the ball is in the midfield, he can use his peripheral vision more to locate the ball, since he may be the backup man on a dodge down the middle of the field.

13. A basic rule for any defender playing a man on the crease: he should play between his man and the ball.

14. A minimum distance of 1 to 2 feet from his man should be maintained by the crease defender when the ball is behind the goal. This prevents the offense from executing a pickoff play on the crease, because the teammate has room to slide through the pick.

15. When confronted with an offensive pickoff play, the defenders should talk to one another and favor the "slide-through" technique as opposed to the switch. The switch is used only when the defender playing the ball is unable to get by the pick and needs help.

16. The defender playing the pick man quarterbacks the defensive movement and is the one to call for the switch when it is needed.

17. The defenders must identify a stackup maneuver and then react to it methodically and not hastily. Verbal communication is essential.

11

man-
down
defense

Whenever a player is sent to the penalty box, so that his team must operate with one less man than its opponent, a great challenge is presented to the man-down defense. However, if the unit has a thorough understanding of the situation and complete confidence in its ability to handle any extra-man play, it can consistently thwart the offense. Since, as noted in Chapter 8, "Extra-Man Offense," a college team will average between six and ten fouls per game, it must be well prepared for operating shorthanded for an appreciable portion of the time the ball is on its defensive half of the field.

Developing a pride in this specialty unit goes a long way toward bringing success to a team. The man-down defense of the 1974 Hopkins team played a vital role in our winning the NCAA championship. The three key games of that season were our homecoming game with an undefeated Maryland team, the semifinal playoff game with Washington and Lee, and the second game with the Terrapins in the NCAA finals. In our first game with the Terps, we limited them to only three goals in thirteen extra-man opportunities. The effectiveness of our man-down unit in preventing Maryland scores on ten extra-man plays proved to be a real "shot in the arm" for our team. Even more significant was our success in allowing Washington and Lee only one goal in six attempts. With the score tied at 10–10 and eight minutes to go, extra-man play became crucial. We committed a one-minute foul with five minutes on the clock, but our man-down defense stopped W&L within ten seconds and cleared the ball to the offense. The Generals then fouled us with two minutes remaining, and Rick Kowalchuk fired in the winning goal on the ensuing extra-man play. In the championship game our man-down unit again came through, holding Maryland to two goals in seven extra-man attempts. In those three games our opponents were successful in only six out of twenty-six attempts (23 percent); whereas our extra-man offense was successful in thirteen out of thirty-one attempts (42 percent). This undoubtedly was a key factor in our winning the championship.

The same qualities needed by defensemen to play all-even are required for handling man-down situations. Mental alertness and physical agility are still the most essential qualities. Speed becomes more important because the defense is operating with one less man and consequently more ground must be covered by the defenders. An ability to anticipate helps the defenders to react to the movement of the ball. Talk helps even more, as everyone on the unit must know what is happening. Split vision is also fundamental, because each defender must see both the ball and the player or players in his area at all times. This is different from all-even play, where a player uses split vision to locate both his man and the ball but with primary emphasis on his man unless the ball carrier has moved into the hole area and is threatening the goal. In man-down defense, seeing the ball and the man are of equal importance.

Traditionally most teams have used three defensemen and two midfielders on their man-down unit. In recent years teams have been using four or five defensemen to get players with longer sticks who are more at home operating in the proximity of the goal. The longer stick has the obvious advantage of intercepting or blocking feeds and passes. At least nine players should be taught the man-down defensive system. Five are needed to play it at any one time, but this does not allow for the fact that one of the nine may commit the foul and therefore be in the penalty box, and one or two may be injured and unable to play. Constant practice of the system is necessary. At Hopkins we practice man-down defense between twenty and thirty minutes a day for three days before a game.

THE ROTATION SYSTEM

A number of systems can be used to play the man-down defense. Many teams employ a pure zone defense, which is similar to the 2–1–2 and 2–3 zones used in basketball. The five defenders are given certain areas of responsibility and try to jam up the prime shooting area and prevent close-range shots. The pure zone defense will vary in its play of attackmen behind the goal. When the ball is behind the goal, some zones send two defenders to play the two attackmen. Some send only one at a time, and some do not go behind the goal at all; rather, they play all five defenders in front of the goal. These systems are workable but not as effective as the rotation system.

The rotation system utilizes the same basic principles of defense that are employed when the opponent's offense has the advantage of an extra man in a fast-break situation, whether it be 6-on-5, 5-on-4, 4-on-3, 3-on-2, or 2-on-1. The defensive maneuvers explained in Chapter 15, "Fast Breaks," follow the same pattern in the man-down defense. It is a rotating system whereby one defender plays the ball carrier at a point where he is considered dangerous as a shooter or feeder. In the fast-break defense this point varies according to the number of defenders. However, in a man-down situation (six attackers versus five defenders), the defense plays the ball carrier when he is several yards inside the perimeter—at about the 18-yard mark in front of the goal and about 10 yards behind the goal. The remaining four defenders will cover the five other attackmen according to their location on the field. Since play is stopped when a foul occurs, the defense has time to position its players to cover the most dangerous attackers.

The order of priority is as follows:

1. The ball carrier, when he moves several yards inside the perimeter, is the first player to be covered.

2. The crease attackman is always considered dangerous because of his proximity to the goal. He must be covered, and if there are two men on the crease, both must be covered.

3. The two attackers on either side of the ball carrier are next in order of priority. The two defenders guarding them sag off about 4 to 5 yards to the inside.

4. The two attackmen who are farthest from the ball are the least dangerous and are therefore covered by only one man.

Thus, the key to man-down coverage is to play the ball carrier, the man on the crease, and the two attackers adjacent to the ball, while the fifth defender covers the two attackers farthest from

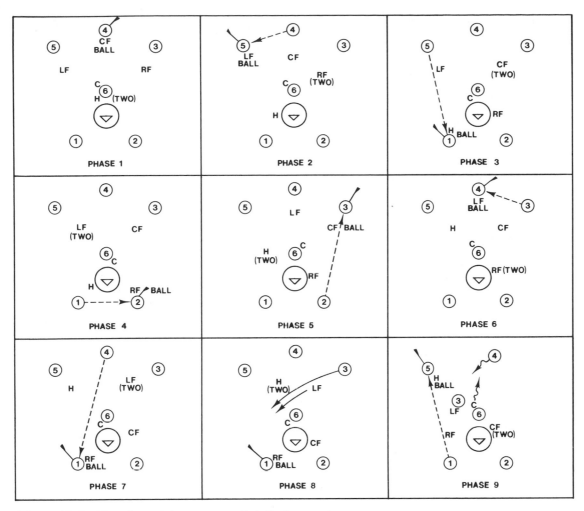

Figure 11–1 Man-down defense versus 3–1–2 alignment.

the ball. Figure 11–1 shows the defense in the proper positions to cover a 3–1–2 extra-man play. With the foul being initiated from the middle position in the midfield, as shown in Phase 1 Figure 11–1, the defenders assume their positions and call out accordingly:

Center Front (CF):	"I have the Center Front and I'm playing the ball."
Left Front (LF):	"I have the Left Front."
Right Front (RF):	"I have the Right Front."
Crease (C):	"I have the Crease."
Hole (H):	"I have the Hole and I'm playing two."

If the play is initiated by two attackers behind the goal, one defender is identified as Left Behind (LB) and the other as Right Behind (RB). If there are two attackers on the crease, one defender is referred to as Left Crease (LC) and the other as Right Crease (RC). If there are three on the crease, the defenders are called Left Crease (LC), Crease (C), and Right Crease (RC). The goalie is responsible for calling out the offensive alignment before the official blows his whistle to start the play. First he identifies the number of players on the crease and then the complete lineup. For example, in Phase 1 of Figure 11–1, the goalie sounds off, "One on the crease, it's a 3–1–2."

The defender who is covering two attackers has the most difficult assignment of all five defenders. He must know not only where each is located but also the position of the ball. To do so, he must keep turning his head. In Phase 1 of Figure 11–1 the Hole Man is covering both O1 and O2 when the play starts. If either cuts toward the goal, he must play him, because he is obviously more of a scoring threat in the crease area than behind the goal. The Hole Man gets help from the Right Front

and Left Front defenders, because they sag to the inside to jam up the hole area. Their sticks are to the inside not only to discourage passes but also to block or intercept them. Notice the defender who is playing the ball has BALL next to him and the defender farthest from the ball has (TWO), because he is responsible for two players.

Whenever the offense makes a pass, the five defenders adjust accordingly, with everyone assuming a new responsibility. Figures 11–1, 11–2, 11–3, and 11–4 show the movements of each defender in four extra-man offensive plays. Every

Figure 11–2 Man-down defense versus 2–3–1 alignment.

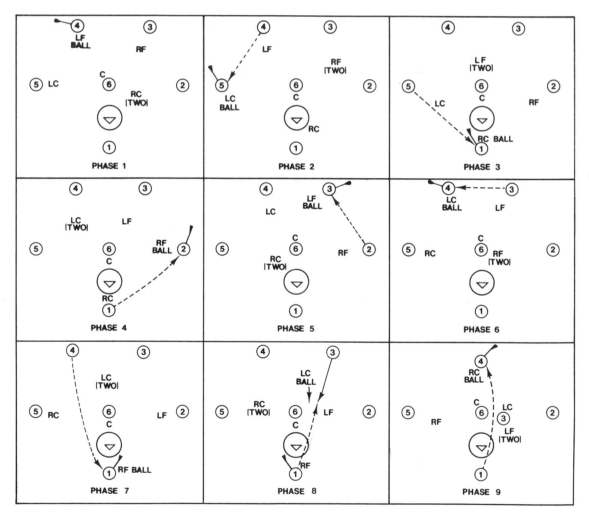

time a pass is made, each defender lets his teammates know who he is covering to avoid confusion. For example, in Phase 5 of Figure 11–1 the following calls are made when the ball is thrown from O2 to O3:

CF: "I have the ball."
LF: "I have one."
RF: "I have one."
C: "I have one."
H: "I have two."

Whenever an attacker makes a cut toward the goal, the defender who is responsible for him must go with him and, almost as important, he must alert his teammates by calling out, "Man cutting; I have him." Phase 8 of Figure 11–1 shows LF going with the cutter. Prior to the cut his responsibility is two men, O3 and O4, because he is not adjacent to the ball and, in fact, is farthest from it. Player H has only one man, O5, prior to the cut. But with the cut, the picture changes for these two defenders—LF has the cutter, O3, and H now has two men, O4 and O5. If LF fails to make the call to alert his teammates that a man is cut-

Figure 11–3 Man-down defense versus 2–2–2 alignment.

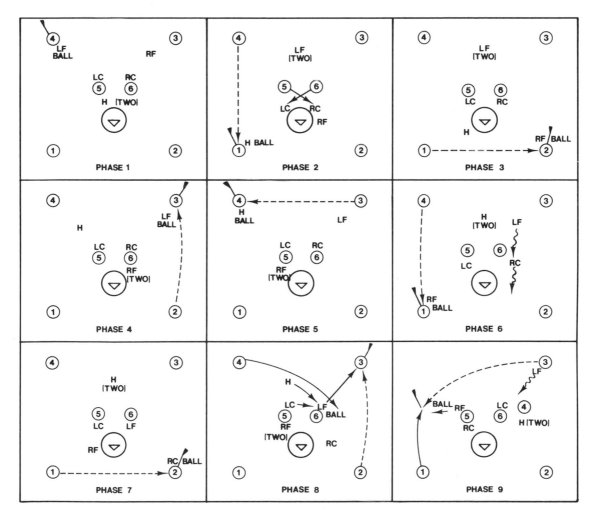

MAN-DOWN DEFENSE

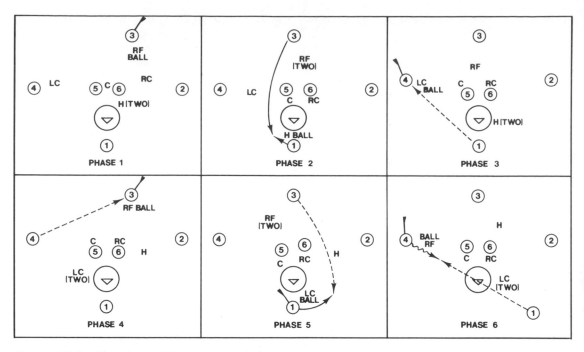

Figure 11–4 Man-down defense versus 1–4–1 alignment.

ting, H may not be aware of it and still cover only one man, O5, leaving O4 completely wide open for a sneak or cut down the back side. Since quite a few extra-man plays try to make use of a cutter to confuse the defense, it is imperative that the defense calls out the cutter and knows how to handle him.

When the ball goes behind the goal and the offense has two men there, the man-down defense has several ways of playing them. It can send only one defender at a time behind the goal, with the other defender waiting near the crease on the offside. In Phase 3 of Figure 11–1, H is playing O1 and RF is waiting at the plane of the goal. When O1 passes to O2, H hustles back to the crease area and RF moves to O2 when H approaches the plane of the goal. The positive aspect of this alternating method is that it jams the crease area with four defenders playing four offensive players. However, its disadvantage is in not putting enough pressure on the feeders and allowing them too much time to pick out an open man cutting for the goal as they pass the ball back and forth. If the defense plays both attackmen hard,

giving them constant pressure, it can disrupt their feeding and control of the ball behind the goal. Our Hopkins teams have used this pressurizing method primarily and have achieved considerable success with it. In addition to the alternating and pressurizing methods there is the soft method, in which neither defender applies pressure to the ball carrier. The one playing the ball goes no farther than the back edge of the crease, and the other is even with the plane of the goal. The soft and alternating methods can be incorporated into the man-down defense as change-ups to the pressurizing defense.

One of the best ways to teach the rotation system is to use poker chips on a table in a meeting room. A circular piece of paper simulates the crease. The white chips are numbered for the offense and the red chips are lettered with the abbreviations for the various defensive positions. A coin is designated as the ball and is placed on one of the white chips. The coin is moved with each pass, and the defense adjusts accordingly. After the basic extra-man plays have been defended, the coach can use all sorts of unusual

TECHNIQUES AND TACTICS

plays that cover just about every offensive possibility. It helps the defensive players immeasurably to watch the various adjustments that the man-down defenders make on every offensive maneuver. From the classroom setting, the man-down defenders are ready to move out on the field for practical work around a goal. Over the course of one week they will be exposed to the basic extra-man plays. Man-down defense is a phase of the game that can be practiced extremely well in a gymnasium during inclement weather.

BASIC RULES

1. All defenders keep their sticks in the high-port position above their heads and in the passing lanes of the extra-man offense. Many passes can be blocked or intercepted if the defenders' sticks are placed high and to the inside.

2. The defender playing the crease attackman concentrates on the location of the ball as much as on the position of his man. In all-even play, the crease defenseman plays his man almost completely eye to eye, but this is not so in the man-down situation, because he must enter into the overall team defense and help out even more.

3. A defender on the crease, whether the crease defenseman or any of the man-down defenders, should leave the crease to play the ball when it is passed from behind the goal to an attacker in a dangerous shooting position in the midfield about 15 yards or closer to the goal. If there is no defensive teammate between himself and the ball, he leaves the crease area and hustles to the shooter to prevent him from moving in even closer to the goal for a point-blank shot. When he rushes at the shooter, he keeps his body directly in front of the shooter's stick, trying to make the save with his body. It is surprising how often the shooter will hit him with the ball if he is in just the right position. The defender must also be under control when he reaches the shooter to avoid being dodged. Phase 8 of Figure 11–3 shows LF first playing O6 on the crease, but when O2 passes to O3, leaving the crease to cover O3.

4. A defender on the crease should be reluctant to leave a man on the crease to play a man behind the goal because he is moving away from

a potential scorer to play a potential feeder, who is obviously less dangerous. There are times when he does make this move, but he must be covered by a teammate before going. Phases 6 and 7 of Figure 11–3 show LF moving to the crease area and directing RC to move behind the goal to play O2; RC does not actually leave until LF tells him, "Go ahead, Doug; I have the crease." This move always takes place from the off side of the field.

5. An onside crease defender never leaves the crease to play the ball behind the goal. Phases 6 and 7 of Figure 11–2 show RF, the offside crease defender, leaving O2 to cover O1 on the pass from O4. LF has enabled him to make the move by sliding to the crease to cover O2. If RC, the onside crease defender, were to leave O5 to cover O1, he would open up an excellent scoring opportunity for O5, because no one would be able to cover him on a quick pass from O1.

6. The defender playing the ball carrier behind the goal must respond quickly to a pass from his man to an attacker in front of the goal. As he follows the flight of the ball with his eyes, he sprints to the crease area. He is ready to move toward the offside crease, because the extra-man offense normally tries to move the ball with speed and take advantage of a slow-reacting defense. Phases 4, 5, 6, and 7 of Figure 11–1 show RF moving from O2 to the crease and finally to O1 on the side opposite his original position in Phase 4. In Phases 4, 5, and 6 of Figure 11–2, RC moves from O1 to the crease area opposite the pass and eventually covers O5 when the pass is made to O4.

7. The defender playing the cutter not only makes his call that a man is cutting but also tries to read the play in order to determine whether the cut is meaningful or not. Often the extra-man offense will use a cutter just to cause confusion in the defense and to make a defender play him. Granted, the cutter must be covered when he breaks for the goal, because an open stick in the crease area can result in a goal, but as soon as the feeder passes the ball to another attacker, the defender releases the cutter to get into the regular rotation. Often the defense makes the mistake of staying with the cutter too long in man-for-man coverage.

8. The defender playing the ball carrier can afford to be considerably more aggressive in the

MAN-DOWN DEFENSE

man-down situation than in the all-even, because the extra-man offense is not geared to dodging. However, a certain amount of caution must prevail to avoid a second foul.

9. After a shot is taken and the offense regains possession of the ball, whether in bounds or out of bounds, the man-down defense must regroup. Frequently the extra-man offense will set up another play in this situation, and the defense must be ready to adjust to it.

10. When time has elapsed on a penalty, the defender entering the game runs at full speed to get inside the defensive perimeter. He plays the nearest man who is unguarded and calls out, "All even." Players entering the game from the penalty box frequently make the mistake of calling too soon, and this causes the defense to relax, thinking all the men are covered when actually they are not.

11. The distance from the center of the field to the defensive perimeter is shorter than the distance from the penalty box to the defensive perimeter. Therefore the player entering the game from the penalty box usually should head toward the attack half of the field, releasing a fast midfielder at the center of the field to take the shorter route back to the defense.

TWO- AND THREE-DOWN SITUATIONS

When two members of a team are in the penalty box, the offense has a 6-on-4 advantage. The keynote to the two-down defense is the defenders' jamming the crease area and encouraging the offense to take shots in the area between the perimeter and the hole. Each defender approaches the offense with the idea of trying to cover two men. Even the defender playing the ball does not concentrate fully on the ball carrier; rather, he tries to anticipate where he will be throwing the ball so he can react quickly and adjust his position. The ball carrier is not played until he is at about the 16-yard mark in front of the goal. Phase 1 of Figure 11–5 shows LF playing O4 at this position and the other three defenders jamming in close to the crease area. If the ball carrier is behind the goal, the defender does not go to him at all. He avoids making the move behind the goal, because it would create in front of the goal a 5-on-3 offensive

advantage, which would be very difficult to stop. When the ball carrier reaches the plane of the goal, the nearest defender then plays him in order to prevent him from taking a close-range shot. Phase 3 of Figure 11–5 shows RC playing O1 when he reaches this point. Phase 4 of Figure 11–5 shows RF moving to O4 when O1 makes the pass to him. When the ball is in the hole area, the closest defender plays it.

When three defenders are in the penalty box, the offense almost always gets a good shot at the goal. However, with a little bit of luck or a spectacular save by the goalie, the defense can prevent the score. The same basic principles that apply to the two-down defense can be adapted to the three-down situation. The three defenders set up in a triangle, with the point man, the defender closest to the restraining line, not going any farther than about 10 to 12 yards from the goal. The other two defenders jam the crease. If the ball goes behind the goal, all three move in close to the crease, trying to entice a shot from the wing areas.

CLEARING IN MAN-DOWN SITUATIONS

When the man-down defense gains possession of the ball, it must try to clear the ball to its offensive half of the field. This is especially important, because, according to a rule instituted in 1969, players are released from the penalty box when the man-down team clears the ball into the attack-goal area. On an inbounds play the defense tries to use speed and dodging ability to clear the ball. When the goalie makes a save, he tries either to pass the ball to a teammate in the midfield area, to make the break himself to the front of the goal, or to go behind the goal in an effort to use the crease to gain an advantage over the riding crease attackman. If the crease attackman follows him behind the goal, the goalie goes to the opposite side from him. If the crease attackman stays in front of the goal, the goalie merely goes behind the goal and waits for the crease attackman to make the first move. When he does, the goalie moves to the opposite side and just keeps going around the goal with the attackman chasing him. This allows the penalty time to run out and the man in the box to reenter the game. If

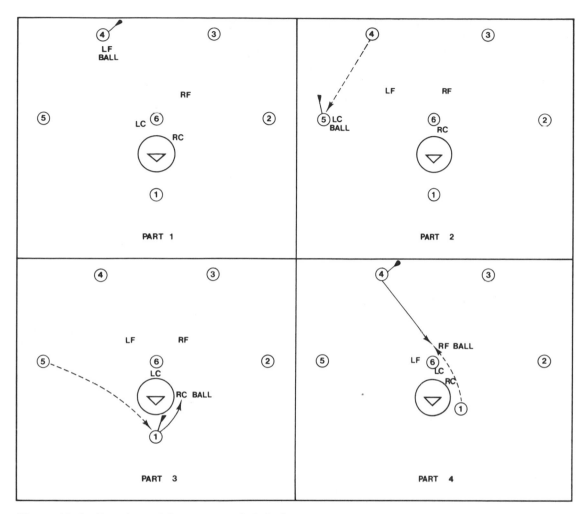

Figure 11–5 Two-down defense versus 2–3–1 alignment.

a riding attackman tries to double-team the goalie when he is being chased around the goal, the goalie then passes off to the defender who has been left unguarded. The defense should have no trouble clearing the ball in this situation. Anytime the defense finds itself in a position in which it may lose the ball, it should throw the ball upfield toward the center line and give the attack the opportunity to fight for possession.

When the man-down defense gets the ball in an out-of-bounds situation, the team's fastest and best-dodging midfielder should bring the ball into play. If this person is not in the game when

the whistle blows, the coach must have him enter as a substitute. Under no circumstances should a slow defenseman or a slow goalie bring the ball into play from out of bounds, because he probably will lose it. As soon as the ball is given to the dodger, all other defenders should move to positions away from him. When the official blows his whistle, the man with the ball drives at his defender and either dodges him or uses sheer speed to go by him. This is the easiest and most effective clear in the book when a team is operating with a man in the penalty box.

If the ball goes out of bounds on the end line,

MAN-DOWN DEFENSE

the goalie can position himself in front of the goal but just inside the crease. When the whistle blows, he breaks close to the pipes in order to get the pass behind the goal, in the crease, and on the side opposite the riding crease attackman. Once the goalie receives the pass, he can run the ball up the field or play cat-and-mouse with the attackman around the crease.

When a defender gains possession of the ball in a two- or three-down situation, he should immediately throw the ball toward the center line, where his attackmen will battle for it. It is foolish to try to clear the ball by running it out or passing it to another defender when the riding team has such a definite advantage.

SPECIAL DEFENSES

Although the rotation system can be used exclusively in man-down situations, the defense can gain an advantage by using a special or changeup defense on occasion. A pure 2–1–2 or 2–3 zone can be disguised to look like the rotation system to confuse the extra-man offense. Another zone defense that can completely disrupt the offense is a box-and-one. In this play four defenders execute the same maneuvers they normally use when two men are in the penalty box. The fifth defender plays the most dangerous shooter or feeder on the offense. He covers him man for man and goes wherever he goes on the field. He can either shut him off completely, try-

ing to prevent him from even getting the ball, or he can play him closely when he doesn't have the ball but allowing him to get it only out near the perimeter and away from prime feeding or shooting territory. The box-and-one defense is especially effective against a team that relies primarily on the offensive capability of one player. When an extra-man offense is dependent mainly on two players, the triangle-and-two defense can be used. Three defenders play the basic triangle, which they use whenever three men are in the penalty box. The other two cover man for man the opponent's most dangerous offensive threats, using either shutoff techniques or just close, pressurized coverage. The special man-down defenses are often used more effectively in thirty-second penalties rather than in one-minute penalties, because the offense doesn't have as much time to identify the different defensive maneuvers.

A pure 1–3–1 zone defense can also give a 1–4–1 extra-man play considerable difficulty. Figure 11–6 shows the three basic maneuvers of this zone defense. One defender (the front point man) is assigned to play the offensive player in the midfield area, and another defender (the rear point man) plays the attackman behind the goal. Either of these defenders may shut off the offensive man he is guarding. This often upsets the strategy of the extra-man offense. The three defenders across the crease play three zones and cover the four offensive players in the crease area. They jam the inside area to prevent a shot

Figure 11–6 A 1–3–1 zone versus 1–4–1 alignment.

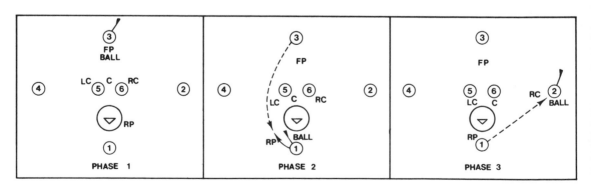

from directly in front of the goal. They encourage the offense to shoot from the wing areas, where they have a poorer angle.

Regardless of the style of man-down defense a team uses, it must continually strive to improve its effectiveness. A man-down unit that prides itself in meeting the extra-man challenge can bolster the overall attitude and morale of a team. It is especially reassuring to every team member to have the confidence that its defense can handle not only the all-even play but also the man-down play.

MAN-DOWN DEFENSE

goal tending

12

The goalie is the backbone of a team's defense and probably carries more responsibility on his shoulders than any other player on the field. There have been few championship teams, if any, with a mediocre goalie. To the contrary, almost every championship team has had a goalie whose performance has been either above average or superior. This has certainly been the case with each of my seven Hopkins champions, and especially so with my last team in 1974. When freshman Kevin Mahon moved into the starting role for the last game of our regular season, he sparked us to a stunning upset of the undefeated defending champions, the University of Maryland, by a 17–13 score. He lead us through the first two games of the NCAA playoffs and then, in what many people considered another upset, was a key performer in our 17–12 victory over Maryland in the NCAA championship game. He made twenty-five saves in that game, including eighteen in the second half, when Maryland made a spirited comeback, and was all over the field intercepting passes and scooping ground balls. Most upsets in the game of lacrosse are attributed directly to the play of the goalie. This was certainly the case in our two big upset wins over Maryland in 1974.

Although the qualities of a good goalie are described in Chapter 4, they should be repeated just briefly here. The most important is courage, or just plain "guts." It takes a special kind of person to place, without flinching, his head and body in point-blank range of a powerfully thrown lacrosse ball. Regardless of the protective equipment worn, the ball either stings or just plain hurts. The average person cannot take this kind of punishment.

Along with courage the goalie must have a number of other qualities, the most important being quick reflexes and agility. Quick reactions inside the 6-foot-by-6-foot goal are of primary importance, because the goalie must try to get both his stick and his body in front of every shot. Good stick work is essential, because it minimizes the number of shots that rebound out of his stick or off his body to give the opponent additional scoring opportunities. The goalie must exercise positive leadership in directing and controlling his teammates on the defensive half of the field. When a goal is scored, he must be careful not to overreact or to blame one of his teammates. If there has been a defensive breakdown that results in a goal, it is up to the goalie to talk to his teammates in a tactful manner. It is not his job to criticize his teammates but to unify them. The goalie must also keep his emotions from running wild when he misses a ball he feels he should have saved. Ranting and raving about a mistake do nothing for his own steadiness or the general morale of the team. Les Matthews, one of our all-time great goalies at Hopkins and a first-team All-American in 1972 and 1973, remarked that while playing he always watched the reaction of the opponent's goalie when Hopkins scored a goal. He found him to be an accurate measure of the team's cohesiveness and stability. If he threw his stick to the ground or into the goal or started chewing out a teammate, his team was in trouble and usually ended up on the short end of the score. If, to the contrary, he controlled his emotions and spoke in even tones to his teammates, his team was unified and very much ready to play the game.

Size and speed are bonus qualities for the goalie but not essential. The goalie who, with his cleats and helmet, is 6 feet tall or more has the advantage of having his head extend above the top crossbar on the goal. The broader he is, the more of the goal he covers. During my twenty years of coaching lacrosse at Hopkins I was fortunate to work with twelve excellent goalies, nine of whom made one of the All-American teams. Of that group of twelve there were nine who were 5'9" or shorter, and the nicknames of three of them—Mouse, Rat, and Elf—indicate just how small they were.

Although it helps to have size in the goal, speed is more beneficial. The goalie initiates most of the clears, and speed makes his job much easier. Six of my goalies had excellent speed and they certainly made use of it in clearing the ball.

Finally, and possibly just as important as cour-

age and quick reflexes, the goalie must have confidence in himself. This is important to meet the challenge of the opponent's shooters and to command his own defense.

COACHING GOALIES

One of the main jobs of the coach in developing a goalie is to instill confidence as well as instruct him in the proper position in the goal and outside the crease. The coach cannot give a player the fearlessness to stick his nose into a rocketlike shot, the quick reflexes to react to the ball, or the speed to move outside the crease. These qualities must come naturally to him. However, with proper handling of the beginner, one who is basically not afraid of the ball, a coach can develop his skills and give him the confidence to become a first-rate goalie. The goalie realizes he will receive a certain amount of physical punishment from the ball, but the coach can help him to minimize it by teaching him to make as many saves as possible with his stick rather than his body. If the goalie is not given intelligent and meaningful direction, his confidence will be completely shattered, and he will fail. This often happens when the goalie picks up bad habits doing what comes naturally to him or when just listening to advice from other players who really don't know the fine points of playing in the goal.

In working with a beginner who has the desire to be a goalie, the first step is to concentrate on the fundamentals of handling the stick—catching, throwing, cradling, and scooping. Once he has the confidence in handling the ball in the big pocket, he is ready to be instructed in the basic movements to the ball. Rather than starting the goalie on a grass or dirt field, it is probably wiser to work with him in front of a wall, on a surface that gives a true bounce of the ball. A wooden gym floor or a concrete pavement is ideal. The outline of a goal can be painted on the wall or made with adhesive or masking tape. The wall is a better training aid for the beginner than an actual goal, because the ball, when missed by the goalie, merely bounces off the wall and returns to the coach, whereas when the goalie misses a shot while working in front of a regular goal, he has to rake the ball out of the net and throw it back to the coach. This not only takes more time but also can be harmful psychologically to the goalie, as he feels he is spendimg most of his time raking the ball out of the net rather than making saves.

To help the beginner get the feel of proper footwork and movement into the ball, it is advisable to take the stick away from the goalie and give him just a sawed-off broom handle or a lacrosse handle without the head. Instead of using a regular lacrosse ball, the coach can use a tennis ball or sponge-rubber ball to throw bounce shots at the goalie. This type of ball does not sting or hurt the goalie when it hits his body. In this way the goalie gets practice in positioning his body directly behind the ball on every shot and doesn't have to be concerned with the coordination of moving his body and catching the ball at the same time. The coach uses this technique for about twenty to thirty minutes during each of the first few workouts with a new goalie.

After the goalie learns to move properly, the coach can give him a stick and begin throwing a lacrosse ball at him at about half speed and from a distance of about 15 yards. The coach makes all his shots with an over-the-shoulder throwing motion. Rather than starting with bounce shots, which are more difficult to catch, he should keep the ball in the air. First the shots are directed to one side of his body and then to the other side, with emphasis on movement of his body behind every shot. Once the goalie handles these shots with reasonable confidence, the coach can move to low bounce shots near the feet, then high bounce shots. The coach lets the goalie know the shots will be thrown only on one side. The goalie then gets the rhythm of moving into the ball on that side. After he experiences reasonable success, the coach switches to the other side. The coach can use this format for the first three or four sessions with the goalie and then, according to his progress, begin to shoot harder. If he wants to give him full-speed shots but still let him know they will be either in the air or on the ground and on the right side or left side, he should move back to a distance of 18 to 20 yards from the goal. If the goalie handles these shots effectively, the coach can work him on high shots without telling him on which side they will be thrown, then on bounce shots to either side, and finally on a mixture of both high and bounce shots to either side.

Whenever the goalie reaches the point of quick movement and effective handling of shots taken on a true surface, the coach can move him into a goal on a natural turf field. However, he may want to take away his stick and go back to the tennis-ball routine to help him react to the ball on a more difficult surface where the bounce will often be irregular. Then he can move along with the sequence of shots followed in the first few sessions on the true surface. The coach will probably not want to open up with full-speed shots at the 18- to 20-yard mark until the goalie has had at least several practices on the natural turf and is ready for them. Once the goalie has confidence in handling hard shots at this distance, he is over the hump in his development in the goal. The coach can then proceed to teach him how to play the various types of shots other than the over-the-shoulder shot, and also shots that are taken from different locations on the field, including the point-blank shots on the crease. Next he can work with him on the vocabulary he uses to direct the defense, on playing screen shots, on handling ground balls around the crease, and on clearing the ball. All these areas will be covered in this chapter, with the exception of clearing, which will be covered in Chapter 13.

EQUIPMENT

Aside from a helmet and gloves, which are standard equipment required by the Rule Book, the goalie wears a cup supporter and a chest pad. Even though the chest pad is less cumbersome than a baseball catcher's chest protector, some goalies prefer not to wear it because they do not want to be weighed down by extra equipment. However, it should be mandatory for the beginner. Although some of our Hopkins goalies have preferred not to wear one in games, we have required them to wear it in practices, just to give them the additional protection. Very few goalies wear arm pads and collars, because they interfere with the goalies' maneuverability. Some do wear elbow pads for protection from the stick checks of riding attackmen. Most goalies wear sweat pants but few, if any, wear shin or leg protectors. Since it is imperative for the goalie to have complete control of his stick, he will probably cut out the major portion of the palm of his gloves to get the best possible control with his fingers.

According to the Rule Book, the goalie's stick may be of any length and the pocket of any depth. Many average-sized collegiate goalies play with a very long handle, which helps them make the long clearing pass, intercept passes, reach for ground balls outside the crease area, and maintain proper position in the goal by hitting the pipes with either the head of the stick or the handle. Although the length of their sticks is generally between 46 and 60 inches, some goalies prefer a stick shorter than 46 inches, because they can dodge more easily with it. Nonetheless, the majority of collegiate goalies use a stick in the range of 50 to 56 inches. The pocket of the stick should definitely be deep enough for the goalie to be able to keep even the hardest shot in his pocket. If his pocket is too shallow and the ball bounces out, the attackers have an excellent chance for a rebound shot and possible a goal. Controlling the ball is the primary consideration regarding the depth of the pocket, although a pocket with an excessive sag will cause the goalie trouble with his throwing.

BODY AND STICK POSITIONING

Ball in Front of Goal

When the ball is in front of the goal, the goalie places himself in a direct line between the ball and the center of the goal. Since the ball leaves the shooter's stick about 1 to 2 feet from the side of his body, the goalie actually lines up between the center of the goal and the ball carrier's stick side. This places him in a more advantageous position to block the shot than if he were lined up with the center of the ball carrier's body. His feet are shoulder-width apart and his weight is carried in his legs and on the balls of his feet. His heels are just barely touching the ground to give stability. His knees are bent, his upper body leans slightly forward, and his eyes never leave the ball. Although he is responsible for directing the entire defense, he will not try to do so at the expense of taking his eyes off the ball. Figure 12–1 shows the goalie in his basic stance when the ball is in the midfield area near the restraining line.

The goalie grips his stick in a different manner than the other players on the team, because the head of his stick is considerably bigger and heavier. To control it properly and to move it quickly to the ball, he grasps it with his upper hand on the handle next to the head of the stick or just an inch or two from it. His hands are closer together than any other player's hands, because his primary concern is control of the large head. A distance of about 6 to 10 inches is desirable. The grip is firm with both hands, although the upper hand is the dominant one and its position on the stick does not change. The lower hand may slide slightly toward the upper hand on bounce shots above the level of the hips.

The position of the goalie's stick will be determined by the location of the ball. Since the most effective shots taken at the restraining line, or a yard or two on either side of it, are bounce shots, the goalie holds his stick at hip level or slightly above when the ball is in this position. Consequently, he can move his stick into the bounce shot more quickly than if he were holding it above his shoulder. (See Figure 12–1.) The goalie will keep his stick in this position even when the shooter is at the 15-yard mark. However, from this point on to the 10-yard mark the goalie will raise the level of his stick slightly because the probability of a high shot increases considerably as the shooter gets closer to the goal. Figure 12–2 shows the goalie's position when the shooter is 10 yards or closer to the goal.

The key to the goalie's position is his readiness to attack the ball as soon as it leaves the shooter's stick. He can't let the ball play him; he must go after it. With his body weight centered in his legs and the balls of his feet, he is ready to spring at the ball like a panther at his prey. Some goalies bounce continuously in place while waiting for the shooter to release the ball. Such movement can in fact be a handicap, because the goalie could be in the upward motion of the bounce when the ball is shot and thus lose a split second in reacting to the ball. To help keep their legs in a ready-to-move position, some goalies continuously shift their body weight just slightly from the ball of one foot to the other; this is acceptable if not overdone.

As the ball changes location in front of the goal, the goalie must adjust his position accordingly. He moves with short, lateral steps, first with one foot and then the other. His feet never get closer together than about 3 inches as he moves, and he definitely does not hop with both feet leaving the ground at the same time. Figure 12–3 shows the

Figure 12–1 Goalie's position when the shooter is located near the restraining line.

path on which the goalie travels as the ball moves in front of the goal. When the ball is directly in front of the goal, the goalie is positioned at the outer edge of the arc that runs from one goal post to the other. The maximum distance from the goal is 3 feet. As the ball moves away from the center of the field, the goalie moves with it. When the ball is even with the plane of the goal, he is next to the post.

The goalie can maintain proper position better by making several marks on the ground with his stick. The first one is on the crease and directly in front of the center of the goal. He also can draw an arc on the ground with the butt end of his stick in order to check his positioning on it during practice sessions. Since the ball often moves rapidly from one position on the field to another, the goalie must use his stick as a feeler while keeping his eyes on the ball. A right-handed goalie moving from the center of the goal to his left uses the butt end of his stick to hit the left goal post. When moving from the center to his right, he uses the head of his stick to hit the right goal post. This contact helps to keep the goalie on his arc and in the best position to make the save. If he doesn't use the stick as a feeler, he will probably

stray from the arc and lose position. If he turns his head even for an instant to look at the goal instead of using his stick, he may sacrifice the save.

Ball Behind Goal

When the ball is behind the goal, the goalie takes a position about 3 to 3½ feet from the goal and approximately in the middle of it. He is primarily concerned with maintaining the position that will give him maximum coverage of the goal when a feed is made to the crease area. Close-range shots will often be stopped by the goalie just because he is in the right position and the shooter hits him with the ball. If he lines up only 2 feet or less from the goal, he is too close to it and will give the shooter too much room on either side of him, as well as making himself vulnerable to shots that may ricochet off his body and go into the goal. If he is farther than 3½ feet from the goal, he may give the shooter too much room to shoot around him. Three to 3½ feet from the goal is the optimum position. Since he must protect the entire goal when the ball is fed to the crease area, he must be in a position near the middle of

GOAL TENDING

Figure 12–2 Goalie's position when the shooter is located 10 yards or closer to the goal.

the goal most of the time. In Figure 12–4 the goalie is in either Position 3 or 4 when the ball is located behind the goal in Area B. When the ball crosses Line b moving from Area B into Area A, the goalie will move into Position 2. When the ball approaches Line a, which is even with the plane of the goal, the goalie moves into Position 1. The same adjustments take place on the other side of the field when the ball moves from Area B to Area C and then from Area C to the plane of the goal (Line d). The goalie moves from Position 4 to Position 5 and finally to Position 6. Figure 12–5 shows the goalie in Position 3 with the ball behind the goal.

When the ball is behind the goal, the goalie is primarily concerned with calling out the location of the ball to help his defensive teammates in front of the goal who may not be able to see the ball. He also tries to intercept feeds to the crease area. He watches the feeder's eyes and stick, trying to get a jump on the whereabouts of his pass. The goalie holds the head of his stick above his own head and in or near the feeding lane of the attackman. This enables him to get to the ball more quickly than if he were to hold the stick at shoulder level or lower. The goalie must be careful in blocking a feed not to bat the ball into the goal. He should not extend himself to catch a

Figure 12–3 Dotted line shows the arc on which the goalie moves when the ball is in the midfield area.

Figure 12–4 Goalie's position in the crease when the ball is behind the goal.

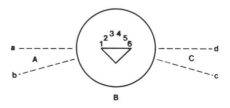

Figure 12–5 Goalie's position when the ball carrier is behind the goal.

feed unless he is 99 percent sure of getting the ball. If he misses, he will not be able to get in position to play the shooter's quick shot.

The goalie must be mindful of the basic rule of keeping his eyes on the ball at all times, even when the ball is behind the goal. He can help himself immeasurably by watching the flight of the ball when an attackman feeds it into the crease area. If he is unable to intercept it, he gets an invaluable tipoff as to the type of shot he can anticipate from the shooter. If the feed is high, the shot probably will be high. If the feed is low, the shot will be low. This guideline holds true in the majority of cases because the shooter is normally under considerable pressure in the crease area and consequently releases the ball in the quickest manner. If the ball is thrown anywhere to the right of the center of the goalie's body, he turns to the right, trying to follow the ball in its entire flight.

If it is thrown to his left, he turns to the left. He never turns his back to the ball, because the failure to see the ball, even for just a split second, can cause him enough delay in reaction to result in a goal. When he makes the turn, he actually steps out about one foot toward the front edge of the crease. This will place him about 4 to 4½ feet from the goal and in good position to stop point-blank shots from the crease.

When the ball carrier gets even with the plane of the goal, the goalie moves to a position where his body is against the goal post. Figure 12–6 shows the goalie with his right foot and the entire right side of his body next to the post. His left foot is several inches from his right foot. His stick is placed just off his right ear to seal off any open area above his right shoulder. The goalie holds this position until the ball carrier is past the plane of the goal by 3 to 4 feet. At this point he starts to

GOAL TENDING

Figure 12–6 Goalie's position when the ball carrier is even with the plane of the goal.

inch away from the post in order to assume a position that will minimize open area for the shooter. It is vital that he does not move too far from the pipe too soon. If he does, he exposes himself to an easy shot by the attackman. Joe Cowan, one of Hopkins' all-time great attackmen, drove home that point emphatically to Les Matthews when he told him that the majority of the goals he scored in his career were aimed at the near pipe.

MAKING THE SAVE

The goalie's prime responsibility is to stop the ball. Both proper positioning and movement into the ball are the keys. To get his body to move in the proper direction, the goalie must concentrate on the ball in the shooter's stick and follow it completely from the instant it leaves his stick. The critical movement is his stepping first with the foot nearer the ball and pushing off with the other

foot. If the ball is shot to the goalie's left side, his left foot is obviously nearer to the ball than his right foot, and he should step first with that foot. Figure 12–7 shows the goalie in his initial move on a shot to his left side. His first step is always toward the ball and forward, not to the side and definitely not back toward the goal. As he pushes off with his right foot and steps with his left, he brings his stick in a sweeping motion from his right side to a position where the head of the stick is directly in front of his body and his body is directly in front of the ball. It is important that the entire head of the stick is opened up to the ball to facilitate the catch. The handle is in a position almost perpendicular to the ground. Figure 12–8 shows the goalie completing his save on a bounce shot to his left side. Notice that his trailing (right) foot ends up several inches from his left foot. The feet do not necessarily come together, although at times they may. The old dictum that the goalie's heels should click together on every save is not correct, because he needs to maintain a firm base in case of a rebound. The feet should be parallel, and most of the time the heels are not touching but are in the normal position.

Once the ball is in the goalie's stick, excessive cradling should be avoided to keep from inadvertently flipping the ball into the goal. Whether in a practice or a game, most goalies have accidentally scored on themselves at one time or other during their playing careers. Geoff Berlin, a two-time All-American goalie at Hopkins, pulled that little trick during his sophomore year, in 1966. We were playing the University of Virginia at Scott Stadium, in Charlottesville, and had a 10–0 lead with only eight minutes remaining in the game when Geoff made a routine save. In his anxiety to pass the ball to a breaking midfielder, he lost control of the ball in his pocket and flipped it into the goal. Since the outcome of the game had already been decided in Hopkins' favor, I really could not have cared less and, in fact, got a good laugh out of the scene that followed. Geoff's reaction was one of complete disbelief, frustration, and anger. I think he displayed more emotion after that goal was scored against him than in any other game during his brilliant career. It would have been the only shutout of his career and also would have been the first shutout registered by Hopkins against major opposition since a 7–0 victory over Army in 1943.

Figure 12–7 Goalie's initial move on a bounce shot to his left.

Figure 12–9 Goalie's initial move on a bounce shot to his right.

Figure 12–8 Goalie's completing the save on a bounce shot to his left.

Figure 12–10 Goalie's completing the save on a bounce shot to his right.

On a bounce shot it is of paramount importance for the goalie to sweep the head of his stick toward the ball with the top of the frame close to the ground. Since some outside bounce shots will skim close to the ground instead of rising, the goalie must guard against this possibility first and then be ready to raise the level of his stick to play the higher bounce. If he fails to do so and the ball gets under his stick, there is a good chance of a score resulting because he has only his ankles and feet to stop the ball. On the contrary, when the ball bounces over the stick, the goalie still has a reasonable chance to stop it, because he has his entire midsection and upper body in front of it.

The sweeping motion of a right-handed goalie moving to his left, and a left-hander to his right, is a very natural motion and normally much easier than a right-hander going to his right and a left-hander to his left. To illustrate this point: A right-handed pitcher or quarterback throws the ball with his weight transferring from his right side to his left side. The same thing applies to a batter hitting a baseball right-handed. A right-handed shortstop usually feels more comfortable playing a ball on his left side because he gets that natural pushoff with his right foot. Although this also applies to the right-handed goalie, both he and the right-handed shortstop must be able to move as effectively to their right side. The motion may not be as smooth but it must be made quickly to get the body behind the ball. Figure 12–9 shows the goalie in his initial move, pushing off his left foot and stepping with his right. Instead of sweeping his stick, he merely directs it toward the ground and in line with the path of the ball. He especially wants to make sure the head of the stick gets close to the ground so that the ball does not get under it. This move is somewhat awkward for many goalies and, in fact, is one of their vulnerable areas—a low bounce shot on their stick side. Figure 12–10 shows the completion of the save with the handle of the stick close to a perpendicular position with the ground and the trailing (left) foot just several inches from the right foot.

On shots that do not bounce and are at a level between the goalie's feet and shoulders, the goalie makes the same move with his body and stick as he does on bounce shots. He even makes the same move on high shots on his stick side, as

Figure 12–11 Goalie's initial move on a high shot to his right.

shown in Figure 12–11. However, on high shots at shoulder level or above and on the side away from his stick, he does not normally use the sweeping motion because it is awkward at this level. Rather, he merely pivots the head of his stick in front of his face and in line with the path of the ball. Figure 12–12 shows the goalie making a save of a shot over his left shoulder.

When the shooter is at close range, the goalie relies primarily on his being in the proper position and moving toward the ball once it leaves the shooter's stick. He tries to anticipate where the shooter will be aiming his shot, and it's amazing how often a shooter will tip off his shot. The goalie mirrors the head of the shooter's stick with the head of his own stick. Often the shooter carries his stick high and shoots high, which makes the goalie's job easier. (See Figure 12–13.) Similarly, a shooter who decides to shoot low may conveniently lower the head of his stick prior to the shot. The goalie has the toughest time against a shooter who either holds his stick high and shoots low and vice versa, or has enough time to fake one way with his stick and eyes and then shoot in the opposite direction. In such situations where the attacker fakes high and shoots low, the goalie may try to stop the ball with his feet, and it is surprising just how many times during a season he will succeed.

Figure 12–12 Goalie's initial move on a high shot to his left.

Figure 12–13 Goalie's position on a high shot taken at close range.

There have been some goalies who have defended against the close-range shot with only one hand on the stick and the other held next to the head on the side opposite the stick. Phil Benedetti, who played for four years at Penn State and then was the "senior citizen" of the Philadelphia Lacrosse Club for many of his twenty consecutive years with them (1952–71), was the master of this one-hand technique. Phil played in a number of the Club All-Star games but was most proud to be so honored in his last year in the nets, at age forty-four. He was extremely quick, but since he was only 5'5", he needed every possible help on shots above his shoulders. Although he was very clever in handling the stick in this manner, he was the exception rather than the rule. It is recommended that the goalie keep both hands on the stick, because his control is so much better.

There are several situations in which the goalie should leave the goal to play an attacker who is moving in for a close-range shot. If an attackman dodges his defenseman behind the goal and for one reason or another no other defensive teammate slides to play him, the goalie should leave the goal to stop him as long as he meets him before he has passed the plane of the goal. If he waits until he has crossed the plane of the goal, he will be too late and consequently give the at-

tackman the opportunity to shoot into an open goal. When the goalie does move out to play him, he must first try to check his stick and then follow through into his body. He will be vulnerable to an easy score if he goes for the body first and doesn't get the shooter's arms and stick. When the offense has a break situation, whether 2-on-1 or any other advantageous combination, the goalie may try to anticipate a particular pass. If the receiver is close enough to the goal, the goalie may leave the goal to check him, but only if he is certain to arrive in time to make the check. The shooter will have a wide-open goal if the goalie is late. If there is any doubt in the goalie's mind as to whether or not he can reach the attacker in time to check him, he should not make the move. Rather, he should stay in the proper position and play the percentages on the shooter either hitting him with the ball or missing the goal completely. Because the pressure is on the shooter to score, he will often make a poor shot.

USING THE CREASE

The crease is the goalie's "home," and he has complete protection within it. The opposition cannot check him or his stick, regardless of whether the ball is loose on the ground or in his stick. The

Figure 12–14 Goalie clamping a loose ball outside the crease.

goalie must be as quick as a cat to pounce on a ball that is on the ground inside the crease because it is a potential goal if the attackman gets his stick on it. In almost every case he uses his stick to control the ball, rather than diving on it with his body. If the ball is bouncing at a height of about 6 inches or higher, he catches it in the air. If it bounces to a height of less than 6 inches or is just rolling on the ground, he clamps the ball to the ground with the back of the head of his stick. The entire stick is flat on the ground or certainly at an angle no greater than 10 degrees. This position prevents the attacker from poking at the ball when the goalie rakes the ball into his pocket. Once the goalie has made his clamp, he must rake the ball immediately or he is penalized for delay of the game, a technical foul that gives the ball to the opposition. When the goalie rakes the ball, the handle of his stick points outside the goal posts rather than inside, where he could inadvertently rake the ball into the goal.

If a loose ball is on the ground outside the crease and within several yards of it, the goalie tries to get possession by keeping one foot in the crease and stepping out with the other (see Figure 12–14). His move is like that of a first baseman in baseball who keeps one foot on the base and stretches out with the other to reach the ball. Although he does not have the protection of the crease when the ball is loose outside the crease (his stick can be checked legally by the attackers), he does have complete protection of it once he gets possession and has one foot inside the crease. If the attacker checks his stick then, he will be penalized thirty seconds for interference with the goalie. About the only time it is desirable for the goalie to dive on a loose ball with his body is when the ball is outside the crease in front of the goal and the opposition has a dangerous crease attackman who is skillful at flicking ground balls into the goal. Once he decides to go for the ball, the goalie must be absolutely certain he will gain control of it, because the goal will be wide open if he fails. Although smothering the ball is a technical foul for which the opposition gets possession of the ball at a distance of 20 yards from the goal, there is less pressure on the goalie in that position than with the crowd of attackers battling for the ball right in front of the goal. If the loose ball is more than several yards from the crease and too far for the goalie to reach it, he merely maintains his position in a direct line with the ball and the center of the goal. His stick is kept close to the ground, because a low shot is most likely if an attacker can direct the ball toward the goal. In this situation the goalie's position is about a foot or two from the front edge of the crease.

When a loose ball is on the ground behind the goal, the goalie moves to the rear of the goal but remains in the crease. If he cannot reach the loose ball with his stick, he calls for a defensive teammate to bat the ball with his stick or to kick it with his foot toward the goal, giving the goalie the opportunity to get possession inside the crease. The defensive teammates should direct the ball toward the goalie on the ground, however, because if they flip it into the air, an attacker may pick off the pass and break for the front of the goal. With the goalie behind the goal in this situation, he usually is caught trailing the attacker to the front of the goal and gives up an easy score.

Some goalies are bold ones who glory in the excitement of action outside the crease. Often they are frustrated infielders who end up playing in the goal. Three of my goalies who could be termed "happy wanderers" were Geoff Berlin, class of 1968; Les Matthews, class of 1973; and Kevin Mahon, class of 1977. Each had excellent speed, quickness in reacting, and judgment. However, at times they nearly gave heart failure to everyone in the stadium, in particular their coach. Although they were outstanding All-American goalies, they did get burned at times and gave up a few easy goals during their careers. Therefore, the goalie should stay at home in the crease and be somewhat cautious—certainly not reckless—in leaving it to make a play for the ball. This applies to his attempts to play ground balls that are more than several yards from the goal and to other situations such as checking dodgers or potential shooters and intercepting passes. Before leaving the crease, he must be absolutely certain of either getting the ball or checking it out of his opponent's stick. If he fails in his attempt, he leaves the goal wide open and subjects his team to giving up an easy goal.

PLAYING THE SCREEN

When the ball is in the midfield area, an effective screen by the crease attackman can cause the goalie considerable concern. Since he must be able to see the ball at all times, the goalie adjusts his normal position to do so. Figure 12–15 shows the goalie looking around the screen in order to keep visual contact with the ball. His right foot remains in position, and he takes a short step to the side with his left foot. The goalie can also make his move to the other side of the screen. If he is having difficulty with the screen, he should alert his crease defenseman. The crease defenseman responds by checking his own position to make sure he is not interfering with the goalie's vision. If he is close enough to the crease attackman when the ball is shot, he drives his shoulder into him, trying to clear the crease for the goalie to see the ball. If the ball is shot and his vision is screened, about the only thing the goalie can do is to move immediately to the spot where he anticipates the ball and hope his positioning will stop the shot.

GOALIE'S VOCABULARY

As the director of the defense, the goalie must talk continuously to his teammates, giving commands and instructions that are invaluable to them. Since every member of the team must know the exact meaning of each command, the coach must take time to make the explanation at the start of the season. The goalie's words of encouragement and reassurance are also very helpful to his teammates. Nonetheless, he does not want to get so carried away with hearing his own voice that he is more concerned about giving orders than he is with stopping the ball.

The following commands are used by the goalie:

"Ball on the left front." Giving the location of the ball in the various defensive positions on the field.

"Who has the ball?" Getting the defender to tell his teammates that he is playing the ball.

"Who has him backed?" Getting his defensive teammates to respond that they have the ball backed up on the right and left sides.

"Drop in, Doug." Telling the defender he is playing his man too far from the goal.

"Move out, Tom." Telling the defender he is too far from his man and he should move out to play him.

"You're good, Harry." Telling the defender his position on the ball carrier is fine.

"Check up." Telling all defenders to identify their men.

"Square up to your right (left)." Telling the defender he is not in the proper position on the

Figure 12–15 Goalie's position as he looks around a screen to locate the ball.

ball carrier and should adjust his position to favor the side to which he is moving.

"Off the pipe." Telling all defenders that the man playing the ball is located at a position in line with the plane of the goal.

"Hold." Telling the defender to stop the penetration of the ball carrier. This call alerts all defenders to the possibility of a slide.

"Slide." Telling all the defenders a teammate has been dodged and now they must move to stop the offensive thrust. The nearest man plays the dodger, and the other defenders move to new men.

"Check." Telling the defenders in the area of the crease to check the attackers' sticks.

"Loose ball." Telling all defenders the ball is on the ground and to be ready to play it.

"Clear the crease." Telling the defenders whose men are on the crease that a ball is loose in the area. They should check their opponents' sticks and use their shoulders to drive them off the crease.

"Here's your help." Telling the defender who has the ball in his possession to pass the ball to the goalie.

"Break," or "Clear." Telling all defenders the goalie has made a save and now wants them to move into their clearing lanes, looking for a pass.

WARMING UP THE GOALIE

It is imperative that the goalie receive a proper warmup before each day's practice and obviously before every game. The coach should be the only one to warm up the goalie. However, if he is handling the team by himself, he may need the assistance of his most reliable offensive player to work with the goalie during some of the practice sessions. This player should receive specific instructions concerning the techniques of warming up the goalie. No other person should ever shoot at the goalie unless the coach is there to supervise. If players are allowed complete freedom to shoot at the goalie without supervision, they will often do more harm than good. In their anxiety to score, they frequently move in too close to the goalie and their bulletlike, close-range shots may cause the goalie to become gun-shy and also expose him to being injured.

About twenty minutes are needed to give the goalie a complete warmup with practice against all types of shots. Since most teams have either two or three goalies, the coach may be able to give a thorough workout to only his number-one goalie and a modified workout to his other one or two. He does not want to slight any of his players, in particular his second-string goalie, because he becomes an important player if the regular goalie gets hurt or is having a bad day. But time is a critical factor at practice, and the coach cannot afford to spend one hour working with three goalies. However, if he uses time both before and after each practice session, he should be able to give about fifteen to twenty minutes to his number-one goalie, ten to fifteen minutes to his number-two, and five to ten minutes to his number-three. Since an intense warmup can be demanding physically on the coach as well as on the goalie, he may want to receive help from some of his best offensive players. Along with utilizing the time before and after practice, the coach can frequently squeeze in about fifteen minutes' work with a goalie when the rest of the team is doing calisthenics or basic stick-work drills. Designated team leaders or an assistant coach can supervise the team at this time.

The following sequence can be used as a guide in warming up the goalie:

1. High shots at three-quarter speed from 15 to 20 yards.
2. High shots at full speed from 18 to 20 yards.
3. Bounce shots at three-quarter speed from 15 to 20 yards.
4. Bounce shots at full speed from 18 to 20 yards.
5. Mixture of high shots and bounce shots at full speed from 18 to 20 yards.

6. Mixture of high shots and bounce shots at three-quarter speed from 12 to 15 yards.
7. Mixture of high shots and bounce shots at three-quarter speed from 9 to 12 yards.
8. Feeds by attackman behind the goal to shooter, who takes a mixture of mostly high and some bounce shots at slightly less than three-quarter speed from 3 to 4 yards off the crease.
9. Dodges by attackman from behind the goal, who takes a mixture of shots at slightly less than three-quarter speed from 3 to 4 yards off the crease.

After the goalie makes a save, he should concentrate on making a sharp, accurate pass to the coach. Once he has had about ten to fifteen minutes of warmup and is reacting well to the ball, the coach can simulate a clearing situation after the save by breaking out and giving the goalie a target with his stick. He can also use midfielders in the right- and left-front positions and have them do the same thing alternately. The coach doesn't want to overemphasize the clearing aspect of the goalie's job, so he may call for the break pass on every third or fourth save. But the goalie must be ready for it on every save and respond with an accurate lead pass when the coach or midfielder makes the break.

PREPARATIONS FOR THE GAME

Since the goalie is the one player on the team whose performance has the most significant effect on the outcome of the game, special attention must be given to his complete preparation, both physical and mental. A scouting report on the offensive capabilities of each opposing player, including his favorite shots and where he tries to shoot them, is very helpful. If the coach or one of his best shooters simulates the various shots of the opponent's star players in the warmup during the practice sessions before the game, the goalie becomes so familiarized with their techniques that he is completely confident when he faces them on game day. The coach should call out the name and jersey number of the player he is simulating and then unload one of that player's most dangerous shots. During my career at Hopkins, our goalies have benefited by being warmed up by some of the best shooters in

GOAL TENDING

the game. Fred Smith, Wilson Fewster, Buzzy Budnitz, Henry Ciccarone, and Joe Cowan are five of the best shooters in the Hopkins lacrosse tradition. When our goalies have had these people firing shots at them during the week, they have gone into the pressure of the game knowing they will probably not see any harder or more accurate shots than they have seen during practice.

If the team is playing an away game on a field different from its home field, it should try to simulate the field conditions during the practice sessions prior to that game. For example, if the crease area on the home field is completely bare of grass, but the team is traveling to a school that has grass in its crease area, the goalie should receive his warmups on grass during every practice before that game. This will just require the goal being moved from its normal position to a grassy location. If it is raining hard the day before the game and rain is forecast for game day, the coach should take his goalie out in the rain and give him a warmup on the wet field. The rest of the team does not have to practice outside, but the goalie must feel confident in the goal, regardless of weather conditions. The goalie may want to use an old stick while practicing in the rain and save his best stick for game day. The position of the sun in relation to the goal may be a factor in considering which goal the team wants to defend. It is desirable to try to avoid placing the goalie so that the sun will be directly in his eyes in the fourth quarter of the game. Since this often is not possible, the goalie should receive practice in a goal facing into the sun.

Since the ball takes varying bounces depending on the playing surface of the field, the goalie must be fully aware of what to expect in each case. On a dry artificial surface the ball will take its truest bounce, but when it is wet, it will tend to skim along the ground. On a dry grassy field the ball may be somewhat cushioned and not bounce as high as on a dry dirt field. When the grass is wet, the ball will skim even more than on a wet artificial surface. On a dry dirt field, the ball will bounce very high; when wet, the dirt may turn into mud, and the ball will stay right on the ground or possibly just get stuck in the mud. The bounce of the ball is also affected by the distance from the goal when it hits the ground. If the ball hits close to the goalie's feet, the bounce will obviously be limited. The farther away from the goalie the ball

hits the ground, the higher the bounce, except in wet field conditions.

The confidence that the team displays in the goalie and the goalie has in himself are vital to the team's success. This confidence can be bolstered, along with the spirit and morale of the team, by the type of warmup given to the goalie on the day before the game. Our players have given us a positive response to the following warmup. The coach gives the goalie a ten- to fifteen-minute workout before the start of practice. The team then moves through a light practice, with the last item on the practice schedule a shootout supervised by the coach but carried out by the team's best shooters and even some of the lesser ones. After giving the goalie about three minutes of three-quarter-speed shots from the 18- to 20-yard mark, the coach places a marker at about the 16-yard spot and turns the shooters loose with full-speed shots beyond that point. The goalie will call out the name of one of his teammates to identify him as the shooter who will fire the ball on the run or just crank up and let it go with all the power he can muster. If the goalie makes the save, he passes the ball to the shooter, who simulates a defensive teammate breaking out on a clear. There is a healthy flow of conversation—the hotshot shooters who are unable to score on the goalie are ribbed, and continuous words of encouragement and praise are given to the goalie. It is somewhat of a relaxed, fun time for the shooters, and it is all work and all business for the goalie, but the whole atmosphere is one of complete support of the goalie.

The goalie's warmup on game day is the same as in a regular practice. The coach shoots the ball with power and accuracy because he wants to sharpen the goalie's reactions. He may not try quite as hard to score on him, because he does not want to affect his confidence. The coach takes him out on the field about fifty to sixty minutes before game time. He may first warm up the number-two goalie for about ten minutes and then follow with the starting goalie for about ten minutes. The coach will then move to the other goal to give the goalies the feel of operating in it. This is important, because there may be a slight difference in both the area in front of the crease and the location of the sun. The coach will give the number-one goalie another ten to fifteen minutes of warmup in this goal. Since he will be overheated and somewhat tired after this workout, the goalie can move to the sidelines to relax for about five minutes while the coach is finishing with the second goalie. If a team has three goalies, the third one may not get a warmup or, at best, may get just a limited one by the coach. The goalies should complete the warmup in the goal on the side of the field their team will be using for the pregame activity. It is up to the coaches to arrange this, making sure the goalies get to work in both goals, however. The goalies should be involved with the defense in making both long and short clearing passes to them. After doing this, the goalies may want to relax for another five or ten minutes; then the coach may want to give the goalie another two or three minutes in the goal right before the start of the game. The goalie is now ready to man the nets. He is prepared both mentally and physically to meet the challenging responsibilities of his position, knowing he has the backing of all his teammates and coaches.

clearing

13

Once the defense gains possession of the ball, it has accomplished the major part of its responsibility, which is to prevent the opponent from scoring. However, before a team can score, the defense must clear the ball from its defensive half of the field to its offensive half. Clearing can be accomplished by either passing the ball from player to player or by just running with it. Since the defense has the advantage of an extra man, its goalie, when it clears the ball, it should be able to be successful on a high percentage of its attempts. Failure to clear the ball with consistency can be both frustrating and demoralizing to a team, because the opponent is afforded opportunities to score easy goals. When the defense loses the ball in its clearing effort, most, if not all, of its players are away from the goal, and the opponent frequently gains a 3-on-2 or 2-on-1 advantage in attacking the goal. Clearing, therefore, is a very important phase of the game.

In fact, the statistics for a team's clearing during a game frequently reflect the outcome of the game. The team that succeeds in 75 percent or more of its clearing attempts in a game will be the winner in most cases, whereas the team that clears in less than 75 percent of its attempts will usually lose. In 1973 Hopkins played the University of Virginia's defending NCAA champions twice and beat them both times. In the first game, a 14–9 victory, we cleared the ball in twenty-seven of twenty-nine attempts, for a remarkable 93 percent of the attempts. In the semifinals of the NCAA playoffs we won by a 12–9 score and cleared the ball in twenty-one of twenty-seven attempts, for a creditable 78 percent. Our only defeat during the regular season that year was a 17–4 loss to the University of Maryland at College Park. Our clearing was so bad that we not only failed in twenty-two out of forty-three attempts but even scored a goal on ourselves. One of our defensemen threw a pass to our goalie and it went several yards off target and into the Hopkins goal. Our failure to clear the ball was certainly a contributing factor to our humiliating defeat.

Several factors facilitate the clear. Of primary importance is the complete organization of the various types of clears a team employs against the different rides used by its opponent. A thorough understanding of each clearing pattern is essential for the entire team; although the goalie, defensemen, and midfielders handle the bulk of the work in the clearing, the close attackmen also are involved. In fact, they become the key to the clear in several situations. Continual practice of the various clears is imperative. Clever stick work and good peripheral vision help considerably, but speed is probably even more important. Some of the most effective clearing takes place when a defender simply runs by his man, not using any fancy footwork or tricky dodges, just sheer speed.

Some of the game's best clearers have been good athletes with limited stick work but with speed. Over the years many Army and Navy defensemen have fitted this description to a T. Two Hopkins defensemen fall in this category, too. Although I never had the pleasure of seeing Pete Reynolds play, I've been told that his forte was his ability to get the ball in his stick and run for daylight. Pete was a football player from Mt. St. Joseph's High School in Baltimore who had never handled a stick until his freshman year at Hopkins. He learned the game quickly and was a regular on the 1932 Hopkins team, which represented the United States in the Olympic games in Los Angeles. Almost forty years later, another football player from Mt. St. Joe came to Hopkins and followed the same script. It was my good fortune to coach Joe Cieslowski, who, as a sophomore, in his second year of playing lacrosse, was a starting defenseman on our 1970 Hopkins team, which shared the national championship with Virginia and Navy. Joe's stick work was shoddy, to say the least, but when the ball was on the ground, he would scoop it and clear it by holding the stick in one hand and just "turning on the jets." It is difficult to beat speed in almost every phase of the game, especially in clearing.

The goalie is the backbone of the defense and the director of the clear. Since he always keeps his eyes on the ball, he knows exactly when one of his defenders gains possession and he is ready to set the clear in motion by shouting, "Break," or "Clear." This tells every defender to move to his assigned position on the field for the clear. Since the majority of clears originates with the goalie, he must have a complete understanding of each clearing pattern and be well drilled in carrying out his responsibilities.

The following guidelines are helpful to the clearing team:

1. Never run with the ball when a teammate who is farther down the field is open. The ball will arrive more quickly at its destination when passed than when carried in the stick.

2. If no one is open to receive a pass, the ball carrier should run for open area, normally toward the offensive half of the field.

3. When a ball carrier who has either speed or clever stick handling or both is confronted by a riding opponent, he can just run by him or dodge him, as long as he has enough room to do so and doesn't have to be concerned about another defender double-teaming him. Midfielders normally are able to dodge much more easily than defensemen, because their smaller sticks present less of a target to the riders' checks.

4. Every member of the clearing team must keep his eyes on the ball at all times. If a player does not know the location of the ball, he is unable to help out in the clear.

5. When a breaking defender is open and wants the ball, he must first call the ball carrier by name to get his attention. For example, "Doug, Doug. Here's your help." Since everyone responds more quickly to the sound of his own name than to any other words, this is the most effective way to gain his attention. This point applies to any situation during a game when an open man wants the ball immediately. It is especially helpful in clearing the ball against a hard-riding opponent.

6. Before calling for the ball, the defender must be sure he is open. The player who continually calls for the ball, even when he is partially covered, will soon find himself being disregarded completely by his teammates.

7. The breaking defender should always give the ball carrier a target with the head of his stick to let him know exactly where he wants the ball. This target is a big help to both the passer and the receiver. The passer has a point at which to

aim his throw, and the receiver has his stick in position to receive it where he can best handle it.

8. Avoid passing the ball to a teammate directly in front of the goal, because if he misses it, an opponent can gain possession and possibly get a "cheap" goal.

9. When a defender gets possession of a loose ball on the ground, he immediately runs for daylight and listens for a teammate's call for a pass.

10. The ball carrier must never allow himself to be forced out of bounds with the ball in his stick and thus lose possession of it. Rather, if he is on his defensive sideline, he should throw the ball toward the attack half of the field in hopes that one of his attackmen will be able to get it. If he is behind the goal and about to be forced out the end line, he should flip the ball on the ground toward the corner of the field, where he can battle for it. At least he has a chance to get possession.

11. When the ball goes out of bounds behind the goal, the goalie should not take the ball unless he is the best dodger and best passer on the team. The goalie should move to a position inside the crease, in front of the goal, where he can use the crease to his advantage. Figure 13–1 shows the goalie making an initial break to his right and then, when O6 follows on the same side, going across the back part of the goal to receive the pass on the side opposite O6. If initially O6 plays behind the goal, the goalie can make his break upfield and away from him. Regardless of how O6 plays the goalie in the crease, he will

Figure 13–1 Goalie's break in crease when ball is being put into play from behind the goal.

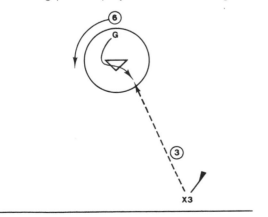

have difficulty in preventing him from getting the ball.

12. When the ball goes out of bounds behind the goal, either the best stick-handling defenseman or the most reliable midfielder on each midfield unit should bring the ball into play. It is important to have predetermined the people who will handle this responsibility. Since the riding team normally uses its best rider to play the person bringing the ball into play from out of bounds, the clearing team will be in trouble if it has one of its weaker, slower clearers in that position. The longer sticks of the defensemen are much better targets for the rider than the smaller midfield sticks. That's why a midfielder is often the best choice to handle the ball, even though he may have to run about 20 yards to the boundary line to get it. Since most teams use a specific midfielder on each unit to move back near the goalie on most clearing situations against a zone ride, these midfielders can easily be geared to taking the ball when it goes out of bounds.

13. If the ball is advanced on one side of the field and is prevented from crossing the center line, the path of the ball can then be reversed and the clearing attempt made on the other side of the field. The ball carrier may also try to clear the ball by making a long, cross-field pass.

14. The player (normally a midfielder) near the center line on the side of the field opposite the ball is responsible for preventing his team from violating the offside rule, which requires four players on the defensive half of the field at all times.

15. The ball carrier will catch his riding opponent by surprise at times with a pass-and-cut play. The rider may tend to relax after the ball carrier has made his pass and consequently lose at least a step or two on him when he cuts by. Goalies and defensemen normally use this maneuver, because riding attackmen frequently overcommit on them when they have the ball.

16. Unless the area is cleared out for a lead pass downfield, a breaking midfielder takes a path that is close to being perpendicular to the sideline as opposed to a path directed more toward the center line. The perpendicular path gives him more protection from a riding opponent.

17. When clearing the ball, always keep one man in the vicinity of the goal to act as a safety

man, just in case the defense loses the ball. Normally the goalie remains in this position, but there are times when he makes a move away from the center of the field and away from the goal. In these situations one of the defensemen must cover for him.

18. Do not throw a "buddy" pass, a lead pass that makes a teammate vulnerable to a body check from a riding opponent. Since the receiver is following the flight of the ball, he is unable to see the opponent who is sliding to a position for the "big crash." Although this pass is called the buddy pass, in reality the thrower is not being kind to his buddy but setting him up for the kill.

There are many different ways to clear the ball. Four basic clears that we have found to be effective in combating just about every type of ride are explained in this chapter.

CLEAR VERSUS INBOUNDS RUNNING RIDE, FIRST PHASE

The most frequently used clear is the one designed to withstand an inbounds running ride. This basic clear normally originates with a shot and a save by the goalie. There is no stop in the action; the ball is inbounds and in play. Figure 13–2 shows the first phase of this clear. The responsibilities of each position are as follows:

Goalie

As soon as the goalie has possession of the ball in the crease, he looks immediately upfield to pass the ball to a midfielder taking a fast-break route. If he is not open, the goalie looks and listens for the other two midfielders. If neither is open, he then looks for the wing defenseman. The goalie must be aware that the crease attackman will attempt to block any pass from the crease. He therefore must try to avoid the head of the creaseman's stick when releasing the ball. He also should not throw the ball from the center of the goal, because if the block is successful, a loose ball directly in front of the goal may result in an easy goal. If the goalie moves just a half step to the side and places his stick outside the pipes when making the pass, he avoids that problem, because a block there is not nearly as dangerous

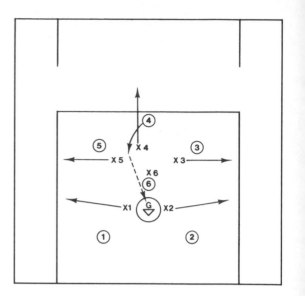

Figure 13–2 Phase 1 of inbounds clear.

as one directly in front of the goal. The goalie is allowed to remain in the crease for four seconds after getting possession of the ball. Frequently goalies do not take advantage of the full amount of time but instead rush themselves and use barely two seconds. This is especially so for the less-experienced goalie. The coach can help him by counting out the time each time the goalie has the ball in the crease. This will give him an awareness of the time element and encourage him to remain in there longer.

If the goalie decides not to pass the ball because no one appears to be open, he then runs with the ball out of the crease. He looks first for an opening to the front of the goal, and if none is there, he breaks behind the goal. When he runs the ball out, he looks for the 2-on-1 opportunity and passes the ball immediately to the open man. He should not be dodge-happy and take too many chances when he doesn't have to. If the crease attackman prevents the goalie from making his break to the front of the goal, he then has to go to the rear. As he makes this move, his eyes are looking for the open man and also for an attackman who might try to double-team him. An inexperienced goalie often makes the mistake of immediately going to the rear of the goal when he gets the ball. His priorities should be:

1. Pass the ball to a midfielder.
2. Pass the ball to a defenseman.
3. Run with the ball to the front of the goal.
4. Run with the ball to the rear of the goal.

Wing Defensemen

The wing defensemen (X1 and X2) make a break toward the sideline and slightly upfield. If the clear is initiated by a shot from the midfield, the attackmen will be behind the goal, and it is therefore unwise for the wing defensemen to break toward the rear of the goal. The break is slightly upfield, or actually as far upfield as the position of the riding midfielder on his side of the field will allow. The wing defenders want to gain as much distance as possible from their riding attackmen, but they can't take an angle that would subject them to a buddy pass. As they break for the sideline, they turn their heads to see the goalie and they give him a target with their sticks. They can catch the ball in either the forehand or backhand position, whichever is more convenient, taking into consideration the position of the riding attackman. If X2 is a right-handed player, he may prefer to break for the sideline looking for a forehand catch, because the backhand catch places his stick a little closer to O2. However, since the difference is so slight and actually can be compensated for by the angle of the break, the wing defender can use his preference. If he is open on the break, he calls the goalie by name to get his attention.

Crease Defenseman

The crease defenseman (X6) remains in the crease area and no farther than a yard from the crease attackman. He keeps his eye on the goalie and is ready to play the crease attackman if the goalie's pass is blocked and the ball is loose. He should also give a quick look to see if a riding midfielder is moving to the crease to play him in what is known as a press, or a 4-on-4 ride. Normally a team will not use this maneuver on an inbounds running situation. However, if it does, the crease defenseman is the one who should inform the goalie and thereby alert him to make his first pass to one of the three midfielders who are being played by only two riding midfielders.

Midfielders

The three midfielders (X3, X4, and X5) have specific responsibilities, depending on their positions on the field when the ball is shot. When a shot is taken by midfielder O4, his defender (X4) follows the ball with his eyes, makes sure the goalie has possession, and then breaks at full speed for the offensive half of the field. As he is running, he looks over his shoulder to keep his eyes on the goalie and calls the goalie by name if he is open. The defender who is playing the shooter is probably the best player to get a fast break, because the shooter is primarily concerned with whether his shot goes in the goal or not and consequently is not thinking at all about riding if the goalie makes the save. The two wing midfielders (X3 and X5) make their break toward the sideline and almost perpendicular to it. If they break more toward the center line, they are moving into their riding midfielders, whereas when they go directly for the sideline they are going away from their riders and consequently creating an opening for the goalie's pass. They, too, give the goalie a target with their sticks and call his name if open.

CLEAR VERSUS INBOUNDS RUNNING RIDE, SECOND PHASE

Figure 13–3 shows the second phase of the inbounds running clear, which begins with the goalie moving behind the goal. The various responsibilities are as follows:

Goalie

As the goalie (G) breaks behind the goal and is receiving pressure from the crease attackman (O6), he looks to make a pass to the wing defenseman (X2) on his side of the field. If he is covered, the goalie passes to either X1 or X6, because there is only one attackman to play these two defensemen. If the goalie is being pressed hard, he should cut by his rider after making the pass. This pass-and-cut maneuver will often free him for a return pass from his teammate. The goalie should try this only if he has average speed or better.

Wing Defensemen

When the goalie moves behind the goal, the wing defensemen (X1 and X2) change their paths, assuming their riding attackmen have covered them on their initial break. They then break back on a slight angle toward the end line, giving a target with their sticks and calling, if open. In Figure 13–3 the goalie passes to X2, who catches the ball and protects his stick with his body. He looks to see if X6 is making his break but is careful not to give him a buddy pass. If X6, the goalie, and he are being played, then X2 knows for sure that either one of the midfielders or X1 is open.

Crease Defenseman

Once the goalie moves behind the goal, the crease defenseman (X6) remains in his position about a yard or two from the crease. He watches both the goalie and the crease attackman (O6). If the goalie is unable to throw to one of the wing defensemen and is receiving pressure from O6, then X6 makes a short break either toward the goalie or the sideline to receive a quick outlet pass. His break carries him away from his original position directly in front of the goal. He never wants to call for the ball there, because a bad pass or missed pass could result in an easy goal. If the goalie makes his first pass to either wing

defenseman (X1 or X2), then X6 makes a break toward the sideline at an angle perpendicular to it or just slightly upfield. If X6 makes his break more toward the center line than the sideline, he is vulnerable to a slide by a riding midfielder.

Midfielders

Once the goalie goes behind the goal, the two wing midfielders (X3 and X5) redirect their paths from the sideline to the center line. The fast-break midfielder (X4) continues in his original path. With the three midfielders being played man to man, they want to carry their men away from the goalie and three defensemen to give them the advantage of four clearers versus three riders.

CLEAR VERSUS INBOUNDS RUNNING RIDE, THIRD PHASE

Figure 13–4 shows the third and final phase of the inbounds running clear. The various responsibilities are as follows:

Goalie

The goalie (G) stays about 5 yards in front of the goal, and if he is not played closely he is ready to call for the ball in an emergency situation.

Figure 13–3 Phase 2 of inbounds clear.

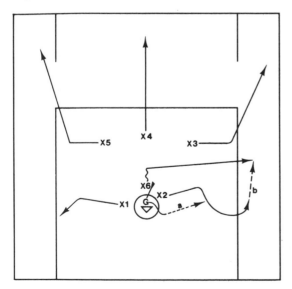

Figure 13–4 Phase 3 of inbounds clear.

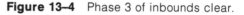

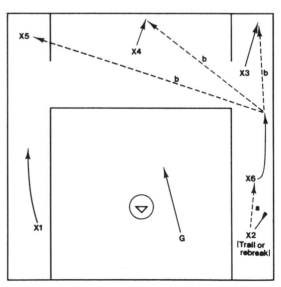

Onside Defenseman

The onside defenseman (X2) makes his pass to X6 and then either trails the play, acting as an outlet, or breaks by his rider (O2), looking for a return pass.

Crease Defenseman

The crease defenseman (X6) catches the pass from X2 and turns his body to protect his stick from a sliding opponent. If no one is sliding to him, he just runs with the ball toward the center line but favoring the sideline rather than the middle of the field. He tries to take advantage of a 2-on-1 opportunity with X3 and his riding midfielder and may have to go 10 yards or more over the center line to do so. He does not have to worry about a violation of the offside rule, because that is the responsibility of X5. If a riding midfielder slides to X6, he must be alert to passing the ball quickly to the open man. If the riding midfielders make an effective slide that covers X3 and X4, the open man will be either the offside midfielder (X5) or the offside defenseman (X1).

Offside Defenseman

The offside defenseman (X1) moves upfield as the ball advances, staying about 5 yards from the sideline. He is ready to receive a cross-field pass anytime there is a bottleneck on the other side of the field.

Onside Midfielder

With the pass to the crease defenseman (X6), the onside midfielder (X3) moves down the field and over the center line to clear out the area for him. If O3 leaves X3 to play X6, then X3 immediately calls to X6 to alert him to the slide and tell him if he is open. For example, "Doug, watch the slide. Here's your help." Midfielder X3 stays close to the sideline in this situation in order to open up as much distance as possible from O4, who could make a slide to cover him. Too often clears are broken by O4 when X3 tries to catch the ball about 10 yards from the sideline. In like manner, X3 should not drift too far downfield near the attack-goal area, where an opposing defenseman could make a slide to him.

Center Midfielder

The center midfielder (X4) stays in the middle of the field unless he feels he can get open by breaking to the sideline. If his rider (O4) makes the slide to X3, he should definitely break to the sideline to get the pass directly from X6 before O5 can slide to cover him. If X6 carries the ball over the center line and works the 2-on-1 play with X3, then X4 remains in the middle of the field away from this maneuver.

Offside Midfielder

The offside midfielder (X5) is located on the off side of the field, and he does not go over the center line. He is primarily responsible for preventing a violation of the offside rule, which requires four players on the defensive half of the field. There are occasions when the clear is jammed and the pass will be made cross-field to him. He must move to meet the ball when it is thrown to him and then turn properly to protect it. If the cross-field pass is made to X1, then X5 is no longer considered on the off side of the field and he therefore can break over the center line to receive a pass. Player X3 now becomes the offside midfielder.

CLEAR VERSUS DROP-BACK ZONE RIDE

Clearing the ball against a drop-back zone ride is usually more difficult than the inbounds running ride. The riding team will normally set up this ride when the ball goes out of bounds and the defense gets possession at the end line or up to the 15-yard mark on the sideline. Also it is used when the ball is in play but the action is almost at a standstill because the goalie has the ball behind the goal and the crease attackman is playing him from the opposite side of the crease. In this situation the riding team may drop back into a zone ride. The defense must be prepared to meet the zone ride from a position anywhere from a yard or two in front of the goal to a point several yards from the center line. Regardless of where the riding team picks up the ball carrier, the clearing team takes the same relative positions. Since most zone rides are set up on a 3–3 basis with three attackmen in the first wave and three midfielders in the second wave, the defense must position its players in the most effective way to break this zone ride. The 3–1–3 alignment shown in Figure 13–5 is the most popular method of clearing against it. The 3–1–3 alignment can be adjusted very simply into a 3–2–2 by breaking X5 from a position in the middle of the field to a point on line with X3 and about midway between the goalie and X2. Both of these alignments spread the clearing players across the field and position them where they can take advantage of the zone ride. Another possibility is a 3–4 alignment, with X3 and X5 either on line with X4 and X6 or in a tandem with one breaking to the right and one to the left. The latter actually ends up in a 3–2–2 alignment.

Let's take a look at the locations and responsibilities of each player in the 3–1–3 alignment, as shown in Figure 13–5. The distance between the first line of clearers (X1, X2, and the goalie) and the second line of clearers (X4, X5, and X6) is about 20 yards. The pivot midfielder (X3) is in the middle and no farther than 10 yards from the goalie and 3 yards to his left.

Goalie

When the ball goes out of bounds, the goalie directs the clear initially from his position in the crease. If the opponents have dropped back in a

Figure 13–5 Drop-back clear.

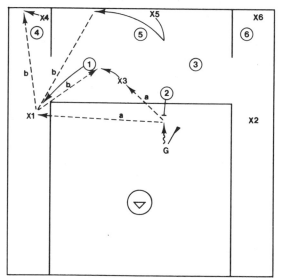

zone ride, he calls, "It's a drop-back ride; set up our clear." After the whistle blows, he calls for the ball from the teammate who is bringing it into play. He then brings the ball up the field, 3 or 4 yards to the right of the middle, sizing up the positioning of the riders. If he sees the three riding midfielders covering his three clearing midfielders, he knows his first pass will probably go to X1, X2, or X3. When he moves to a point about 10 yards from O2, he prepares himself to make a pass as soon as O2 commits to him. He should release the ball before O2 is close enough to check his stick but certainly no farther than 4 to 5 yards away. When making the pass to either X1 or X2 he steps to the side to avoid O2's check. If, as a right-handed goalie, he wants to pass to X3, he should sidestep to his left just before releasing the ball in order to get the head of his stick away from O2's stick. The goalie may have to fake the three-quarter-arm pass and to throw sidearm if X3 breaks to the goalie's right. He must be careful not to throw the ball into the rider's stick. A block of the pass gives the rider a chance for an easy goal.

Wing Defensemen

Both wing defensemen (X1 and X2) should be good stick handlers, since they will probably receive the first pass. Initially they move up the field with the goalie, keeping about 1 to 2 yards in front of him and about 3 yards from the sideline. If the goalie makes his first pass to X3, both X1 and X2 will move toward the center line, looking for the next pass. If X1 receives the goalie's first pass, he looks first to pass to X3, then either to X4, X5, or X6. He uses the goalie or X2 as an outlet if the others are covered. If the goalie makes his first pass to X2, he has the same options as X1, although X3 is farther removed from him.

Pivot Midfielder

The pivot midfielder (X3) is usually the midfielder who can best handle the ball under pressure. His position is in the middle of the 3–1–3 alignment, and the clear revolves around his play. He also has a primary responsibility to stay onside in the event he does not receive the ball. In effect, he has changed positions with the crease defenseman (X6), because he is more skilled at clearing the ball. He maintains a distance of no more than

10 yards from the goalie and about 3 yards to his left. He keys the movement of the riding attackman (O2) to the goalie. As soon as O2 moves, he makes his break for open area according to the position of O1, O3, and O5. If he receives the goalie's first pass as shown in Figure 13–5, he turns properly to protect his stick with his body and looks to pass off to the open man as soon as he is pressured. If O1 were to slide to him, he would pass to X1. If O5 were to slide to him, he would pass to X5 or possible X6 or X2 if the riders were sliding in some fashion. However, if he receives no pressure when he catches the ball, he runs toward the center line and clears the ball himself. If the goalie's first pass goes to X1 or X2, then X3 makes his break toward the ball and at a slight upfield angle, looking for the second pass. If X1, X2, or the goalie runs the ball over the center line on a solo clear, then X3 must definitely remain on the defensive half of the field to prevent an offside violation.

Upfield Defenseman

The upfield defenseman (X6) may be any of the three close defensemen, but frequently it is the crease defenseman, because his stick work may not be as good as that of the other two. Over the years we have hidden a number of mediocre stick handlers in this position. Even though our opponents may have been aware of the weakness of the player in this position, they still were forced to use a rider to cover him. This was necessary because no other clearer was close enough for one rider to attempt to cover two clearers, as in the case with X3 and the clearers near him. Player X6 lines up about 5 yards from the sideline and reacts to the position of the ball. If the ball is located anywhere between the middle of the field and the opposite sideline, he is ready to move to the defensive half of the field to keep from violating the offside rule. If the ball is located on his half of the field, he does not have to be concerned with staying onside and can go over the center line. He remains near the sideline and looks for a pass from one of his teammates, normally X2. If X2 runs the ball over the center line on his side of the field, X6 still goes over the center line, keeping a distance of about 10 yards from him. Two midfielders (X3 and X4) are responsible for staying onside in this situation.

Wing Midfielder

The wing midfielder (X4) has the same responsibilities as X6 and plays in the same relative position on the opposite side of the field.

Middle Midfielder

The middle midfielder (X5) plays in the middle of the field, no farther than 20 yards from the goalie. When X3 makes a break to his right, X5 can make a break for open area to his left, giving the goalie the choice of passing to either one. If the goalie passes to X2, he can break to open area toward the center line or near the sideline. If the goalie's pass goes to X1, then X5 breaks back to his original position and goes for open area over the center line and with a slight angle to the sideline. When either X4 or X6 receives the pass, he breaks toward them and looks for the ball. He does not have any responsibility for staying onside, regardless of the position of the ball.

CLEAR VERSUS TEN-MAN RIDE

If the clearing team does not have a specific plan to combat the ten-man ride, it will spend most of the game on its defensive half of the field. The ten-man ride, with the goalie moving out of the goal to cover an opposing attackman, was popularized in the 1970s. But when the opposition is prepared for it, the clear can result in an easy goal, because the goalie, as well as one or two defensemen, can be caught fairly far from the goal. The classic example of this took place in a game between the University of Maryland and the University of Virginia at Charlottesville in 1971. Maryland used a ten-man ride successfully throughout the game, as evidenced by Virginia's failure to clear the ball seventeen times. However, by an ironic twist of fate, the ten-man ride was Maryland's undoing. With less than one minute remaining in the game and the score tied at 8–8, Virginia got possession of the ball on the end line behind its defensive goal. The Cavaliers made several passes in a vain attempt to clear the ball, and then passed it to their goalie, Al Hirsh. Hirsh realized time was running out. More important, he saw the Maryland goal unattended and unleashed a 75-yard shot straight down the middle of the field. It took two bounces, dented the Maryland net, and gave Virginia a 9–8 victory. Without a doubt this was the most dramatic goal ever scored by a goalie.

Long shots, taken at a goal left open by the ten-man ride, figured prominently in the outcome of two other key games, in 1973 and 1975. In the 1973 NCAA championship game at Franklin Field in Philadelphia between Maryland and Hopkins, Rick Kowalchuk, in a prearranged play in a clearing situation, took a shot from about 50 yards from the Maryland goal when the Terps were in a ten-man ride. He missed by inches, and we ended up losing the game by a 10–9 score in overtime. We were about 6 inches away from pulling off one of the game's biggest upsets. Charlie Brown, Washington and Lee's goalie, scored an important goal from 60 yards out against Hopkins' ten-man ride in the big upset of the 1975 NCAA playoffs when W & L beat Hopkins by an 11–7 score.

Although shooting at the open goal is one way to break the ten-man ride, there are other moves a clearing team may make. The close attackmen must get fully involved with the clear in order to succeed. Figure 13–6 shows one way to clear against the ten-man ride. The responsibilities of each player are as follows:

Goalie

The goalie is the key man in the clear. As soon as he knows the opponents are using a ten-man ride, he shouts it loud and clear so all his teammates will hear. If the riding team allows him to make one pass before moving into the ten-man ride, he should make it to X1. If the riders move into positions to cover the three midfielders and three defensemen before playing him, the goalie then has to make his first pass upfield to one of the attackmen or shoot at the goal. He looks first for attackman X8, who breaks over the center line. If he is covered, he looks for wing attackman X9, who is being covered by the opponent's goalie. If neither X8 nor X9 is open, he passes to X7 or takes a shot at the goal, with X7 ready to hustle for the back line to be closest to it when the ball goes out of bounds, thus gaining possession. This is an easy way to clear the ball.

Wing Defensemen

If the riding team does not put the ten-man ride in

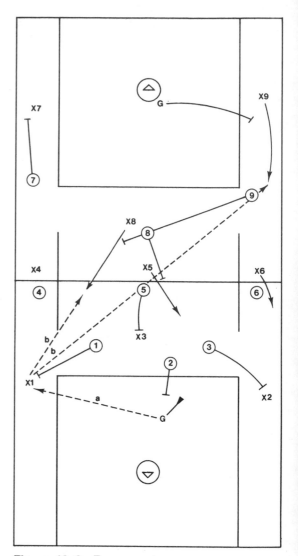

Figure 13–6 Ten-man clear.

effect until the clearing team makes its first pass, the clear should be designed to place its best stick handler in the position of X1. This can be the regular defenseman who plays this position on the drop-back clear, or it can be the midfielder who plays the X3 position. If this is done, then X1 and X3 just exchange places. When X1 gets the pass from the goalie, he has several options. He can pass the ball to X8 breaking over the center line; he can throw a cross-field pass to X9 near the restraining line; he can clear the ball himself by running at O1 and dodging him. If the riding team forces the ball to X2, his courses of action are the same as X1's. However, X8 will have to make his break to the opposite side of the field—between X5 and X6. Player X2 will make the long pass to either attackman X7 or X9, depending on which one is being played by the goalie.

Midfielders

When either the goalie or X1 has the ball, midfielders X3 and X4 remain in their original positions without making any breaks in order to open a cutting lane for attackman X8. Midfielder X5 breaks slightly to his left when the goalie is played by O2. This move also opens an alley for X8.

Crease Defenseman

The crease defenseman (X6) remains in his regular position, on line with X4 and X5. When the goalie is played by O2 or when he passes to X1, X6 makes a short break back toward his goal to bring O6 with him and thus out of position for sliding to cover X9 on the cross-field pass to him.

Point Attackman

The point attackman (X8) is normally the most skilled attackman, and he plays a vital role in the clear against the ten-man ride. As soon as he sees his defender (O8) move up to play X5, he checks to see if the opponent's goalie is moving out to cover an attackman, and if he is, he then calls out, "Ten-man ride." This alerts the goalie and all his teammates. Player X8 then moves to a point just several yards from the center line. When a rider pressures the ball carrier (either the goalie or X1), X8 breaks for open area on the defensive half of the field between X4 and X5. If X8 receives the pass from either one, he turns his body to protect the stick and looks to clear the ball himself or pass it cross-field to attackman X9, because the goalie probably will be moving back toward the goal at this time.

Wing Attackmen

The wing attackmen (X7 and X9) will take their positions according to the opponents playing them. The attackman being played by the goalie will move to a position outside the attack-goal

area about even with the restraining line and then look for the long pass, normally a cross-field pass. The other attackman will also move outside the attack-goal area but even with the plane of the goal. He is ready to back up a long shot taken at the goal. As soon as the ball is cleared over the center line, both X7 and X9 will run for the goal, looking for a fast-break opportunity.

CLEAR VERSUS PRESS RIDE

The clearing team must be quick to identify the opponent's use of a press ride. The press is used mainly when a ball goes out of bounds and the riders have time to move into position for man-to-man coverage of the ball carrier and the four nearest clearers. The sixth rider plays the two clearers farthest from the ball. This ride is very easy to break once it is recognized. Guidelines 11 and 12, mentioned earlier in this chapter, help to set the stage for the clear against the press ride. Figure 13–7 shows the clearing positions, and the following responsibilities are given to each player:

Goalie

The goalie alerts his teammates to the press ride and takes his position inside the crease. Guide-

Figure 13–7 Press clear.

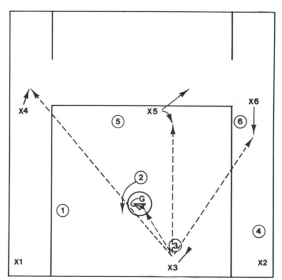

line 11 and Figure 13–1 explain his initial moves. Once he receives the pass, he looks to make an upfield, lead pass to either X4, X5, or X6. This could open up a fast-break opportunity. If X3 tries to dodge his man and clear the ball himself, the goalie should move to the opposite side of the crease once X3 has started to run. This will keep his rider (O2) from double-teaming him. If X3 passes to any other player, the goalie should still remain in the crease.

The Ball Carrier

Guideline 12 gives background information about this position. As soon as the whistle blows, the ball carrier (X3) must be ready to react quickly to put the ball into play. He looks first to the goalie, then to X4, X5, or X6. He passes the ball to the open man. If he is unable to determine the open man right away and is getting considerable pressure from the riding attackman (O3), he can just start running with the ball and try to dodge his man. Speed is a big asset for X3. I prefer the ball carrier to be the midfielder (X3) who handles the pivot position in the drop-back clear.

Wing Defensemen

The wing defensemen (X1 and X2) move to positions as close to the corners of the field as possible. They want their riding attackmen (O1 and O4) to cover them and therefore be well removed from the action. If their riders sag too far from them, the ball carrier can use them for an outlet pass, if he so desires. If either receives the first pass from X3, he looks to make his pass to either X4, X5, or X6.

Players at the Restraining Line

Players X4, X5, and X6 are the same ones who operate on the second wave of the clear against the drop-back and ten-man rides. They handle the same relative positions against the press ride; the only difference is in their location on the field. They must not go any farther than the restraining line, because the farther they move down the field toward the center line, the easier it is for two riders (O5 and O6) to play them. They must respond quickly to the call that a press ride is being used. The onside player (X6) lines up about 3 to 4 yards from the sideline and breaks about 5 yards toward the back line when the whistle blows. The middle man (X5) lines up just a few yards from the middle of the field on the side of the ball. When the whistle blows, he either remains in position or breaks a yard or two for open area, toward either the ball or the center line. The offside player (X4) lines up about 5 yards from the sideline and eases a few yards toward the center line when the whistle blows, looking for a long pass from X3.

The main advantage to the clearing patterns diagramed in this chapter for the drop-back, ten-man, and press rides is the similarity of each clear. Regardless which of these three rides is used, the wing defensemen (X1 and X2) and the second wave of clearers (X4, X5, and X6) go to the same relative positions on the field. Only the goalie and X3 make slight adjustments, but these two players should be the most capable clearers on the team and able to handle the added responsibility.

Clearing is such an important part of the game that it requires special emphasis during practice sessions. In making preparations for an upcoming game, about ten to fifteen minutes are needed to brief the team on the types of rides the opponent has used and the clearing patterns that will be used against them. Then another twenty minutes are needed to practice them. In addition, the team should spend about twenty minutes during each of two other days to practice clearing. Actually, the team is practicing its riding as well in these two sessions, because the second team simulates the opponent's rides and clears on a full-field basis. A well-organized and well-drilled team will have little difficulty in clearing the ball and will remove considerable pressure from its defensive unit.

riding 14

When Charlie Wicker or Joe Cowan went after a clearing defenseman or goalie, the pressure was on the defensive team, even though it had the ball and an extra man. Concern, if not at times fright, could be seen in the eyes of the ball carrier. He knew what was coming from a tough, hard-checking, and clever rider who could run down the clearer like a cheetah attacking its prey. In effect, the tactics of such outstanding riders as those All-Americans Wicker at Maryland in 1953–56 and Cowan at Hopkins in 1967–69 were purely offensive in nature. They went after the clearer with the simple objective of taking the ball away from him. They were exceptional athletes who had great success with this approach. The good athlete, who hustles and anticipates the moves of the clearing team, may not accomplish what Wicker or Cowan did, but he can cause the defense considerable difficulty in clearing.

Riding is the maneuvering by the attacking team, once it loses possession of the ball, to prevent the defensive team from clearing the ball to its offensive half of the field. Although some aspects of the riding game boil down to 1-on-1 confrontations, riding is primarily a team proposition. Even though attackmen and midfielders do the bulk of the work in riding, the defensemen and goalie have definite responsibilities, too. Every team member must carry out his assignment if the ride is to be successful. When all ten players function with precision and cohesiveness, the clearing team may get very frustrated because the players realize they cannot cope with their opponents, even with an extra man, the goalie, to clear the ball. Loss of the ball to the riders can further demoralize the clearing team because they may have given up an easy goal. Often the goalie or a defenseman is caught out of position when the ball is lost, and a 3-on-2 or 2-on-1 fast break results. This scoring opportunity places an undue burden on the defensive team.

155

The effective rider has a number of attributes. Speed and hustle are probably the most important. Persistence and a "never-quit" attitude can cover up a lack of speed. The rider must have excellent control of his body and stick when he encounters the ball carrier. He assumes a basic defensive position with good balance and uses a variety of checks. The rider can act aggressively to get the ball and take the risk of being dodged as long as he is quick in delivering his stick checks and in reacting to countermoves by the ball carrier. Mental alertness is essential, because the rider must have a thorough understanding of the riding strategy.

The following guidelines will bring success in riding:

1. The basic defensive fundamentals on positioning and stick checks as explained in Chapter 9, "Individual Defense," are applicable to the attackman when he rides a clearing defenseman or goalie.

2. After running at top speed to reach the ball carrier, the rider must bring his body under control to avoid being dodged.

3. The "one-shot" rider can destroy the effectiveness of the ride. If he moves aggressively into the ball carrier and makes one hard check or over-the-head maneuver, he either knocks the ball out of the stick or misses it completely and gets dodged. Unless the rider is like Wicker or Cowan (and there haven't been too many close to their level), he should approach the clearer with the idea of applying pressure more than of actually taking the ball away. A rule of thumb is the three P's—pressure, but with position and patience.

4. The riding attackman can use over-the-head and wraparound checks to try to get the ball. However, his body weight should be controlled so that he is able to regain position if he fails in his attempt to check the clearer's stick. If he overcommits himself, he will be dodged.

5. A thorough understanding of the opponent's clearing pattern helps the rider anticipate the next pass. A keen sense of anticipation of the pass will allow the rider to make the proper move to break up the clear.

6. The rider's eyes should light up when he sees a buddy pass en route to a nearby clearer. He makes his slide to the ball anytime he is certain he can check the receiver's body and stick prior to his catching the ball and passing it to a teammate. When making the contact, he should drive his shoulder into the chest or shoulder of the receiver, hitting him high rather than low. If he checks below the waist, he usually falls to the ground and is almost as much out of the play as his opponent.

7. At times the rider can bait the ball carrier into throwing the ball to the man he is covering by lagging a yard or two farther than a normal distance from him. When the pass is on the way, he bursts full speed and arrives in time either to check the receiver's stick or to put pressure on him.

8. Each member of the riding team must keep both the ball and the nearby clearer in sight at all times. He must continually turn his head and eyes to do this, because he will be in trouble if he follows one and not the other.

9. The midfield riders who are not playing the ball carrier must maintain a topside position (between their man and the ball) on the player they are covering. This enables them to make a slide to cover another defender if a poor pass is thrown to him. If they play alongside or behind their man, they will lose this opportunity and also will not be able to prevent their man from breaking back toward the ball carrier to receive the pass.

10. The proper distance between a midfielder (not covering the ball) and his man is determined by the proximity of the ball. If the ball carrier is fairly close to the rider (about 10 to 15 yards), the rider must remain almost next to his man. If he is 20 or more yards away, the rider will move as far from his man as the distance he could cover if a long pass were to be thrown to the man he is covering. The sag position enables the midfielder to help out on the ride by making a slide to another man.

11. One of the most disheartening happenings for the riding team is the failure of one of its defensemen to shut off his attackman and thereby allow him to receive a clearing pass from a ball carrier who is under considerable pressure. It is very upsetting to the three attackmen and three midfielders, who are doing an excellent job of delaying the clear and pressuring the ball carrier, to have a teammate on their defensive half of the field "fall asleep" and allow his attackman to receive an outlet, or release, pass. This turns an effective ride into an easy clear.

12. Once a rider gains possession of the ball, he looks immediately to the hole area to see if

there is an open teammate. If so, he passes the ball to him for the point-blank shot. If there is no one open, he bursts at full speed for the goal and looks for a fast-break opportunity.

13. Since close to half of a team's rides are delayed, as opposed to the inbounds running rides, it can position its personnel to get maximum use of their talents. It is not too difficult to design a ride that gives the easiest assignment to the weakest rider and the most important one to the best rider. If the opponent's goalie is only an average clearer and brings the ball up the field against any type of drop-back ride, a weak rider can be assigned to him. The weak rider can also be given the job of shutting off a specific person as soon as the ball goes out of bounds. Not much skill is required in either of these assignments. Alternatively, the ride can be designed to cover six of the seven clearers, leaving the opponent's weakest clearer wide open. When the ball is thrown to him, the riders shift their positions, placing the best rider on the opponent's weakest clearer and the other five riders shutting off his outlet passes. They give him, as his only possibility, a long cross-field pass. This pass is difficult to make because he is being pressured hard by the toughest rider.

14. When an attackman is riding a defenseman or goalie with the ball near the center line, he anticipates crossing the center line if the ball carrier does. Since a teammate has to remain onside to allow the clearer to go over the center line, a teammate on the riding team should also stay onside to allow the rider to go over. He can remove any doubt in the mind of the rider by calling out, "I'm back, Doug. Go over." At times inexperienced attackmen will not go over the center line and consequently will give the defense an easy clear.

15. If an attackman on the clearing team breaks over the center line trying to get a pass, the defenseman on the riding team should take a quick look to see if he has a teammate staying onside. If so, he should go over the center line, too, and continue to stay with his man.

16. Considerable talk is necessary at the center line in order to keep the pressure on the clearing team by allowing riders to cross it. In addition to verbal communications, the basic rule that requires a rider to stay on the same side of the center line as the clearer he is guarding can ease the uncertainty of crossing the center line. In certain

rides, specific instructions are given to the riders in this situation.

There are two basic categories of rides. One involves fast action when the ball is inbounds and the goalie initiates the play. Normally, the goalie gets possession of the ball by making a save or by scooping a loose ball in the vicinity of the goal. He then tries to clear the ball as quickly as possible to the offensive half of the field. The other type of ride stems from either an out-of-bounds situation or one where the inbounds clear is delayed because the goalie goes behind the goal and the riding team drops back. In either case, the riding team has time to place its players in specific positions for the various rides. Although there are different types of rides within each of the two main categories, only five of the most effective rides will be explained in this chapter.

INBOUNDS RUNNING RIDE, FIRST PHASE

The success of the inbounds running ride depends on the quickness of the offensive team in changing from an attack-oriented group to a hustling band of riders trying to prevent the defensive team from clearing the ball. The ride is basically man to-man coverage by the three midfielders, with the three attackmen scrambling to cover the four clearers (the goalie and three defensemen). This is the safest way to prevent a team from getting a fast break on its clear. Once the goalie passes the ball to a wing defenseman, and the ball is moving downfield, a midfield slide can be used to break up the clear, but a certain amount of risk exists with this maneuver. Figure 14–1 shows the movements of the riders on the first phase of a ride that was initiated by a shot from the midfield and a save by the goalie. Their responsibilities are as follows:

Crease Attackman

The primary responsibility of the crease attackman (O6) is to keep the pressure on the goalie as soon as he gains possession of the ball in the crease. He immediately maintains a position directly in front of the goalie to prevent him from running out of the crease to the front of the goal. He also places the head of his stick over his own head, where it can block the goalie's pass to a

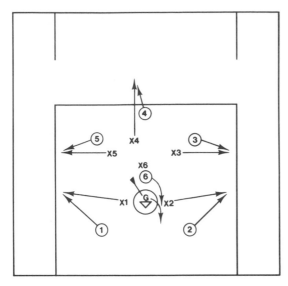

Figure 14–1 First phase of inbounds running ride.

breaking midfielder. By placing his stick in this position, he will frequently discourage the goalie from making the fast-break pass to his midfielder, because the goalie will be afraid of its being blocked and giving the offense a chance for a cheap goal. If O6 prevents the goalie from running the ball out of the crease to the front of the goal or passing it to a midfielder, he then primes himself to ride him hard when he goes behind the goal and out of the crease. The longer the goalie delays in the crease, the more pressure O6 can put on him when he does break out. As soon as the goalie moves outside the crease, O6 should be right on him, delivering poke and slap checks, which may cause him to drop the ball or make a bad pass.

Wing Attackmen

The wing attackmen (O1 and O2) hustle to cover their defensemen (X1 and X2) and prevent a quick outlet pass from the goalie to either of them.

Midfielders

The three midfielders (O3, O4, and O5) shut off their midfield defenders to keep them from getting a fast-break pass from the goalie. They should keep their eyes on their men as well as on the ball, because sometimes the goalie will try to

force the pass to the breaking midfielder even when he is covered. If the riding midfielder doesn't keep his eyes on the ball, the pass can be completed even though he is right next to the receiver.

INBOUNDS RUNNING RIDE, SECOND PHASE

In the second phase of the inbounds ride, as shown in Figure 14–2, the responsibilities are as follows:

Crease Attackman

The crease attackman (O6) keeps harassing the goalie until he passes to X2. Then he moves away from him and toward X6. He obviously won't be able to prevent X6 from receiving the pass, but he can keep running to place pressure on him in the event of a poorly thrown pass or his failure to catch it.

Wing Attackmen

After stopping the quick outlet pass to their defensemen, the wing attackmen (O1 and O2) may not be able to prevent their men from breaking back toward the end line and receiving a pass

Figure 14–2 Second phase of inbounds running ride.

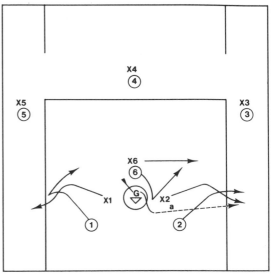

behind the goal. In fact, it may be desirable to have the ball on one side of the field and near the corner, especially if the team's best rider is playing the ball carrier. If the goalie is "running for his life" behind the goal with O6 in pursuit, O1 and O2 should shut off their men and force the goalie to make a hurried pass to X6 in front of the goal. A failure to complete this pass could result in an easy goal.

With the goalie's pass to X2, player O2 moves in to play him aggressively but without fouling him or allowing him to dodge. Player O1 runs at full speed toward the middle of the field to help out in covering X6.

Midfielders

The three midfielders (O3, O4, and O5) remain in man-for-man coverage but move to a topside position between their men and the ball. They keep their eyes open for a possible buddy pass to the crease defenseman (X6).

INBOUNDS RUNNING RIDE,
THIRD PHASE

Figure 14–3 shows the third phase of the inbounds ride with a coordinated midfield slide. If the opponent has excellent stick work and speed, the riding team may be wiser not to make the slide and just stay in man-to-man coverage by the midfielders. However, it a team is able to work the slide, it can cause the clearers some problems. Here are the responsibilities for each position:

Attackmen

Once defenseman X2 passes the ball to the crease defenseman (X6), player O2 follows the flight of the ball and starts to move toward X6. Player O1 sprints toward the center line to cover both X5 and X1. The crease attackman (O6) keeps hustling for X6. If, on the pass from X2 to X6, the sliding midfielder (O3) is able to check X6, the ball may end up on the ground near either O2 or O6. If this happens, one of them scoops the ball and looks to pass it to the other, who should be breaking for the goal.

Midfielders

The middle midfielder (O4) directs the slide by alerting first the offside midfielder (O5) and then

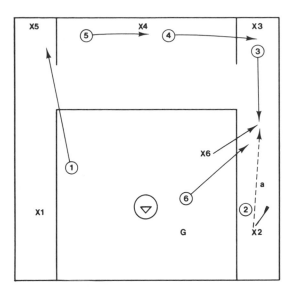

Figure 14–3 Third phase of inbounds running ride.

the onside midfielder (O3). He gives O3 two commands: "Get ready to slide" and, "Go ahead." All three midfielders start to inch farther and farther from their men and toward the ball, anticipating the slide. When the "go ahead" call is made, they burst at full speed to their new men—O3 to X6, O4 to X3, and O5 to X4. Player O3 tries to check X6 as he is reaching with his stick to catch the ball. If he has the opportunity to body-check X6, he certainly does so if it will enable him to get the ball. Getting possession of the ball is most important, not punishing the clearer with a hard hit. Players O4 and O5 will try to prevent their new men from receiving a pass from X6 if he does catch the ball. In the event that the sliding midfielders fail in their attempt to break up the clear and the ball is passed to either X3 or X4, then O1 may have to go over the center line to play X5 and prevent a 6-on-5 fast break. Player O3 must stay back onside to allow O1 to go over; he should call to him, "Go over, John; I'm back."

JUMP RIDE

The jump ride is really just a changeup maneuver by the three close attackmen on an inbounds running ride. Figure 14–4 shows their movements,

RIDING

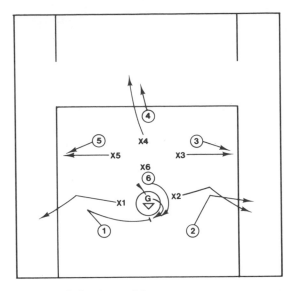

Figure 14–4 Jump ride.

which, at the outset, are the same as those in the inbounds running ride.

The crease attackman (O6) plays the goalie tough and forces him to go behind the goal. If he is a right-handed goalie, he normally looks to pass the ball to his right. Since his primary target is X2, it is up to O2 to hustle to get to a shutoff position on him and to prevent this outlet pass from the goalie. The crease attackman keeps pressure on the goalie and forces him toward the point of the goal. When the goalie makes the turn to go in this direction, he will be double-teamed on his blind side by O1. Player O1 initially breaks toward X1 as if he were going to play him, but when the goalie starts to move toward the rear of the goal, he leaves X1 and drives for the point of the goal, where he hopes to catch the goalie by surprise with his double-team or jump maneuver. The three riding midfielders have the same responsibilities on the jump ride as they do on the inbounds running ride.

In the 1964 Army-Hopkins game, Jim Adams, Army's great coach, used this ride very effectively against us and our goalie, John Dashiells, Jr. John was a right-hander, and the script outlined in the preceding paragraph was followed exactly. On about six occasions during that game, John was jumped and Army gained possession of the ball. Their riding played an important part in their 13–10 victory on Homewood Field, as we failed to

clear tne ball sixteen times. However, the following year we prepared John for the jump ride and went up to West Point ready to break it. We were successful, and our clearing helped us upset the Cadets by a 6–3 score. The surprise element of the jump ride can completely frustrate the goalie in his attempt to clear the ball after a save. However, the jump ride cannot be overworked, because it will lose its effectiveness if it is expected.

PRESS RIDE

The press ride is also known as the "four-on" ride, because the goalie and three defensemen are covered by three attackmen and a midfielder. It is a 4-on-4 situation, with the other two midfield riders trying to cover the three clearing midfielders. The press ride is best used as a changeup. Constant use of it can give the clearing team too many fast-break opportunities, because it will be prepared to look for the open midfielder and ready to pass the ball as soon as the whistle blows. The best time to employ the press ride is when the ball goes out of bounds on the end line or on a sideline no farther than 20 yards from the corner of the field. If the clearing team anticipates a drop-back ride when the ball goes out of bounds but instead is surprised with a press ride, it may lose its composure and fail to clear the ball. The press ride can also be used when the goalie makes a save on an inbounds play, but only if the goalie prefers to handle the ball himself and is quick to go behind the goal with it. If the goalie is alert in making the upfield pass to a midfielder immediately after getting control of the ball, the riding team will probably give up a fast break if it moves in one of its midfield riders to play a defenseman. Let's take a look at the positioning of each rider as shown in Figure 14–5. The riders' responsibilities are as follows:

Attackmen

When the ball goes out of bounds, the crease attackman (O6) plays the goalie wherever he goes on the field and tries to put the shutoff move on him. The other two attackmen (O1 and O2) play the ball carrier (X2) and the nearest behind-the-goal defenseman (X1). Player O2 lines up 5 yards, and no farther, from X2 and is ready to go

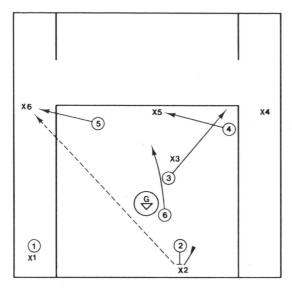

Figure 14–5 Press ride when ball is being put into play from behind the goal.

after him as soon as the whistle blows. He wants to apply immediate pressure on him to force him to make a bad pass or to drop the ball. Player O1 shuts off X1. If X2 makes the pass to X6, all three attackmen start to move upfield with the ball, and they keep running until the ball is cleared over the center line.

Press Rider

One midfielder is designated on each midfield unit as the press rider (O3). Since his job is the easiest and requires only average speed, the least able of the midfielders is given this assignment of shutting off the crease defenseman (X3). If the crease defenseman were to change positions with one of the midfielders on the clear, the press rider would play the midfielder. The key to the press ride is to cover the goalie and the three players nearest the end line.

Midfielders

The two remaining midfielders (O4 and O5) have the difficult job of splitting the three clearers (X4, X5, and X6). They favor X4 and X5 because they are closer to the ball than X6. The best midfield riders are placed in these positions. They keep a close eye on the ball carrier and try to anticipate his pass. As soon as the ball is released, they move at full speed to cover the two midfielders

nearest the ball. If X2 passes to X6, player O5 slides to X6 and tries to check his stick as he catches the ball. Player O4 slides to X5, and player O3 slides to X4.

DROP-BACK ZONE RIDE

The drop-back zone ride is normally set up when the ball goes out of bounds anywhere on the end line or on the sideline from the corner of the field to the restraining line. It can be used during an in-bounds play when the goalie goes behind the goal and the riders have a chance to drop back. The drop-back zone ride can be set up at varying positions on the field. In the regular drop-back zone ride, the ball carrier is played when he is about 15 yards in front of the goal. This ride allows for a fairly large area in which the riders keep delaying the clear by a considerable amount of running, in hopes of pressuring the defense into making a mistake. The deep drop-back zone ride draws the goalie away from the goal area and fairly close to the center line. This causes him considerable anxiety, especially if he is slow or has only mediocre stick work. The clearing team must also be concerned with staying onside when combating the deep drop-back zone ride.

The drop-back zone ride must be ready to cope with clears that bring the ball up the field with either three or four players in line. For illustration purposes, the regular drop-back zone ride will be described against both the three-across and four-across clears. (The deep drop-back zone ride is very similar; it just plays the ball at a point 10 yards or less from the center line.) Figure 14–6 shows the positions for the first phase of the regular drop-back zone ride versus the three-across clear.

REGULAR DROP-BACK ZONE RIDE VERSUS THE THREE-ACROSS CLEAR

The responsibilities for the six riders are as follows:

Point Attackman

The point attackman (O6) initially lines up about 3 yards past the restraining line. When the goalie

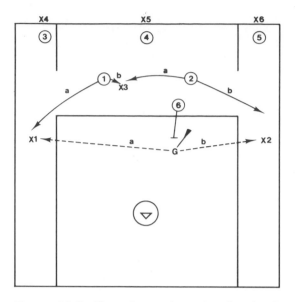

Figure 14–6 First phase of regular drop-back zone ride versus three-across clear.

reaches the 15-yard mark, O6 bursts at him at full speed but then gets under control when several yards away. He holds his stick over his head to interfere with or possibly block the goalie's pass. Once the goalie passes the ball to either X1 or X2, player O6 stays on the goalie to prevent him from getting a return pass. Since this assignment requires little speed or cleverness on O6's part, the least able riding attackman can play this position.

Deep Attackmen

The deep attackmen (O1 and O2) line up about 5 yards deeper than O6. Player O1 is responsible for covering X1, but he must also be close enough to X3 to discourage the goalie from throwing to him. Player O2 is responsible for covering X2 if the goalie's first pass goes directly to him, but if the goalie's first pass goes to X1, he covers X3. He therefore must line up not quite directly behind O6 but close to this point. When the goalie passes to X1, player O1 can delay for just a second to allow O2 to get close enough to cover X3. Then he takes the proper cutoff angle to get to X1. If the goalie's first pass goes to X2, then O2 plays him, and O1 plays X3. Player X3 must be shut off when the ball is thrown to either X1 or X2. With the goalie being shut off by O6, the only

opening for a clearing pass is to the offside defenseman.

Midfielders

The three riding midfielders (O3, O4, and O5) shut off their men with topside positioning. If anyone makes a break back to the goalie, he must be played. If the goalie's first pass goes to X1, then O3 and O4 remain tight on their men but O5 starts to slide down the back side, where he is responsible for covering both X2 and X6. If X1 tries to clear the ball himself, O5 stays back onside to allow O1 to go over the center line and keep playing X1. If X1 does not try to run with the ball but is looking to make a pass, O5 keeps a close eye on him in order to try to anticipate it. If his pass is made to X2, as shown in Figure 14–7, then O5 will play him, and O3 and O4 will slide across the field to play X5 and X6. With this move, O1 is now the back-side slider and responsible for both X1 and X4.

Basic rules for the midfielders:

1. Stay in man-to-man coverage until the first pass is made.

2. With the first pass, the offside midfielder becomes the slide man, who splits two men.

3. If the cross-field pass is made (from one

Figure 14–7 Midfield slides in regular drop-back zone ride versus three-across clear.

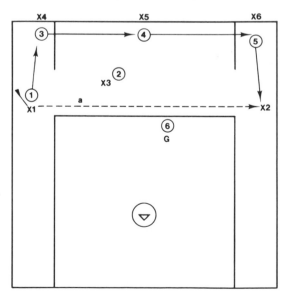

sideline to the other), all three midfielders make a slide.

REGULAR DROP-BACK ZONE RIDE VERSUS FOUR-ACROSS CLEAR

See Figure 14–8 for the basic positions of the riders. Their responsibilities are as follows:

Attackmen

The point attackman (O6) and the two deep attackmen (O1 and O2) reverse their positions from those used in the three-across clear. Players O1 and O2 line up about 3 yards past the restraining line and even with the two inside clearers. When the ball reaches the 15-yard mark, they quickly move in to play the goalie and X3. If X3 is their best clearer, O1 can play him when he is at the 10-yard mark just to shut him off from the ball, or the riding team can place its best rider in O1's position and let the two of them battle it out. When the goalie passes the ball to either X1 or X2, both O1 and O2 stay with their men and maintain a shutoff on them.

The point attackman (O6) lines up about 5 yards deeper than O1 and O2 and at a point equidistant from X1 and X2. He reads the ball carrier's eyes and his stick in order to get a jump on the

Figure 14–8 Regular drop-back zone ride versus four-across clear.

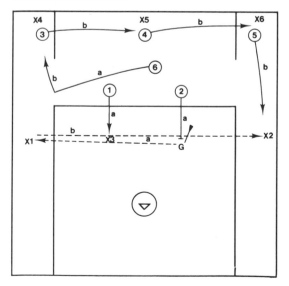

pass, because he has a lot of ground to cover. He must be able to cover either X1 or X2 when the pass is thrown. Usually the best rider handles this position, because he must have speed to get to his man and then he must exert pressure on him once he is there.

Midfielders

The midfielders (O3, O4, and O5) have the same responsibilities on this ride as on the regular drop-back zone ride versus the three-across clear.

TEN-MAN RIDE

Like the press ride, the ten-man ride should be used as a changeup ride where the surprise element can disrupt the clearing pattern. A steady diet of the ten-man ride can backfire on the riding team. If the clearing team is well prepared to break the ride and faces it throughout an entire game, it probably will have little difficulty with it and will possibly score a goal. Diagram 14–9 shows the players' positions in a ten-man ride versus a three-across clear. The ten-man ride treats the four-across clear the same as the three-across. The players have the following responsibilities:

Attackmen

The three attackmen (O1, O2, and O6) have the same responsibilities in the ten-man ride as in the regular drop-back zone ride.

Midfielders

Midfielders (O3 and O4) have the same responsibility on the first pass of the ten-man ride as they do in the regular drop-back zone ride. On the goalie's pass to X1, they cover X4 and X5 man to man. However, on the cross-field pass from X1 to X2, they do not slide; they stay with their men. Although their assignment is simple in the ten-man ride, they do have one additional responsibility, which is very important. On the cross-field pass from one defenseman to the other, the off-side midfielder must go to the defensive half of the field to allow the riding defenseman on the onside to go over the center line, if necessary. Figure 14–9 shows O3 going to his defensive

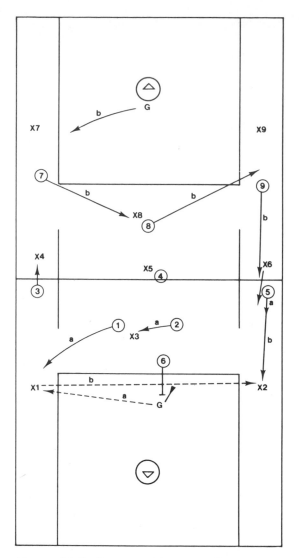

Figure 14–9 Ten-man ride versus three-across clear.

half of the field when X1 makes a cross-field pass to X2, thus allowing O9 to go over the center line to cover X6.

Midfielder (O5) is the offside midfielder when the goalie passes to X1. He does not have to be at all concerned with X6 and makes the back-side slide to X2 when the cross-field pass is thrown to him. He actually baits the cross-field pass, because this is where the riders want the ball to be thrown. When it is on the way, he sprints to X2 and pressures him

with aggressive checks. He still maintains good position on him to prevent the dodge. At this point X2 should be in trouble, because every member of the clearing team should be covered.

Defensemen

The three defensemen (O7, O8, and O9) remain in an upfield position on their three attackmen when the first pass is made from the goalie to X1. However, as soon as X1 is about to make his cross-field pass to X2, who is the only open man, all three defenders start to move to cover their new men. When the ball reaches X2, they should be tight on their men and maintaining a topside, shutoff position—O9 covering X6, O8 on X9, and O7 on X8. If either X6 or X8 breaks over the center line to get the ball, the defenseman covering him must go over, too, because the shutoff is essential.

Goalie

The goalie (G) remains in the goal when the first pass is made to X1. But as X1 starts to make the cross-field pass to X2, the goalie moves out of the goal to cover X7. He doesn't have to be right next to him; in fact, he can be about 5 yards or more from him, just as long as he can reach him if X2 tries to make a long cross-field pass to him. The closer X7 moves to the middle of the field, the tighter the goalie must play him. If X7 moves up to the restraining line, the goalie will still stay with him up to, but not beyond, that point. It is enough of a gamble for the goalie to go that far from the goal; any farther would be too much of a risk. The goalie keeps his eyes on the ball at all times and is ready to scramble for the goal if X2 tries to take a long shot. He might be able to make the save. If the shot misses the goal, he wants to be nearest to it when it goes out of bounds. His team then gets possession of the ball, and the ride is successful.

In conclusion, teamwork must be stressed in the riding phase of the game. If everyone does his job, the clear will be broken often enough to demoralize the opponent. In addition, the riding team gains the big advantage of ball control and continuous offensive pressure. The longer the ball remains on the opponent's defensive half of the field, the less his chance of scoring.

Several key points to remember:

1. Plan the ride carefully.

2. Practice it to the point where the movements are automatic.

3. Vary the rides and use changeup rides.

4. Be willing to concede a reasonable percentage of clears. After all, the clearing team has an extra man on its defensive half of the field. But make it tough on the clearing team by riding hard and intelligently.

15

fast breaks

The most thrilling plays in lacrosse take place when a team gains possession of the ball on its defensive half of the field and bursts for the goal with a fast break. The offensive players are moving at top speed, trying to take advantage of a lagging defender and consequently gain an extra-man advantage for a scoring attempt. The defensive players are scrambling to get back into a closely knit unit that will be able to handle the offensive thrust. Fast breaks give the game excitement because the end result is normally a goal that comes from a hustling, pinpoint passing effort by the offense, a spectacular save by the goalie on a point-blank shot, or a breakup of the scoring attempt by quick-reacting defenders who are outnumbered by the offense.

Since each team will normally average at least one fast break during each quarter of a game, and sometimes even two or three, it is imperative that a team knows how to handle break situations, both defensively and offensively. We will treat each phase of play separately, starting with the defense.

FAST-BREAK DEFENSE

Defending the 4-on-3 Fast Break

The fast-break alignment that occurs most frequently is the 4-on-3. The defense must meet the challenge of an opponent racing ahead of his man toward the goal. This places the three defensemen in a difficult situation, because they must defend against four attackers. The key to an effective fast-break defense is training the three defensemen to form a closely knit triangle within 12 yards of the goal. By forming a tight triangle the defense is jamming the hole area and preventing openings on the crease, which would give the offense point-blank shots at the goal.

The goalie is the director of the defense, and he identifies the fast break by shouting instructions. He will designate which of his three defensemen will play the point position (closest to the restraining line) in the triangle. An example of his commands to the defense: "Fast break, fast break. Drop in. Doug, you've got the point." In response to the goalie's command, each of the three defensemen will make a call. As shown in Figure 15–1, X1 will sound off, "I've got the point"; X2, "I've got the right crease"; X3, "I've got the left crease." Communication helps to minimize any uncertainty or hesitation by the defenders; it is imperative that each knows which position he will be manning and the responsibilities of the position.

Before analyzing these responsibilities, let us consider the general principles that apply to all three defensemen:

1. When a fast break is identified, all three defenders immediately run at full speed to their positions in the triangle. As they are running into position, they should turn their heads and try to keep the ball in sight.

2. Once in the tight triangle, the defenders are more concerned with watching the ball than the man. Since the offense has an extra man, zone principles are in effect, not man-to-man defensive principles. Eye the ball and not the man.

3. All three defenders should hold their sticks

slightly over their heads and in position to block the offense's passes. Keep the sticks in the passing lanes.

4. A keen sense of anticipation of the next pass will aid the defense tremendously and often foil the attack.

5. The defender playing the man with the ball must move quickly to him, but under control. He must be careful not to rush at him and overcommit. If he does, the attacker has an easy opportunity to either face-dodge or roll-dodge the defender and take a point-blank shot at the goal.

6. When a shot is taken, the goalie and all defensive players should be ready to follow the ball, and if it is headed for the boundary line, they should race to it. The man closest to the ball when it goes out of bounds will gain possession of it. Often attackmen are not in a favorable position to back up a shot and can be beaten to the boundary line.

7. Once the fast break is stopped, each defender must be alert to identify the jersey number of the man he is guarding. Frequently defenders end up playing a different man than the one they were originally guarding. The identification of men is referred to as a "checkup" and is very important, because it avoids the common error of two defenders playing the same man.

Figure 15–1 shows the fast break coming down the left side of the field with the point attackman (O1) on the right side. The maneuvers for the defenders will be explained for this particular alignment.

Figure 15–1 Alignment of both offensive and defensive personnel in a 4-on-3 fast break.

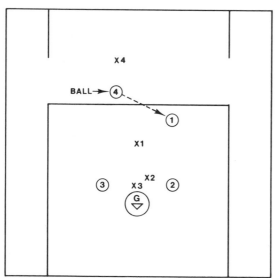

Responsibilities of Each Defensive Position
Point Defenseman (X1). The goalie determines the point defenseman—normally the man closest to the ball as it is advanced by the opposition on a fast break. The point man can be predetermined when there is a center faceoff. In this case, the middle of the three defenders takes the position.

The point man moves to a position halfway between the restraining line and the goal and directly in front of the goal. From this spot he moves out no more than 2 or 3 yards to meet the ball carrier at about 12 or 13 yards from the goal. The most crucial mistake on fast-break defense occurs when the point defenseman commits to the ball near or beyond the restraining line. When he plays the ball at the 12- or 13-yard mark, he assumes a crouched defensive position with his legs ready to move. If the ball carrier moves close enough to him, he will shoot a poke check or slap check into him, trying to dislodge the ball. He must be careful about making his move too aggressively and opening up the opportunity for a successful dodge that would result in a point-blank shot.

About 90 percent of the time, if the point man is in good position, the ball carrier will pass off to one of the attackmen, and the point man should be geared to blocking the pass. He has the best chance of blocking it if he holds his stick at the high-port position, where the head of his stick matches up with his opponent's stick. Since most middies or defensemen carrying the ball on the fast break will look exactly where they are going to throw the ball, the point man can gain an advantage by watching the eyes of the ball carrier.

Once the ball leaves the stick of the break man (the offensive player initiating the break), and the block is unsuccessful, the point man must turn and run at full speed for the crease area. He keeps his stick up and toward the goal. If the first pass in Figure 15–1 goes to the point attackman (O1), the point defenseman pushes off with his legs and turns toward the goal, keeping his eye on the ball at all times. A common mistake for the point man is to turn his back to the ball for even a full-second count. This will prevent him from intercepting the pass from the point attackman (O1) to the left creaseman (O3). If he picks up the ball at the 12-yard mark, turns properly on the passoff to O1, and hustles toward the crease with a high stick, he will either discourage the second pass, a cross-feed to O3, or he will make the block if it is attempted.

If the first pass goes to O2, the point man follows the flight of the ball and is ready to play O4 or O1 if either cuts toward the goal. If the first pass goes to O3, he will play O4 or O1 if either cuts toward the goal.

If the first pass goes to the point attackman (O1) and he then makes the second pass back to O4, the point man will stop moving toward the goal and move back out to play O4. If O1 makes the second pass to O2, the point man will continue to the crease to play O3, who may be cutting across the crease for a feed and a left-handed shot. If O2 has the ball and feeds it to O4, who is cutting for the goal, the point man will leave O3 and try to break up the play to O4.

Right Crease Defenseman (X2). With the fast break coming down the left side of the field, the right crease defenseman (X2) takes his place approximately 1 or 2 yards to the right of the right goal post and about 3 to 4 yards from the front edge of the crease. He is responsible for covering both men, O1 and O2, who are on his side of the goal. He watches the eyes of the break man (O4) as well as the head of his stick to find out where the next pass is going. Player X2 plays with a high stick to the inside to discourage the diagonal pass from O4 to O2. If this pass is completed, the offense will have an excellent scoring opportunity, because O2 will be moving into prime shooting territory. Therefore X2 must make sure he doesn't leave too much room between himself and O2 as he moves out from the crease area.

However, X2 must move out about 6 or 7 yards from the goal in order to be able to play the point attackman (O1) if the first pass goes from O4 to him. With the flight of the ball from O4 to O1, player X2 bursts toward O1, trying to get to him as quickly as possible but making sure he is under control when he reaches him. If O1 is in a position too close to the goal, X2 may be able to check his stick as he tries to catch the ball. If O1 is in the proper position, where he cannot be checked when he receives the ball, X2 must be careful not to lunge out at him and allow him to face-dodge or roll-dodge for a point-blank shot or a passoff to an open teammate on the crease. Player X2 should approach O1 with a high stick for blocking purposes because O1 will often telegraph where his pass is going to be thrown.

If O1 passes the ball to O2, then X2 moves away from O1 and toward the goal. He follows the ball and is ready to jam the hole area. He plays O4 or O1 if either cuts toward the goal and becomes a scoring threat. If O1 passes the ball back to O4, player X2 reverses his position and moves back to cover O2 in the crease area. If O4 then passes the ball to O3, player X2 guards O2 but is mindful of the possibility of O1 cutting toward the goal. If O1 makes this cut and receives the pass, X2 is ready to help out in stopping his shot.

If the first pass goes from O4 to O3, player X2 is still responsible for both O1 and O2 but will favor O2, since he is closer to the goal and consequently more dangerous. If O2 cuts across the front of the crease, X2 must play him. If O2 does not cut but O1 does, then X2 must play O1 as he moves into the hole area.

Left Crease Defenseman (X3). When the fast break comes down the left side of the field, the left crease defenseman (X3) moves to a position directly in front of the left goal post and about one yard from the edge of the crease. He is responsible for covering O3 but also mindful of the position of O2. He responds to, or keys, the ball, and when the break man (O4) passes to the point attackman (O1), he moves across the crease to play O2. When the ball is in O1's stick, he should be no farther than 1 or 2 yards to the right of the right goal post. If he moves too fast and goes much farther than this point, he will open up O3 for a diagonal pass from O1 and a point-blank shot. Player X3 moves under control and plays with a high stick, anticipating the diagonal pass and trying to intercept it.

If O1 passes the ball to O2, then X3 hustles to get to a squared-up position on him but is cautious not to overcommit and give him a dodge. Often O2 will shoot the ball right away, and if X3 is in good position with his body and stick covering the shooter's stick, the ball will hit him and the scoring attempt will be broken. If O1 passes the ball to O3, then X3 moves back to play him, maintaining a squared-up position and trying to block his left-handed shot. Player X3 must be geared to stopping the forehand shot with a good angle on both sides of the goal—O2 shooting right-handed and O3 shooting left-handed. If O1 passes the ball back to O4, then X3 moves back across the crease to play O3.

Trailing Defensive Midfielder. The defensive midfielder who is trailing the man carrying the ball on the fast break tries to catch up to him and stop the break. If he does, he calls out, "No break, no break." The goalie echoes this call, and each defenseman responds by calling out the number of the man he is guarding. Frequently the defenders are playing different men than they were originally. If the trailing midfielder is unable to stop the break, he runs at top speed for the hole area, tries to intercept or block a pass, and just generally jams the area. He will play the first man he can, and normally it will be the break man (O4) after he has passed the ball to one of the attackmen.

Defending the 5-on-4 and 6-on-5 Fast Breaks

The same principles of defending against the 4-on-3 fast break apply to the 5-on-4 and 6-on-5 situations. The three defensemen still drop into their triangle position and then react to the play of the offensive midfielders. When one of them has the ball inside the restraining line and is moving toward the goal, the point defenseman will play him at about the 13-yard mark, and the other two defensemen will make the same slides they use in defending the 4-on-3 fast break. It is the responsibility of the defensive midfielders who are hustling to stop the 5-on-4 and 6-on-5 fast breaks to get inside the restraining line before playing the ball. The longer they can delay the offensive opening, the better it is for the defense. The scoring percentage is considerably lower in the 6-on-5 fast break than in the 5-on-4, in the 5-on-4 than in 4-on-3, in the 4-on-3 than in the 3-on-2, and in the 3-on-2 than in the 2-on-1. Obviously the offense has the best chance of scoring in a 2-on-1 situation of all the fast-break plays. The defense must try to avoid being placed in this position.

Defending the 3-on-2 and 2-on-1 Fast Breaks

When two defenders are confronted with three attackers moving toward the goal, they must drop into a position no farther than 8 or 9 yards from the goal (see Figure 15–2). The defenseman (X1) who is closer to the man with the ball plays him at this point, trying to block either his pass to his team-

Figure 15–2 Initial alignment and movement of both defensive and offensive personnel in the 3-on-2 fast break.

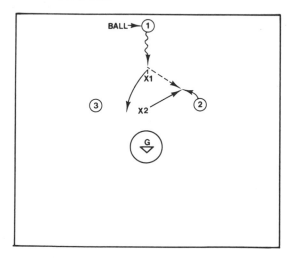

mate or his shot at the goal. As soon as O1 passes the ball to O2, player X1 retreats toward the goal, trying to cover both O1 and O3. The defenseman (X2) who is farther from the ball drops in a few yards closer to the goal than X1. He keys O1's eyes and the head of his stick, anticipating his pass. If the ball goes to O2, he moves quickly to cover him, trying to block O2's shot or pass to O3 or back to O1. He must be careful about rushing too hard at O2 and giving him a dodge and a point-blank shot. If O1 should throw his initial pass to O3, then X2 would move to him in a similar fashion.

If the 3-on-2 fast break approaches the goal from the side rather than the middle of the field, as shown in Figure 15–3, the two defensemen play side by side. If O1 has the ball, then X1 will play him at about 8 or 9 yards from the goal and X2 will be ready to play both O2 and O3. If O1 passes to O2, X2 starts a move at him, trying to force him to pass off to O3. Player X1 will slide off O1 and also try to place some pressure on O2. If O2 passes to O3, then X2 will try to move over to play O3. If he cannot, and probably X1 cannot either, the goalie can move out from the goal to play O3, trying to cover the head of his stick with his own stick. If the goalie cannot reach him in time to make the check just as he catches the pass or within one second thereafter, he should stay in the goal and attempt to stop the shot. The offense should get a

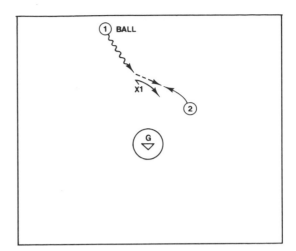

Figure 15–4 Alignment and movement of defender in playing the 2-on-1 fast break.

good shot at the goal in a 3-on-2 situation. However, if the defense can make use of its long sticks and block a feed or a shot, or make the offense shoot hurriedly or from a poor angle, it has accomplished its job.

When one defender is placed in a position in which he must play two men, he is in real trouble (see Figure 15–4). The only thing he can do is to drop into a position about 7 or 8 yards from the goal, fake at the man with the ball (O1), and try to force him to pass to O2. When he does, the defender tries to block it. If he is unable to do so, he then moves with the pass and tries to play O2. If O2 passes back to O1, he will then turn back to play him. The defender tries to draw out from the two attackers as many passes as possible, with the hope that one will not be completed. The goalie is ready to move out from the goal to help his defenseman in a 2-on-1 situation but only does so if he is confident of getting to the man receiving the ball just as he catches it or one second later.

The keynote of fast-break defense is to place the primary emphasis on following the ball and not the man, since the offense actually has an extra-man advantage. The hole area must be jammed to prevent the point-blank shots and also to intercept or block passes into this area. The close defense will always set up in the basic triangle position regardless of the alignment of the opponent's attackmen and the type of play

Figure 15–3 Initial alignment and movement of both defensive and offensive personnel in the 3-on-2 fast break that originates from the side.

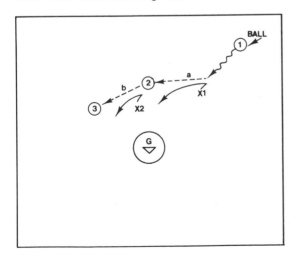

they use. The defense can adjust to any offensive pattern from the triangle.

FAST-BREAK OFFENSE

Most fast breaks originate on the defensive half of the field when the goalie makes a save or a defender gains possession of the ball. In either case the ball is passed upfield to a midfielder who is breaking out and calling for the ball. The ball can be advanced more quickly from the defensive to the offensive half of the field by passing rather than by running with it. The defense tries to get a fast break every time it gets possession of the ball. The ultimate is to have the ball move upfield quickly and to gain the extra-man advantage with the fast break, resulting finally with an offensive man going head to head with the opponent's goalie. The next ideal situation is the 2-on-1, then the 3-on-2, then the 4-on-3, then the 5-on-4, and finally the 6-on-5 fast break.

There are a number of basic principles that apply to all these fast-break situations:

1. Make a defender commit himself to the ball to open a passoff to an offensive teammate. The farther the defender is from the goal when he commits, the better the attack's chance of scoring.

2. The stick work must have pinpoint accuracy to advance the ball toward the goal as quickly as possible.

3. The man receiving the ball should give the passer a target with the head of his stick to let him know exactly where he wants the ball.

4. As soon as the three attackmen see the fast break developing, they should run at top speed, watching the ball as they move into their positions.

5. Once the ball crosses the midfield line, the fewer the passes, the less opportunity for a mistake.

6. Once the ball is within 5 yards of the restraining line, the three attackmen should be ready to receive the ball. Each should have his feet placed in a position to give him a full view of the goal, the defenders, and also his offensive teammates when he catches the ball. He will then be better able to decide whether he will shoot the ball or pass off to an open teammate.

7. Each attackman should move toward the ball when it is passed to him instead of waiting for it to come to him.

8. The offense must anticipate the moves of the defense and occasionally use a fake pass to draw the defense out of position.

Attacking with the 4-on-3 Fast Break

The most frequent fast break is the 4-on-3, which normally starts when a player gains possession of the ball on the defensive half of the field and bursts at full speed for the goal. Midfielders usually carry the ball on fast breaks, although there are times when a defenseman or even the goalie will lead the break. Some breaks occur from the center faceoff at the midfield line.

There are a number of offensive patterns that can be used on 4-on-3 fast breaks. The most common and most effective is the box, or rectangular, alignment. Since the defense will normally use a triangular setup, the box makes use of a 2-on-1 situation on the point defenseman. When the defense slides to cover the attackmen, the offense is spread in such a manner as to take advantage of the extra man.

Since each of the three attack positions on the fast break requires special skills, it is advisable to identify which position each attackman will play. Whenever possible—and this will include the majority of the fast breaks—each man should go to his designated spot. Practice sessions should give each man the opportunity to work at perfecting the necessary skills for his position. However, there are occasions when the attackmen will not be able to get to their regular positions, so a small portion of practice time should be set aside for playing the other fast-break positions.

Let's take a look at the responsibilities of each of the four men involved in the 4-on-3 fast break (see Figure 15–1).

Man Carrying the Ball (O4). The man carrying the ball on the fast break (O4) must run at top speed, because an opponent will be trying to catch up to him to stop the break. Once over the midfield line, he looks at the positioning of the three defensemen. If any of them leaves his man to play him, he should then pass to that defender's man immediately. This will open up a 3-on-2 situation. which is better for the offense than 4-on-3. It is the job of the break man to get one of the defenders to commit himself to the ball. If the defense reacts properly to the break and drops into a tight triangle, the break man will carry the ball to a point several yards inside the restraining line, at which time the point defenseman (X1) will normally start to move toward him. If, however, all three defensemen keep dropping in toward the goal and no one picks up the breaking middie when he gets to the 10-yard mark, he should take the shot himself. In the majority of fast breaks, the point defenseman will play O4, and he will then pass off to the point attackman (O1). After doing this he can keep moving toward the goal, looking for a return pass from O1.

However, if O4 sees X2 anticipating his pass to O1 and getting too far away from O2, then O4 will fake the pass to O1 and cross-feed it to O2, throwing behind X2's back. If O4 notices X3 starting to move across the front edge of the crease and getting too far from O3, then O4 can fake the pass to either O1 or O2 and throw the ball to O3. Once O4 has passed the ball to either O2 or O3, he can cut toward the goal and look for a return pass in the hole area.

Point Attackman (O1). The point attackman is the director of the fast-break offense. He should be the smartest of the attackmen and have the ability to react quickly under pressure in determining the open man, and his stick work should be excellent. Usually the best all-round attackman will play the point position.

As soon as a fast break is started, the point man moves to the side of the field opposite the man carrying the ball. If the break comes down the left side of the field, he moves to the right side about 2 to 3 yards inside the restraining line and about 3 to 4 yards from the center of the field. This position allows him to attack the defense most effectively. If he receives the ball at the restraining line or beyond it, he is too far from the goal, and his diagonal pass to O3 has a greater chance to be blocked or intercepted. He is also not in as good a position to gain the 3-on-2 advantage on X2 and X3. If he receives the ball at the 16-yard mark or nearer to the goal, he is too close to the goal and is vulnerable to X2's slide. If he does catch the ball before being checked by X2, he just does not have enough time to make the right decision. His position 3 to 4 yards from the center of the field gives him better vision of

both O2 and O3 than he would have from the center of the field.

The point attackman has the following options after he receives the ball:

1. Make a diagonal pass to the left side of O3.
2. Make an onside pass to the right side of O2.
3. Give a return pass to O4.
4. Drive for the goal and either shoot or pass off.
5. Dodge the charging defender and go to the goal.

Player O1 gives the break man a target with his stick, and when he receives the ball, his body is in a position in which he can quickly read the defense's reaction and determine the next pass. After catching the ball, he turns his head and eyes to the inside and actually moves toward the goal to draw the slide from X2. This creates a difficult situation for X3, who, if he moves too quickly to cover O2, leaves O3 open. Player O1 then makes the pass to O3 for his left-handed shot. If X3 is slow making his slide across the crease, O1 makes the pass to O2 for his right-handed shot. Often X2 will be overanxious to make his slide to cover O1 and will rush out at him. In this case O1 should pass the ball to O2 or O3 immediately after receiving it or, if it is obvious to him that X2 is not under control, dodge him and go to the goal for a point-blank shot. If, on the other hand, X2 is late in making his slide or doesn't come out at all to play him, O1 should drive for the goal and take the shot himself. If the trailing defensive midfielder is late in catching up with O4, and the three defensemen execute an effective slide in jamming the hole area, O1 can give a return pass to O4, who can drive for the goal and take the shot. If O4 makes his first pass to either O2 or O3, the point man should make a break toward the ball and look for the next pass and a possible shot directly in front of the goal.

Right Creaseman (O2). On a fast break the right creaseman is primarily a shooter and should have an excellent right-handed shot. He positions himself in line with the front edge of the crease and about 5 yards from the center of the field. When the ball is thrown to him, he moves toward it, rather than waiting for it. By so doing he will normally be in a position about 5 yards in front of the goal and 5 yards from the center of the field. This position will give him an excellent shooting angle but at the same time give him a little cushion from X3, who will be making the slide across the crease to play him. If he were to remain too close to the crease, the goalie would also be able to check him when he receives the pass.

When receiving the pass on the fast break, O2 should be facing the ball with his feet staggered —left foot back and right foot forward. As soon as the ball hits in his stick, his head and upper body turn toward the goal. He will then be able to get the shot off quickly, since he will be looking at the goal. The shot will also have power because when shooting right-handed, the body weight is initially on the right leg and then transfers to the left leg as the ball is being released. He should be in this position and ready to receive the ball as soon as the break man is within 10 yards of the restraining line, because O4 may make his first pass directly to him.

The right creaseman has the following options after he receives the ball:

1. Shoot the ball with power, aiming for open area on the goal.

2. Make a pass to the left side of O3, who is moving into position for a left-handed shot.

3. Make a pass to either O1 or O4 cutting for the goal.

4. Dodge the charging defenseman and go to the goal.

If the ball is passed to O3 from either O4 or O1, the right creaseman makes a cut toward the goal, looking for a feed from O3 and a point-blank, right-handed shot. If O1, O3, or O4 takes the shot, O2 is ready to race for the back line if the shot misses the goal and goes out of bounds. If he fails to move quickly in backing up the shot, the goalie or a defenseman may beat him to the ball and gain possession of it. It is important for the attack to maintain control of the ball.

Left Creaseman (O3). On a fast break the left creaseman has the same responsibilities and assumes the same relative position as the right creaseman except on the left side of the field. He is primarily a shooter and should have an excellent left-handed shot. When he is receiving the ball his feet should be staggered—right foot back and left foot forward. His head and upper body turn toward the goal once the ball is in his stick. The left creaseman has the same options with the ball as the right creaseman, except that the pass across the crease will be directed for a right-handed reception by O2, who will be looking for

the right-handed shot. Player O3 must also be ready to back up a shot by O1, O2, or O4.

Attacking with the 5-on-4 and 6-on-5 Fast Breaks

The offensive alignment used in the 5-on-4 and 6-on-5 fast breaks is basically the same as in the 4-on-3. In a 5-on-4 break the man carrying the ball on the break, either a midfielder or a defenseman, drives toward the goal, and when a defensive player commits himself, he passes the ball to his teammate, who in most cases is a midfielder. This action takes place before they reach the restraining line. If it were a 6-on-5 break, there would probably be one more pass as the ball approaches this point.

The three attackmen move to the same relative positions as in the 4-on-3 break. The left and right creasemen go to exactly the same locations. The point attackman adjusts his position so that he maintains at least 5 yards' distance from the midfielder nearest him so as to prevent one defensive man from covering two offensive men. Instead of receiving the ball at about 2 or 3 yards inside the restraining line and about 3 or 4 yards from the center of the field, the point man will be as far as 8 or 9 yards from the restraining line and about 6 or 7 yards from the center of the field. However, his exact position will be determined by the commitment of the defensive players. If the defensive players pick up the ball just after it crosses the center line, the point man's position will be identical with his 4-on-3 position. If the defensive players do not pick up the ball until it is within several yards of the restraining line, the point man will definitely have to move closer to the goal and farther from the center of the field in order to take advantage of the extra-man situation on the break. If he does not alter his position from the one he uses on the 4-on-3, the advantage will be lost.

Attacking with the 3-on-2 and 2-on-1 Fast Breaks

In attacking the goal with three offensive players against two defenders, the most effective play is to give the ball initially to the middle of the three attackers. As shown in Figure 15–2, player O1 drives with the ball until he is played. As soon as a defender commits to him, he passes off to the open man. If X1 plays O1, player X2 is left in a bind, since he has to try to cover both O2 and O3. The fewer the passes, the better; therefore O1 should react quickly to X1's commitment and the position of X2 in trying to determine his next pass. It is desirable to make just one pass and then have the shot taken. If necessary, two or three passes can be made in trying to get the point-blank shot.

In the 2-on-1 situation the man with the ball should drive directly toward the goal. If the lone defender commits to him, he should veer off slightly to the side to pull the defender away from the teammate to whom he will be passing the ball. He should not telegraph his pass or do anything that will allow the defender to block it. He should also avoid giving his teammate a lead pass that will carry him in too close to the goal and give the goalie the opportunity to check him. If the defender tries to draw out the pass from the break man, the break man should be alert enough to detect this maneuver, to fake the pass, and to drive to the goal himself for the point-blank shot.

faceoffs 16

Play is initiated at the beginning of each quarter and after each goal by facing the ball at the center of the field. The top picture of Figure 16–1 shows the faceoff men, known as centers, each in position on the same side of the center of the field as the goal he is defending. Their sticks are resting on the ground with the pockets in a back-to-back position. Both hands must be on the handle of the stick and in contact with the ground. The feet may not touch the stick. No portion of either stick may touch, and the walls of the two sticks must be approximately one inch apart, so that when the ball is placed between them, it does not touch the ground. Both hands and both feet must be to the left of the throat of the stick, and the hands must be at least 18 inches apart. When the official places the ball between the two sticks and sounds his whistle to start play, each center tries to direct the course of the ball by a movement with his stick and body.

Control of the ball at the center faoooff is an important factor in determining the outcome of a game. In order to score, a team must get possession of the ball, and normally the team that dominates the faceoff is the winner. Over the years, the national championship lacrosse teams have had outstanding faceoff men. Some of the great ones of recent champions have been Navy's Neil Henderson in 1965, Hopkins' Jerry Schnydman in 1967, and Maryland's Doug Radebaugh in 1973 and 1975. What a psychological lift is given to the team that has confidence in the ability of its faceoff man to get the ball most of the time!

The most essential qualities of a good faceoff man are quickness and strength. Agility is necessary to give body control and balance while contesting for the ball. The faceoff man must concentrate fully on the job at hand, and once the ball is on the ground, he must be relentless in his pursuit of it. When size complements strength and quickness, the faceoff man is almost unbeatable. This

Figure 16–1 Four phases of the clamp maneuver used on a faceoff.

FACEOFFS

was certainly the case with Neil Henderson, who did not play lacrosse until he arrived at the Naval Academy. Neil was an excellent tight end on the Navy football team, and at 6′2″ and 210 pounds he developed into a great faceoff man on two national-championship lacrosse teams. Although his stick work and offensive ability were limited, he completely dominated the faceoffs and was honored as a first-team All-American in 1965.

If the little man has strength and quickness, he, too, can be an effective faceoff man. One of Hopkins' best was Jerry Schnydman. Although only 5′1¾″ tall, Jerry took great pride in his ability to get the ball on the faceoff. He practiced his maneuvers religiously and thrived on the challenge of competing against larger opponents. In his seven years of playing lacrosse at Hopkins and Mount Washington, he was successful in over 80 percent of his faceoffs. This is quite a record and would have been considerably higher if it weren't for the day he met his match against Neil Henderson in the 1965 Navy-Hopkins game. In their head-to-head battle, Neil completely overpowered Jerry and controlled sixteen out of seventeen faceoffs. It was simply a case of a skillful big man beating a skillful little man.

BASIC POSITION

The basic position of the faceoff man is illustrated in the top picture of Figure 16–2. The feet are placed hip-width apart. The right foot is even with the right hand and slightly behind the left foot, in about a toe-instep relationship. This places the right foot in a position from which it can make a natural step forward and toward the top of the stick when the whistle sounds. The right hand grasps the handle at the throat of the stick, right next to the head, and exerts downward pressure to get the wall of the stick completely flush with the ground. The left hand is placed in a comfortable position on the handle but normally no farther than the minimum distance of 18 inches from the right hand. The right elbow should be inside the right knee and pushing against the knee. The right knee, in like manner, pushes into the elbow, creating considerable pressure on the right hand and arm. The body is kept low to the ground in a crouch position, with the body weight leaning slightly to the right, and the right hand and right

foot are ready to spring forward when the whistle blows.

GUIDELINES FOR THE FACEOFF MAN

1. Keep your head down and your eyes on the ball during the entire faceoff maneuver, until the ball is under control.
2. Respond immediately to the official's whistle. Try to anticipate it to get a jump on the opponent.
3. Never stand up. Stay low to the ground.
4. Keep the handle of the stick low to the ground. If it is at an angle greater than 45 degrees with the ground, it will tend to force you to stand up, and this weakens your position.
5. Keep turning your body and try to screen off your opponent by placing your body between him and the ball.
6. Don't tip off the maneuver you are planning to use by adjusting your stance. Use the same basic position for all maneuvers.
7. Scoop the loose ball with two hands on your stick and then protect it with your body. The one-hand, snakeout maneuver is often very effective. (See Figure 5–9 in Chapter 5.)
8. When you have control of the ball, be ready to pass or flip it immediately to an open teammate as soon as a wing defender moves in to play you.

FACEOFF TECHNIQUES

There are a number of techniques that can be used in the faceoff, but the two most popular are the clamp, and the half-clamp and rake.

Clamp

Figure 16–1 shows the movement of the center as he executes the clamp. When the whistle blows, the right foot and the right hand move simultaneously. The right foot goes to a position next to the top of the head of his stick. The right hand turns the head of the stick flat to the ground with as much force as possible, trying to cover the ball completely and clamp it to the ground. The left hand lifts the handle about 12 inches from the ground to add more pressure to the clamping motion. As the ball is being clamped, the center turns his backside into the opponent and pushes into him with all of his strength. Since the center will have a difficult time scooping the ball at his feet, his backing-in maneuver places the ball in a position from which he can scoop it. If he is unable to drive the opponent back, he pushes the ball with the head of his stick to a point that is normally to the right rear of his original position. He may also use his foot to kick the ball away from his body. He then scoops the ball with two hands on the stick and is ready to use the one hand, snakeout maneuver to avoid the opponent's stick check.

Half-Clamp and Rake

The half-clamp and rake is shown in Figure 16–2. The initial movements of the right foot, right hand, and left hand are the same as in the clamp maneuver. However, instead of clamping the head of the stick flat to the ground, the faceoff man turns it only about halfway, pushing the opponent's stick back slightly and causing the ball to drop to the ground. Once the ball is on the ground, the center rakes (or pushes) the ball with the head of his stick to a left-side or left-rear position with a sweeping motion of both hands. The right hand drives across the front of the body to the center's left side, and the left hand moves to his left rear. The entire half-clamp and rake is one continuous motion. Once the ball has been raked away from his body, the face-off man moves quickly to it and scoops it with two hands on the stick. He is then ready to use the one-hand, snakeout maneuver.

Rake

The rake without the half-clamp is also a standard maneuver. All of the mechanics are the same as the half-clamp and rake except that the faceoff man makes his raking motion with the head of his stick in its original position.

Flip

For many years the rules required sticks to be touching on the faceoff, and this made the flip technique one of the most popular. Since 1955 the sticks have been separated at least an inch, and the flip has become more difficult to execute. However, it can be worked against an opponent who is somewhat lacking in quickness. When the whistle blows, the faceoff man delays his movement for just a fraction of a second rather than stepping forward into his opponent. His feet ac-

tually remain in their initial position, and he anticipates the opponent's pushing the ball into the back of his stick with a clamp or half-clamp move. As soon as this happens, the center flips the ball by snapping his hands forward and pushing the ball to the left front of his body. The head of the center's stick may be directed either under or over the head of his opponent's stick. His step with his right foot is simultaneous with the flip action. In addition to the front flip, the center can flip the ball back to his right rear by taking a short step in this direction with his right foot and flipping the ball back toward the goal he is defending.

Counter for Rake

If the opponent has an effective rake maneuver, the center can counter it in several ways. First, his initial step with his right foot helps to block the opponent's rake partially with his foot and leg. If the center doesn't make the step, the opponent should have little difficulty in completing the rake. Another counter for the rake is accomplished by the center's moving at the sound of the whistle to the point at which his opponent has been raking the ball. He makes no attempt to control the ball initially but lets the opponent make the first move and then tries to beat him to the ball. If the center doesn't get to the ball first, he will at least be there to check his opponent's stick and thus prevent him from scooping it.

Counter for Clamp

Against an opponent who uses a clamp with repeated success, the center can counter with another maneuver. When the whistle sounds, he quickly slides his stick under his opponent's stick. This forces the opponent to clamp the ball into the back side of his stick. The center then drives his entire body weight in an upward motion to lift the opponent's stick. He keeps his eye on the ball because it may be flipped in the air or just drop to the ground. Regardless, he is ready to play it immediately.

Counter for Flip

The easiest way to stop the flip action on the faceoff is to move the stick back rather than pushing it forward. The flip is difficult to execute when the ball is on the ground and not in the stick.

Figure 16–2 Four phases of the half-clamp and rake maneuver used on a faceoff.

FACEOFFS

ALIGNMENT AND RESPONSIBILITIES OF THE WING MIDFIELDERS

Proper positioning of the two wing midfielders is essential in controlling the ball on the faceoff. Figure 16–3 shows the standard positioning of all six midfielders on a faceoff, but for explanation purposes we will consider only the moves of O3 and O5. They can line up anywhere behind the wing-area line, which is 20 yards in length. Their legs are primed for the sprint as soon as the whistle blows.

Wing Midfielder O3

Wing midfielder O3 has defensive responsibilities because he is on the side of the field where the opponent's center (X4) will be trying to control the ball in most cases. The location of O3 is determined by the position on the field where X4 is consistently directing the ball. Player O3 wants to line up where he can take the shortest route to the ball. He needs speed to get to the opponent's center before he scoops the ball, and once he reaches him, he must be aggressive and tenacious in the battle for ball control. He can body-check his opponent as long as he can keep on his feet and play the ball. However, if he loses his footing and falls to the ground, the body check is useless. Gaining possession of the ball is the primary consideration.

The best wing defender I coached at Hopkins was Bob Barbera, better known as "The Panther." He was fast and tough and used a long defense stick to give him extra reach. As a sophomore in 1972 he saw only limited action as a substitute defenseman. Our regular season ended with a 13–12 loss to the University of Maryland in a game that was highlighted by Maryland's control of faceoffs. We got another crack at the Terps two weeks later in the NCAA semifinal game at Col-

lege Park. If we were to beat the Terps, we certainly had to minimize their domination of face-offs. The Panther was the answer to our problem, and we used him at the defensive-wing position on every faceoff. He harassed the Maryland face-off men, got a number of ground balls himself, and was a key factor in our 9–6 victory. We gained possession of the ball in eleven faceoffs, compared with seven for the Terps. In the last game of his college career, the Panther did an outstanding job in pressuring the Maryland face-off men again and led us to a 17–12 victory in the NCAA finals at Rutgers University in 1974. He even scored a goal on a play that resulted from his getting the ball on a faceoff. What more can a defensive wing midfielder do?

If the opponent's center is so skillful that he can get control of the ball before O3 can get to him, O3 should play at the very end of the wing-area line on the defensive half of the field. Doug Rade-baugh, one of Maryland's premier faceoff men (1972–75), was especially effective with initiating quick scores within ten seconds after the whistle had blown. About the only way to stop his burst for the goal after his quick control of the faceoff was to place O3 at the end of the line. When the whistle blew, O3 would sprint for the defensive goal area to try to stop the fast break.

Wing Midfielder O5

Wing Midfielder O5 has offensive responsibilities in most cases, because he is on the side of the field where his center (O4) will be trying to direct the ball. Player O5 positions himself closest to the point to which he expects O4 to direct the ball. He starts to move toward the center of the field when the whistle blows but is ready to read the play and react quickly. If O4 can get to the ball before he does, O5 stops and starts to move for the offensive half of the field. If his defender (X5) continues toward O4, O5 calls for the ball. If the ball is on the ground, O4 can either kick it with his foot or push it with his stick toward O5, who should be open. If O4 scoops it, he can either pass or flip it to O5. Player O5 may have a fast-break opportunity.

If O5 can get to the loose ball before O4 or X4, he scoops it and runs for daylight. He is ready to pass or flip the ball to an open teammate who is calling for it. If the opponent's center (X4) is able to control the ball himself and initiate a fast break,

Figure 16–3 Positioning of wing midfielders on a faceoff.

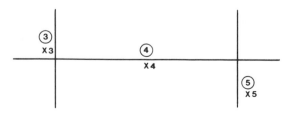

à la Doug Radebaugh, O5 can line up at the very end of the wing-area line on the defensive half of the field, in the same manner as O3. This position will help stop the fast break.

RESPONSIBILITIES OF OTHER PLAYERS

Every player on the field has certain responsibilities on the center faceoff. The three defensemen, the three attackmen, and the goalie must remain in their respective goal areas until possession is determined by the official or the ball crosses either restraining line. Then they can make a play for the ball. Prior to the whistle, they should gear themselves for a possible fast break from the faceoff. The goalie checks with his three defensemen to determine their positions in the event of a fast break. Normally the defenseman who is in the middle will identify himself as the point man; the man on his left will be the left crease defender; and the man on his right, the right crease defender. The three attackmen on the offensive half of the field will do the same. The man who normally plays the point position will be in the middle of the field, and the right and left creasemen will be on their respective sides.

FACEOFF WITH PLAYER IN PENALTY BOX

When a team has one or more players in the penalty box in a center faceoff situation, it can make an adjustment of its personnel to cover the two wing midfield positions. Normally a team will move its best all-round attackman from the attack-goal area to the offensive wing position to battle for the ball, because control of the ball will mean the opponent cannot make use of his extra man. Figure 16–4 shows the point attackman (O1) lining up in the wing position but on the offensive half of the field, because he must avoid going over the center line. If he does, his team will be penalized for being offside. This is one of the problems in the man-down faceoff situation. Another concern is the need for the center (O4) and defensive wing midfielder (O3) to play man-down defense. If they fail to get possession of the ball on the faceoff, they must know how to handle those responsibilities.

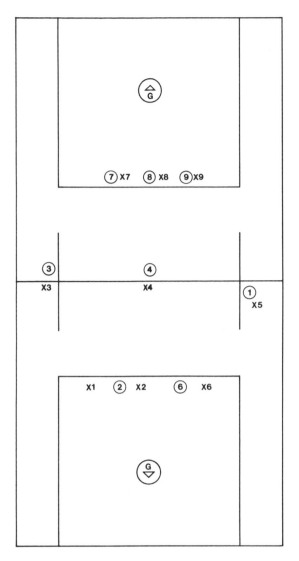

Figure 16–4 Positioning of players with a man in the penalty box.

If, in a man-down situation, a team wants to play three midfielders who know how to play man-down defense, it can take one of its attackmen, usually the weakest, out of the game. Both wing midfielders line up at the center line but on the offensive half of the field. When the whistle sounds, they drive toward the center of the field, but the one who is farther away from the ball must maintain the offside rule by staying on the offensive half of the field. The one nearer the ball can go over the center line to play it. This maneuver gives better coverage of the loose ball on the faceoff but does require the wing midfielders to make a decision about staying onside. Using an attackman on the wing solves the offside problem, because the attackman knows he cannot go over the center line. He can play a loose ball only on the offensive half of the field. When the ball is loose on his side of the field, but on the defensive half, he is unable to play it.

CONCLUSION

A team should have at least three players who are skilled in the techniques of controlling the ball on faceoffs. It helps to have one in each midfield unit. They should practice their maneuvers for at least 10 minutes every day because they must continually strive to improve. Since strength is so important, faceoff men can make use of various weight-training exercises to build up their muscles, especially in their wrists, arms, shoulders, and legs. Throughout his high-school career, Jerry Schnydman carried a small sponge-rubber ball in his right hand. By constantly squeezing it, he strengthened the muscles in his hand and wrist to the point where they were strong enough to give him an advantage over many of his bigger opponents. The faceoff is very demanding, both physically and mentally, and complete dedication and concentration are required for success in this important phase of the game.

17

drills

As you practice, so you play. Never underestimate the importance of well-planned practice sessions that emphasize fundamentals, physical conditioning, and every possible situation a team will face in a game. Drills are necessary to develop meaningful practices that improve individual skills as well as team play. Through repetition in drills, players will "muscle-memorize" certain responses, which enable them to act automatically in game situations.

It is the coach's responsibility to make use of a variety of drills to condition his players both mentally and physically. The following guidelines can help the coach get maximum effectiveness from his drills.

1. Don't run the same drill for too long a period. Monotony can cause loss of enthusiasm.

2. Try to avoid long intervals between a player's participation in a drill. If a player spends too much time watching and not playing, he often loses interest in the drill.

3. But then again, don't overwork a player in a drill. Make sure there are enough people so that maximum effort can reasonably be demanded throughout the player's time of involvement.

4. Make sure the drill is explained thoroughly and each player knows the purpose of the drill.

5. Some drills can be fun for the players. The coach should make an effort to try to invent new drills that accomplish the same results as the regular ones, but with a different look.

6. Fit the drill to the skill level of the players. Drills that require complicated maneuvers should not be prescribed for players with limited stick work.

7. Enthusiasm must be shown by all players during a drill—those waiting for their turns as well as those actually in the play.

I have found the following drills to be useful. Most of them are as appropriate for a college varsity team as for a little-league team. However, several may be too complicated for beginners.

189

WEAVE—FIGURE 17-1

Six to eight players divide into two lines with three or four players in each line. The first players in each line should be about 20 yards apart. Player O1 starts with the ball, runs several yards, and passes to O2, who initially calls for the ball, "Doug, here's your help," gives a head-high target with his stick, and moves forward to meet the ball. After he catches it, he passes it to O3. Player O3 must not break for the ball until O2 has control of it in his stick, because forward passes are desired, not lateral ones. After passing the ball, the player goes to the end of the opposite line. If the players are advanced in their stick work, they can handle the ball right-handed for several minutes, then left-handed. The coach should be the one to signal for the change.

From this same alignment, the coach can change the drill from catching and throwing to scooping a ground ball. The scooper controls the ball in his stick, making the designated call (whether it be "Take the man, drop off" or "Ball"), and then he rolls it toward the next player. No passing is used in this drill, just scooping and rolling the ball. The player who is in line behind the scooper should call to him, "I've got you backed." If the ball goes past the scooper, the backer should then play it.

The normal length of time for this drill is five minutes.

SCOOP TO—FIGURE 17-2

Four to six players get in a line, and another player with the ball positions himself about 20 yards away. Player O1 rolls the ball on the ground toward O2, who moves toward it, makes his appropriate call, and scoops it. As O2 is about to scoop the ball, O1 breaks toward O2 and several yards to the side, where he can receive a backhand flip from O2. If O1 is a right-hander, he catches the ball in a backhand position, makes a half circle, and throws a lead pass to O2, who is making a break and who catches it over his shoulder. Player O2 then moves to a position near O1's original location, makes the proper turn, and rolls the ball toward O3. At this time O1 is moving to the end of the line. The player who is in line behind the scooper is ready to back up the play and tells his teammate so.

The normal length of time for this drill is five minutes.

CIRCLE DRILL—FIGURE 17-3

Five or six players form a circle with a diameter of 15 to 20 yards. A player (O1) moves into the center of the circle. The action starts when O1 makes a break and calls for the ball, and a player on the rim of the circle passes it to him. When O1 catches the ball, he passes it to any of his team-

Figure 17-1   Weave drill.

Figure 17-2   Scoop-to drill.

mates, who in turn passes it back to him. About four or five circles spread over the entire field can be in operation at the same time. The coach blows his whistle when he wants to change the middle man. The players on the circle can also roll the ball to the middle man and make him scoop it. Thus, for a minute or two a player gets a vigorous workout of catching, scooping, and passing from many different angles. All the appropriate commands are given during this drill.

The normal length of time for this drill is ten minutes.

DODGE THE DUMMY—FIGURE 17–4

Five or six players form in two lines with 15 to 20 yards' distance between the leaders of each line. Either a coach or a player positions himself in the middle to play the role of a defensive player (dummy), who allows the player with the ball (O1) to dodge. After O1 executes a predetermined dodge, he flips the ball to O2 who moves toward the dummy and uses the same dodge. All three dodges (roll, face, and bull) should be practiced. It is the coach's responsibility to signal for the change from one dodge to another. The dummy doesn't give the ball carrier much pressure; he actually tries to help him through the dodge. If players man the dummy position, they should be rotated every two minutes or so.

The normal length of time for this drill is ten minutes.

SCOOPING AROUND THE CLOCK— FIGURE 17–5

Four to six players line up in a column with another player (O1) several yards to the side and in front of O2. Player O1 rolls the ball about 5 yards in front of O2, who scoops it, sprints 5 yards, circles (keeping his body between his stick and an imaginary defender), and passes the ball to O1. Player O1 rolls the ball out for O3 and goes to the end of the line. Player O2 moves to O1's original position while O3 scoops the ball. All the appropriate talk is utilized.

After about two minutes of scooping the ball from this position (at seven o'clock), the coach signals for the roller to move to the nine o'clock position, then twelve o'clock, and finally three o'clock.

The normal length of time for this drill is eight to ten minutes.

SPRINT AND SCOOP—FIGURE 17–6

Five or six players are in a line (three at one restraining line and two or three at the other restraining line, which is 40 yards away). Four or five lines are spread across the field from sideline to sideline. There is one ball in each line. On the whistle the action starts with O1 scooping the ball and sprinting to the opposite line. When he gets about a yard from O2, he rolls the ball away

Figure 17–4 Dodge-the-dummy drill.

Figure 17–3 Circle drill.

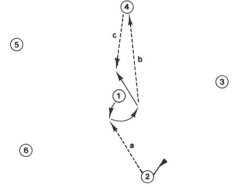

from O2, who scoops and sprints. This drill is good for conditioning as well as scooping, because the action is continuous. After three or four minutes, the coach can signal for the ball to be rolled toward the scooper when the ball carrier is about 5 yards from him.

The normal length of time for this drill is six to eight minutes.

SCOOP AND SHOOT
(MIDFIELDERS 1-ON-1)—FIGURE 17–7

Eight to ten midfielders divide into two lines about 2 yards apart at the center line, facing in the same direction. There is a goalie in the goal. The coach rolls the ball, and the first two men in line battle for it. The player who scoops the ball (O1) passes it back to the coach and breaks for the goal. The other midfielder (O2) trails O1 but allows him to catch a pass from the coach. Player O1 takes a shot no closer than 15 yards from the goal. (A scrimmage shirt can be used as a marker at a point 15 yards from the goal.) If the goalie makes the save, he passes the ball to O2, who makes a break for the opposite goal. This completes the action for these two players, and the next two players are ready to go.

The normal length of time for this drill is eight minutes.

PRESSURE SCOOP
(DEFENSE VERSUS ATTACK)—FIGURE 17–8

Five or six defensemen form in line 1 and five or six attackmen in line 2. The lines are about 10 yards behind the goal and about 2 yards apart. The coach rolls the ball toward players O1 and O2. If the defenseman gets control of the ball (as shown in Figure 17–8), he tries to clear it by running over the center line. The attackman rides him and tries to turn him back. If he is successful in so doing, the goalie leaves the crease area, calls to his defenseman for the ball, and then executes a 2-on-1 maneuver to clear it. The riding attackman delays the 2-on-1 clear until the goalie is near the restraining line. Then he drives at the goalie and tries to block his pass.

If the attackman gets control of the ball, he drives for the goal and shoots. The defenseman tries to stop him from taking a close-range shot with a good angle. If the shot is taken and the goalie makes the save, he looks to pass the ball to his defensive teammate, who makes a break into his appropriate clearing lane.

After four or five minutes, the lines should be

Figure 17–6 Sprint-and-scoop drill.

Figure 17–5 Scooping drill around the clock.

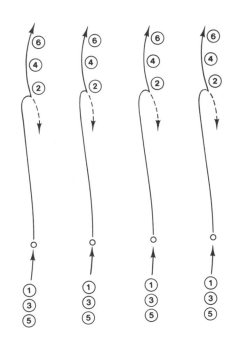

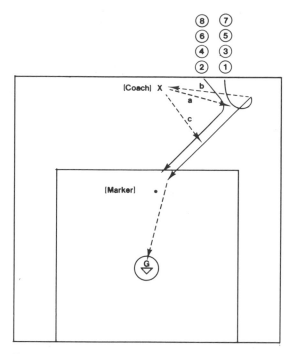

Figure 17–7 Scoop-and-shoot drill (midfielders 1-on-1).

Figure 17–8 Pressure scoop (defense versus attack).

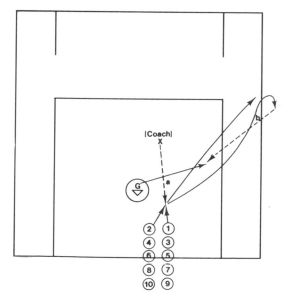

switched to the other side of the goal. This gives the attackmen the opportunity to shoot from the left side and the defenders to clear the ball from that side. The attack line still takes a position nearer to the goal, with the defenders lined up on the outside. The coach can change his position and roll the ball away from the two players instead of toward them.

The normal length of time for this drill is eight to ten minutes.

FULL FIELD, 4-ON-3 FAST BREAKS—FIGURE 17–9

Defensemen and attackmen take their respective positions at each goal area. Ten to twelve midfielders are divided into two lines near the sideline and about 20 yards from the center line. One line wears the appropriate scrimmage vest to distinguish it from the other. Player O1 initiates the action by carrying the ball for a fast break. Player O2 chases him after having given him a head start of several yards. After the 4-on-3 play is completed, the goalie initiates a fast break toward the other goal by passing the ball to O2, who makes a break as soon as the ball is shot. If the shot misses the goal or the goalie is unable to get control of it, he uses one of about five balls that he has in reserve in the goal. The action should be continuous.

After O2 carries the ball (with O1 chasing) to the other goal, the 4-on-3 attempt is made at this goal. After the shot is taken, O1 and O2 are out of the play and go to the end of their respective lines. The goalie then passes the ball to O3, who is calling for it from a position about 15 yards from the center line and about 15 yards from the sideline. Once O3 catches the ball, he carries the fast break with O4 chasing him, and the same routine follows as described for O1 and O2. After five to eight minutes of action, the midfielders can switch to the other side of the field to practice the fast breaks from a different position.

The normal length of time for this drill is ten to fifteen minutes.

HALF-FIELD FAST BREAKS

All the various fast-break opportunities (from 6-on-5 to 2-on-1) can be practiced on a half-field

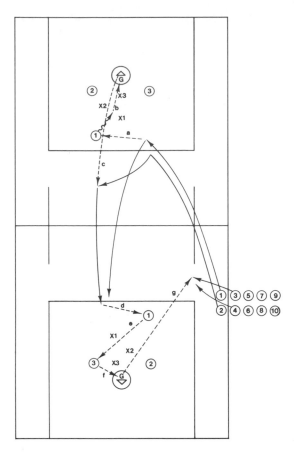

Figure 17–9 Full field—4-on-3 fast breaks.

basis. The play should be started from about 10 yards on the opposite side of the center line with an offensive player scooping a ground ball and driving for the goal.

The normal length of time to practice any one of the various fast-break combinations is ten minutes.

STICK PROTECTION

This drill is designed primarily for attackmen, although midfielders may use it, too. Players team up in pairs. One player has the ball and tries to protect it by reacting to the defender's pressure. The ball carrier holds the stick with one hand and keeps one foot in place. He pivots on that foot and tries to prevent the defender from checking his

stick. The defender moves anywhere he desires and uses any type of check. After about one minute, the ball carrier grasps the stick in his other hand and changes his pivot foot. After another minute, the two players change positions.

The normal length of time for this drill is four to five minutes.

GOALIE REACTION

There are several reaction drills a goalie can use by himself. He can throw the ball against a wall and make the save. When he has control of the ball, he can simulate a clearing pass by throwing the ball at a particular spot on the wall, striving primarily for accuracy. When on the practice field, he can practice his positioning by moving on his arc and feeling for the pipes with his stick as he maintains position on an imaginary ball carrier moving in the midfield area. The goalie can also practice his turns on an imaginary feed from behind the goal to the crease. By reviewing his footwork and stick positioning by himself for several minutes each day, he can improve his techniques and quickness.

At the start of the season or when inclement weather forces indoor practices, the coach can give the goalie a concentrated workout in the gymnasium. The goalie assumes a position about 6 to 8 yards from a wall and faces it. The coach stands several yards behind him and throws the ball against the wall (inside two lines, which are 6 feet apart). The goalie keeps his eyes on the wall, and when the ball hits it, he reacts quickly to play it. Once he has control of it, he flips it back to the coach, assumes a ready position and waits for the next shot. The coach gives the goalie practice against both bounce shots and those thrown in the air. From his position behind the goalie, he is in an excellent position to observe the goalie's movement into the ball.

FACEOFF REACTION

There are several reaction drills that can help the faceoff man. First, from his crouched position and without opposition, he responds to the whistle and plays a ball that is thrown by the coach to various positions within 5 yards of the center line. If the ball is too close to him, he pushes it with the head of his stick or kicks it with his foot. After scooping the ball, he listens for a call from his teammate in the wing area and makes a pass or flip to him.

The second drill requires just the faceoff man and one other player. The ball is placed on the ground in front of the faceoff man. The opponent is positioned directly behind him. When the whistle blows, the faceoff man tries to screen off the opponent from the ball by using his body to protect it. The opponent moves in any way and from any position to try to get the ball. When the whistle blows again, the faceoff man kicks the ball and then scoops it, with the opponent continuing to apply pressure.

DEFENSE VERSUS OFFENSE

Concentrated work can be given to both offensive and defensive players, plus the goalie, by using drills with 1-on-1, 2-on-2, 3-on-3, and, with two players on the crease, 4-on-4. Close attention can be given to each player's reactions.

lacrosse
at
Johns
Hopkins

the eighty-seven-year record

As we saw in Chapter 2, Johns Hopkins neither introduced lacrosse into the United States nor brought the game to Baltimore. (Many Hopkins lacrosse fans believe firmly that it did both.) But in the larger sense these myths have more than a grain of truth in them. Almost from the beginning Hopkins has been recognized as the center of college lacrosse in the United States.

Staying power has been the reason. From 1889 right up to the present, Hopkins lacrosse teams have been a force to be reckoned with. In other sports Hopkins, with its small student body, has learned to be content with playing opponents in its modest class. In lacrosse it has always contended with the best and come out well—32 national championships, either won outright or shared; 62 winning seasons and 10 all-even ones out of a total of 87; 29 out of 118 members of the Lacrosse Hall of Fame; and 106 first-team All-Americans since the selections first were made in 1922. And Hopkins was the United States representative in the only two Olympic Games at which lacrosse was played.

On the other side of the coin, lacrosse has always been important in the life of a generally unsportsminded university. Visitors at almost any game at Homewood Field will see—in addition to the students—deans, professors, emeritus professors, old and young alumni, and a cross section of other Baltimore fans.

These are the reasons why I want to say something about lacrosse at Johns Hopkins before my final chapter on the twenty Hopkins teams I have coached.

The first game of lacrosse known to have been played in Baltimore was in 1878, only two years after the founding of the university. Four years later the Johns Hopkins Lacrosse Club was organized on October 10, 1882, by Elgin R. L. Gould, a University of Toronto man who had earned a fellowship at Hopkins. The club's first game was played May 11, 1883, when the Hopkins team lost a 4–0 decision to the Druid Lacrosse Club. After that game, Hopkins students had to be content to play with the Druids at their home field in Druid Hill Park and did not field a team of their own again until 1888. Clinton L. Riggs, a former Princeton player who was doing postgraduate work at Hopkins, was captain and coach of that team. On April 19, 1888, Hopkins started its first official season, losing to the Druids 4–1. The only other game that season was against the Patterson Lacrosse Club of Baltimore, and Hopkins registered its first victory by a score of 6–2. Since that time, Hopkins has fielded a team every year but one, 1944, when World War II curtailed intercollegiate athletics.

In 1889, Hopkins had its first unbeaten team. The Jays were undefeated in collegiate play by virtue of a 6–0 win over then-powerful Lehigh, their only collegiate opponent. Ties with two club teams, the Druids and Philadelphia, rounded out their abbreviated season.

Hopkins joined the Intercollegiate Lacrosse Association in 1890, and the Blue Jays won one game and lost two. The *Hopkinsian,* an early student yearbook, reports that the team's losing record in league play was caused by "careful and long-continued abstinence from training and practice, which has become proverbial in Johns Hopkins athletics—we blush to own it, the team had what is vulgarly known as 'swell head.' " The *Hopkinsian* also attributed a measure of the team's uninspiring record to "an umpire who only had his Hopkins eye open for fouls."

After such a season, interest in the new sport began to wane at Hopkins. But Brantz M. Roszel, who served as captain and coach for four years, persisted. In 1891, Hopkins' second season as a member of the Intercollegiate Lacrosse Association, the team won the championship, defeating the University of Pennsylvania twice as well as Lehigh and Stevens.

Up until the '91 season, teams customarily made long passes to get the ball to attackmen before the opposition's defense could get set up. Hopkins' championship team resorted to a more deliberate type of play, passing to a man stationed near midfield and then attempting to maneuver the ball into scoring position by running with the ball as well as passing it. This was the beginning of the modern carrying game.

After a lapse of six years, the intercollegiate championship returned to Hopkins in 1898. The *Hullabaloo* (then the new and still the present name of the student yearbook) eulogized on the event:

And that old banner of '91
Which lonely in our gym has hung.
At last has found its sequel, mate,
In the championship banner of '98.

The championship banners of 1899 and 1900 soon hung in the gym as well, largely because of the efforts of William H. Maddren, who, though only a freshman, was elected captain and coach in 1897. Bill Maddren had taken up the game in 1892 when a student at Brooklyn Polytechnic High School and had later played for the Crescent Club of New York. He instituted what later became known as the Hopkins System of play: that of taking the ball down the middle of the field with short diagonal passes and developing preset "crisscross" plays.

The 1902 team, which won the intercollegiate championship, was captained and coached by William C. Schmeisser, later affectionately known to generations of Hopkins men as "Father Bill." He coached the Blue Jays to further championships in 1903, '06, '07, '08, and '09. Father Bill also was instrumental in the early organization of the Mount Washington Club team. His interest in coaching lasted until his death in the summer of 1941; throughout all this time he never asked or received any pay for his coaching. He worked with the Hopkins varsity during his entire adult life and helped to introduce lacrosse to many other schools. He was with the Johns Hopkins team of 1928, which represented the United States in the Amsterdam Olympics, and accompanied an all-star team to England in 1937. He was for a long time active in the affairs of the United States Intercollegiate Lacrosse Association, serving at various times on the rules committee, as chief referee, and as president. He was one of the first men elected to the Lacrosse Hall of Fame.

Lacrosse had become so popular nationally, and Johns Hopkins such a byword of championship play, that in 1905 the June 24 issue of *Tip Top Weekly,* "an ideal publication for the American youth," was devoted to "Frank Merriwell's Lacrosse Team, or, The Great Tussle with Johns Hopkins." In this story the Hopkins captain attempts to take away Merriwell's girl (she's faithful to Frank), to get Merriwell drunk (Frank doesn't drink), to get Merriwell to smoke (Frank politely declines), to get Merriwell beaten up by a pug (Frank kayos the fighter in the third round), and to knock Merriwell out of the lacrosse game by breaking a stick over his head (Frank's injury is quickly dressed and a bandage tied around his head, and he goes on to score the winning goal). At the end of it all Frank Merriwell tells the villainous Hopkins man, "I don't know how you happened to be chosen the captain of the Hopkins team. You can play lacrosse, but you are a dirty fellow."

The championship Hopkins team of 1908 played for the first time at Homewood Field. The Blue Jays were invited to participate in the Olympic Games in London but were unable to make the trip. As a result, the United States was not represented in lacrosse that year.

Hopkins alumni, playing either for the alumni team or for one of the club teams, had a way of coming back to haunt the varsity team. This was certainly the case in 1911 when Hopkins, coached by G. Pitts Raleigh, again earned the collegiate championship but was denied an undefeated season by the alumni team. The old grads beat the varsity 2–1, and that was the last time Dr. Ronald T. Abercrombie, captain of the 1900 team, played for the alumni.

Reaney Wolfe, one of the great players of the 1911 team, coached Hopkins to three championships in 1913, 1915, and 1919. In the crucial game of the 1913 season with Harvard, Johnny Knipp, all 115 pounds of him, made his presence felt as he scored three goals in a 6–3 victory. The 1915 team was unbeaten, but it did have one tie on its record, a 3–3 game with the Carlisle Indians. That game was played at Homewood Field during the period of the inaugural ceremonies of the third Johns Hopkins president, Frank J. Goodnow. Dr. Goodnow showed his interest in lacrosse by sitting on the Hopkins bench during the entire game with the Indians. After that game he frequently attended home games. (Among the more recent presidents, Milton S. Eisenhower and Steven Muller have been enthusiastic fans.) Hopkins won the Southern Division championship in 1918. In 1919 C. Herbert Baxley led the Blue Jays to victories over the Crescent Club of New York and the Mount Washington Club. It was the first time since 1901 that Hopkins had beaten the Crescents. At the opening game of that season, Father Bill Schmeisser presented the team captain, Herb Baxley, with a gold-star flag commemorating three former Hopkins lacrosse players who had lost their lives in World War I: Theodore Prince, Warren B. Hunting, and the captain's brother, W. Brown Baxley. The flag was fastened to the goal net before the game. To this day flags commemorating Hopkins lacrosse players who died in both world wars and in Vietnam are hung on the Homewood Field nets at the beginning of each season and remain there for all home games.

In 1922 the first All-American lacrosse team was selected. Hopkins' representative on the first team was Douglas C. Turnbull, Jr. This name became legendary at Hopkins as Doug made the first All-American team four straight years, and up through 1975, no one has equaled his record. Doug led Hopkins to a championship in 1923 and 1924, and he received strong support from two other All-American midfielders—John Murphy and Howard Benedict. Doug's younger brother, Jack, was a three-time All-American in 1930, '31, and '32 and is considered one of the game's best players.

Ray Van Orman was head coach from 1926 through 1934. Father Bill worked with Ray during this period, in which Hopkins won three championships and was the leading team in the country for three years when a champion was not named. The Blue Jays twice represented the United States in the Olympic Games. The 1926 team went undefeated with a 9–0 record. Its defense, headed by Thomas N. Biddison and team captain Karl Levy, limited its opponents to just eleven goals for the season, while Norman Robinson and Walker Taylor led the offense, which tallied 103 goals. Norm Robinson captained the 1927 team to another unbeaten season (8–0). Tom Biddison and John Lang were first-team All-Americans, and Bill Logan scored thirty-two goals during the season, nine against the University of Virginia.

To decide who would represent the United States in the 1928 Olympic Games at Amsterdam, a playoff of the country's top six teams was arranged. Mount Washington was the decided favorite, and Johns Hopkins was ranked sixth. The Hopkins team had lost to both Army and Navy during the regular season and would not have been in the playoffs at all had it not been for a startling win over previously undefeated Maryland. Hopkins' first-round game was with the Mount Washington Club, the only unbeaten team to enter the Olympic playoff series. The club team had a 3-to-2 halftime lead, but Hopkins came on to win 6–4. In the semifinal round Hopkins beat Army 4–2. The finals were played in Baltimore Stadium, and Hopkins defeated Maryland 6–3. The leading Hopkins players that season were goalie Ray Finn, defensemen Gardner Mallonee and Carroll Leibensperger, midfielders Johnny Lang and Benny Boynton, and attackmen Tom Biddison and Bill Logan. After making the first All-American team as a defenseman for two years, Biddison was a first-team All-American attackman in 1928.

At the Olympics, the Americans took the measure of Canada, 6–3, but the next day lost to Great Britain 7–6. When Canada beat Britain 9–5, it looked like a three-way tie. The United States offered to play another series; Canada agreed, but Britain declined.

Sandwiched between the two Olympic squads were three Hopkins teams, two of which were very successful. In 1930, Purnell Hall and Jack Turnbull were first-team All-Americans at defense and attack respectively and the key figures in a 7–2 season. Turnbull and Lorne Guild led the 1931 team to an 8–1 record.

In 1932 Hopkins won all nine of its regular season games. However, the playoff system was again used to determine the American representative at the Olympic Games. Eight teams were selected, and Hopkins won its first two games with St. John's, 5–3, and the Crescents, 10–2. In the final game with the University of Maryland the Terps led 3–2 at halftime, and Hopkins did not take the lead until the last three minutes of play. The final score was 7–5. Jack Turnbull and Don Kelly were first-team All-American attackmen, and Lorne Guild, Millard Lang, and George Packard were first-team All-American midfielders.

The Olympic Games of 1932 were played at Los Angeles, and Canada was the only other nation entered. The teams met three times, on August 7, 9, and 12, and the total attendance was an unbelievable 145,000. The Americans won the opening game 5–3, Canada the second 5–4, and the Americans the deciding match 7–4. The play of Jack Turnbull at attack and Fritz Stude in the goal earned special commendation.

Although a national collegiate champion was not selected in 1932, 1933, or 1934, Hopkins was considered by many the leading team each year. The 1933 team, captained by James "Moke" Merriken, was undefeated with a 7–0 record. Four Blue Jays made first-team All-American: Don Kelly and James "Boots" Ives (attack), Millard Lang (midfield), and Church Yearley (defense). The 1934 team compiled a 7–1 record, losing its last game of the season, 10–9, to Mount Washington, a team it had already beaten 8–6. Henry Beeler, a fine center, joined Kelly, Lang, and Yearley on the first All-American team.

Dr. W. Kelso Morrill succeeded Ray Van Orman as the head coach in 1935. The Hopkins record was not impressive during his first four years, although several players were selected as first-team All-Americans: Lou Ruhling (goal) in 1935, Pete Swindell (defense) in 1935, '36, and '37, and Don Naylor (defense) in 1936 and '37.

In 1938, under Dr. G. Wilson Shaffer's leadership, Johns Hopkins University took a dramatic step in intercollegiate athletics in an attempt to distinguish between recreation for college students and public amusement. The most important feature in this venture was the elimination of gate receipts. From 1938 to 1970 admission was free to all athletic events, and it is interesting to note that during this period Hopkins won or shared the national lacrosse championship eleven times.

The 1939 team got Hopkins back in its winning ways with a 7–2 record, which included a 6–3 upset victory over the University of Maryland, the national champions. John Tolson was the defensive star of that team as well as of the 1940 team (8–2) and of the undefeated 1941 team (12–0). He was a first-team All-American each year.

The 1941 Hopkins team, under Kelso Morrill's direction, was one of Hopkins' greatest. Gardner Mallonee coached a superb close defense of Tolson, Nelson Shawn, and Benjamin "Bud" Kaestner, Jr. LeRoy "Toy" Swerdloff was the goalie. This unit registered five shutouts and permitted the opposition only thirteen goals for the entire eleven-game regular season, which ended with a 10–3 victory over Maryland. Jack Williams scored three goals in that game, but the offensive leadership throughout the season was provided by George D. Penniman III. He was ably supported by Charlie Thomas, Dick Green, and Edgar Spilman. Mount Washington was also undefeated and had a string of twenty-four consecutive victories when it challenged Hopkins to play a postseason game for the benefit of the

British War Relief Society. The Blue Jays were un-decided until Father Bill Schmeisser spoke to the team. It would be the last time he would ever ad-dress a Johns Hopkins lacrosse squad, for he died two months later. He assured them that this was the year they could beat the Wolfpack. The challenge was accepted, and the Blue Jays jus-tified Father Bill's confidence in them. Dick Green scored the winning goal, with a little over one minute remaining in the game, to give Hopkins a 7–6 victory.

Charlie Thomas and Bud Kaestner were the first-team All-Americans who led the 1942 team to a 9–2 record. Henly Guild (midfield) and George Riepe (defense) were also first-team All-Americans in the 6–2 season of 1943. Although Hopkins did not field an official team in 1944, G. Wilson Shaffer kept the sport alive in the Balti-more area. Players from Hopkins, Mount Wash-ington, and other local affiliations were organized in the Johns Hopkins Lacrosse Club, with Kelso Morrill and Gardner Mallonee as coaches. The service academies were the only teams played. An informal Hopkins student team was organized in 1945, and it split a two-game schedule.

Shortly after the war was over, a second com-memorative service flag bearing seven gold stars was hung in one of the goals for all of Hopkins' home games. It represented the following former Hopkins lacrosse players who had died in World War II:

Frank Cone
Walter J. Fahrenholz
David H. W. Houck
George D. Penniman III
Edward A. Marshall
Peter W. Reynolds
John I. Turnbull

The postwar era started slowly for Hopkins in 1946. The Blue Jays wound up with a 4–5 record, which, however, featured a 12–9 upset victory over Navy, with Gordon "Reds" Wolman scoring four goals. Jerry Courtney and Clarence Hewitt were first-team All-Americans at goal and de-fense respectively.

In 1947 Howard Myers, Jr., entered the Hopkins scene. He combined veteran players with a wealth of new talent from the local high schools, in particular St. Paul's School, where he had just finished a brilliant career with seven consecutive championships. Howdy's three Hopkins teams of

1947, '48, and '49 did not lose a single collegiate game, running up twenty-four consecutive vic-tories. However, each of those years they ended the season with a 6–5, 8–2, and 12–4 loss, re-spectively, to the powerful Mount Washington Club. The closest game of the 1947 collegiate season was an uphill, 8–7 overtime win over Princeton. The equally close Mount Washington game was played under the lights at Homewood Field. A crowd of 9,000 stayed on, despite the at-traction of a large fire at the Roland Park Country School, just half a mile away. Freshmen Lloyd Bunting (defense) and Wilson Fewster (midfield) were first-team All-Americans that year, along with attackman Brooke Tunstall.

The 1948 team again won all eight collegiate games but had several close calls. Army led the Blue Jays until the last forty-five seconds of play, when Hopkins scored the tying goal and went on to win in overtime, 11–9. Against Navy, Hopkins tallied three times in the final five minutes to win 9–8. It was Neil Pohlhaus who tied the score, and Ray Greene whose goal won the game. The Mary-land game was a hard-fought 10–8 victory for the Jays. Brooke Tunstall was a first-team All-American again and was joined in that select group by midfielder Ray Greene. Ironically, these two players had been first-team All-Americans at other schools during the war years, Greene at Drexel in 1943 and Tunstall at Cornell at 1944.

Howdy's last team at Hopkins swept through its college opponents without a close game. Navy and Hopkins did not play in 1949, and since Navy was also undefeated in the collegiate ranks, the two schools were declared cochampions. Lloyd Bunting, Jim Adams, and Corky Shepard were first-team All-Americans.

Before the 1950 season, Howdy left Hopkins to become the director of athletics, as well as foot-ball and lacrosse coach, at Hofstra University in Long Island, New York. Dr. Shaffer called on his good friend Kelso Morrill to coach the Blue Jays one more time. With basically the same person-nel as in the previous three years, the 1950 team defeated all its college opponents but lost a 6–5 heartbreaker to Mount Washington in the last game of the season. Joe Sollers gave a coura-geous performance in the Hopkins goal in that game, playing with a cast on his previously frac-tured right arm and with an ankle that was badly sprained in the first quarter.

The 1950 team, along with the '47, '48, and '49

teams, belongs with the best in Hopkins' history. Eleven of its players made one of the All-American teams at least once during their playing careers. Four already were first-team All-Americans: Bunting, Fewster, Adams, and Shepard; in 1950 Bob Sandell joined that elite group. Fred Smith goes in the record book as the greatest second-team All-American of all time, having been so honored three times. Tommy Gough, Byron Forbush, and Joe Sollers were also second-team All-Americans. Mort Kalus was a third-team selection and Ham Bishop an honorable mention.

With the graduation of so many great players, Hopkins moved out of the championship picture for the next six years. Fred Smith took over the head coaching reins in 1951 and began a career of dedicated service to Hopkins lacrosse. Princeton, led by Don Hahn and Reddy Finney, broke Hopkins' thirty-one-game collegiate winning streak with a 13–11 victory. The score was tied nine times during that game, and Joe Sollers' chest must still have indentations from the hard shots of Reddy Finney. In Hopkins' 13–10 victory over Navy that year, a Blue Jay record was established when Bill Carroll scored three goals in twenty-seven seconds. At the conclusion of the season, Fred Smith left coaching to go into business. But, as we shall see, he didn't separate himself from Hopkins lacrosse.

Wilson Fewster succeeded Fred as head coach in 1952 and did an excellent job. The Blue Jays lost four games, but each was by only one goal, the most exciting being a 13–12 loss to the championship University of Virginia team at Homewood Field. In the Homecoming game with the University of Maryland another royal battle took place. Mike Dix, a fine goalie who had made twenty saves in our 8–7 upset victory over Army, was having difficulty with outside bounce shots by the Terps and was replaced by his substitute, Charles "Chubby" Wagner, at the end of regulation play, with the score tied 10–10. Maryland controlled the ball about 90 percent of the time in the two overtime periods, taking sixteen shots to just two for the Jays, but just couldn't get the ball by Wagner, who had eight saves and was the hero of the game. Hopkins was also unable to score, and the game ended in a 10–10 tie. Emil Budnitz, Jr., Bud McNicholas, and Don Tate were the offensive leaders of the team. The 1953 team had a mediocre record but produced two first-

team All-Americans in Budnitz, his second time, and Eddie Semler. Wilson Fewster left Hopkins after the '53 season to become the coach at the University of Virginia. Fred Smith served as interim coach in 1954 while I was finishing my tour of duty in the army. The '54 team had a 4–4–1 record. An 8–8 tie with the University of Virginia, coached by Fewster, was the feature game.

My twenty years as head coach at Hopkins began with the 1955 season and ended in 1974. Those years will be covered in Chapter 19, "My Twenty Hopkins Teams." So now let us skip to the 1975 season.

Henry Ciccarone directed the '75 Hopkins lacrosse team and gave it great leadership. The Blue Jays were supposed to be in a rebuilding year after losing eleven seniors from the 1974 championship team (including five who were on one of the All-American teams). Freshman Mike O'Neill teamed with Franz Wittelsberger and Richie Hirsch to form a powerful close-attack unit. Dale Kohler, Jim Moorhead, and Kevin Mahon were also outstanding. The team registered ten straight victories—the most impressive being the opener with Virginia, 10–9; Cornell, 16–9; Long Island Club, 20–9; and Navy 16–11. Maryland was primed for the Jays, remembering their two losses to us in 1974, and won decisively 19–11. In the first round of the NCAA tournament Jack Emmer's Washington and Lee team surprised Hopkins with an 11–7 victory. Although the season ended on a disappointing note, overall it was very successful.

However, the success of lacrosse at Johns Hopkins isn't measured only in championships. The game has meant much to the entire university community—students, faculty, alumni, and friends. Sharing in the excitement of the Hopkins lacrosse tradition has been a meaningful experience to many people.

One person who stands out in this regard never attended Hopkins or even played lacrosse. John N. Richardson went to Baltimore City College (a public high school) before the turn of the century. He became interested in lacrosse shortly thereafter and followed the sport closely throughout his entire life. When he retired from his job in 1944 at age sixty-eight, he adopted Hopkins as his team. He hardly missed a practice or home game from the postwar era until his death in 1971 at age ninety-four. He knew every player by name and even the names of their girl friends. The 1950

Hopkins team made him an honorary team member, and "Uncle John" became an integral part of the Hopkins lacrosse tradition. The 1970 championship team named an award in his honor. The John N. Richardson Award is given annually to the person who has made a significant contribution to Hopkins lacrosse. The winners of this award indicate the broad base of interest and support that makes lacrosse a vital part of the Hopkins tradition.

In 1971, on his fiftieth anniversary as director of the Hopkins band, Conrad Gebelein received the first award. "Gebby" has been a spirited booster of our teams, and the Blue Jay band has been right behind him. He has always been with the team, whether in the pouring rain at West Point, the comfort of the Astrodome, or the whipping winds at Pebble Beach, California. Those of us who made the trip to California in the summer of 1974 never will forget the enthusiasm of Gebby, whether it was his counting out the number of goals scored and then shouting, "We want more!" or his trooping up and down the hills of San Francisco on a sightseeing tour at age seventy-nine.

Another early recipient of the Richardson Award was G. Wilson Shaffer, who has served the university in many ways for many years. Dr. Shaffer graduated from Hopkins in 1924, received his doctorate in psychology in 1928, and became a member of the Homewood faculty in 1934. As professor of physical education in 1935, he reshaped the athletic program from one geared to gate receipts and athletic scholarships to one that emphasized increased participation by students in a variety of athletic activities. Dr. Shaffer became dean of the Homewood schools in 1942 and remained in that position until 1967, when he retired as an administrator. He continued teaching through 1974 and still maintains an office in Homewood House, where he counsels students. Hopkins' athletes, lacrosse players in particular, have had a real friend in Dr. Shaffer. I am sure he has helped more students deal with their problems than anyone else on the campus.

Gardner Mallonee was also honored for his long service to Hopkins lacrosse. He played on three championship teams at Hopkins (1926–28) and was one of the best defensemen to play the game. He became a member of the Hopkins athletic staff in 1931 and coached the defense for a number of years. In addition, he served as football and basketball coach, as well as director of

athletics. His wholesome approach to athletics, and to life in general, has had a great influence on his players. "Mr. Mal" is one of the best-liked and most respected sports figures in Baltimore.

Three people who have had no official connection with the university have been honored with the Richardson Award. Mr. and Mrs. Talbott Anderson have been following the lacrosse teams at Hopkins since 1933. They have not missed a lacrosse game, at home or away, for the past twenty years. They are just Hopkins fans, people who have gotten wrapped up in the sport and have given so much in the way of support and friendship to both players and coaches. George Pohler falls in this same category. When his daughter became the athletic department's secretary, George started to attend practices, then backed up the goal, then helped to arrange the layout of our fields with his surveying equipment. Ever since we found out that George left home at 5:00 A.M. on a Saturday to make commercial bus connections to Charlottesville for our game with Virginia, he has been an official member of our travel party.

Fred Smith, another recipient, has been affiliated with Hopkins lacrosse since 1947. He was a great player on four great teams. He was head coach of the varsity team in 1951 and then again in 1954. During the remaining twenty-three years he has been either varsity assistant coach, freshman coach, or chief scout and has given his time and effort without financial remuneration. Not only is he knowledgeable in every technical aspect of the game, but he has also maintained a unique rapport with the players. In earlier years, they referred to him as just plain "Fred," never "Coach Smith," and in recent years "Uncle Fred." He has been admired, respected, and liked by everyone.

Two recent players have also been cowinners of the Richardson Award. Both added a great deal to their teams with excellent attitude, dedication, and loyalty—Phil Calderone as a substitute player who saw limited action, and Dennis Gagomiros, who underwent surgery and consequently was unable to play at all in his senior year.

The lacrosse tradition will live on at Hopkins. The names and faces will change, but the same spirit and enthusiasm will continue for players, coaches, students, alumni, and friends of lacrosse at the Johns Hopkins University.

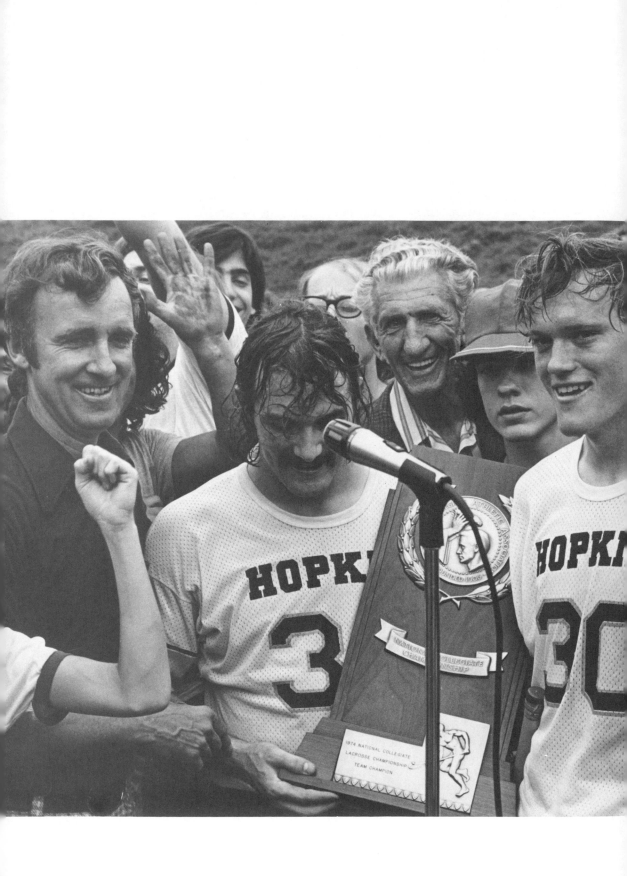

my twenty Hopkins teams

19

For my concluding chapter, I would like to talk about the players, managers, trainers, and coaches who were a part of the twenty lacrosse teams that I had the good fortune to coach at Johns Hopkins University. The players, for the most part, were a closely knit group that enjoyed lacrosse. All of them, I hope, became better people because of their opportunity to play the game. The coaches, managers, and trainers who worked with me could not have been more loyal, more dedicated, and more helpful to me and to Hopkins lacrosse.

First, let me explain how I became head coach at Hopkins at age twenty-four. During my playing days at Hopkins I was just a slightly better-than-average player who hustled and knocked down more people than I scored goals, although, as all of my former players know—because I have told them—I did have the Homewood crowd on its feet when I scored two backhand goals within two minutes against the University of Virginia in 1952, my senior year. I was captain of the team that year and an honorable-mention All-American midfielder. (I only mention the latter to set the record straight, because after twenty years go by, everyone gets to be a first-team All-American.) These were the credentials that landed me the job as head lacrosse coach at Hopkins. Not overly impressive, to say the least!

However, when Wilson Fewster decided to leave Hopkins after the 1953 season, Marshall S. Turner, Jr., director of athletics, called and offered me the job, which was to start in the fall of 1954, after my military tour of duty was completed. I was quick to accept the offer.

It was obvious that I was going to need help—a lot of it—to learn the game from a coach's viewpoint. G. Wilson Shaffer, dean of the Homewood schools at the time, made arrangements with two of the great coaches of the past to instruct me. W. Kelso Morrill had coached championship teams at Hopkins, and William F. Logan had done the same at Princeton. Dr. Morrill had been my coach on the freshman lacrosse team in 1949 and the varsity team in 1950. These two men passed on to me a wealth of knowledge. Any Hopkins person who knew Dr. Morrill can appreciate just how hard he worked me over with my lacrosse lessons—as hard as he had done with many of his mathematics students over the years. With these two men as my assistant coaches, I began my career at Homewood.

The first year, 1955, was not easy for me or my players. I was just learning the game as a coach, and six of my players were freshmen during my senior year at Hopkins and knew me as a friend. One of my former teammates on the Hopkins freshman team of 1949, Allen Klein, had returned from the service and was also on the team. In addition, one of my players, Richard Watts, Jr., was almost two years older than I and was the father of two children. So it made for a bit of a strain at times when I played the tough taskmaster's role and pushed them rather hard. We won only four of ten games, but we did win the season opener with Harvard 14–1. Lou Ruland and Herbert "Buzzy" Williams captained the team. Our two overnight trips to Virginia and Rensselaer Polytechnic Institute turned out to be the highlights of the season, as we came through with 23–9 and 10–6 victories respectively.

Cocaptains Dick Watts and Arlyn Marshall got the '56 team in the winning habit. After one-goal losses to Yale and Princeton, the Blue Jays won six straight games. The pivotal point of the season was a second-half comeback victory over undefeated RPI. The Engineers held a 6–2 halftime lead, but George Breslau's four goals sparked a second-half rally and brought a 10–7 Hopkins victory. The following week Breslau scored the winning goal again in an 8–6 triumph over Navy. Arlyn Marshall, our leading scorer and one of the nation's best faceoff men, was the first of my players to make the first All-American team, edging out a Syracuse junior by the name of Jim Brown.

Billy Morrill and Mickey Webster were the leaders of a group of talented sophomores who were instrumental in guiding the Jays for the next three years. These two attack stars were first-team All-Americans for three years and teamed with John Jory in '57 and '58 to form one of Hopkins' most potent attack units. Walter Mitchell, a first-team All-American for two years, was the leader of the defense and was cocaptain with Jerry Bennett. Wilson Fewster, who had returned to Hopkins the previous year, played an important role in coaching the Morrill-Webster crowd on the freshman team, and he moved up with them to the varsity in 1957. The key game for the undefeated '57 team was with the University of Maryland, the defending national champions for the preceding two years. The Terps were on a thirty-one game winning streak. Although our sophomores were outstanding (in particular Morrill, Webster, Ed Bernstein, Bruce Duffany, Al Seivold, and John McNealey), it was two seniors who stole the show in the 15–10 Hopkins victory at College Park. Pete Banker, substituting for Bob Powell (an excellent goalie who was an honorable-mention All-American for two years), was called upon to tend the goal early in the second quarter. He responded beautifully with twenty saves. Dick Steele was the other standout and scored five goals. The following week the Homewood Field spectators were treated to the battle of the unbeatens—Hopkins versus the Mount Washington Club. It was a classic, as both teams played even-up during regulation play as well as in overtime, the score ending in an 11–11 tie. The '57 season ended when the North-South All-Star game was played on Homewood Field. Midfielders Carl Muly, Jerry Bennett, and Dick Steele represented the Jays on the South team and played well but were overwhelmed by Jim Brown, the Syracuse midfielder, who put on a one-man show in the North's 14–10 victory.

The 1958 season was one of controversy for the collegiate lacrosse world, and Hopkins was in the thick of the action. After rolling through our first seven games of the season without a loss, we took on the undefeated Terps in our Homecoming game. Hopkins dominated play in the first half with a 9–5 score but was unable to score in the third quarter, and Maryland tied it at 9–9. When we went on top, 11–9, with twelve minutes remaining in the game, we executed a slowdown tactic that we had learned from Ferris Thomsen, who had used this maneuver in our game with Princeton earlier in the season. Since John McNealey and Bruce Duffany had just been injured and were unable to return to action, we felt we could not run with Maryland. (McNealey had limited the Terps outstanding attackman, Dick Corrigan, to just one goal; Corrigan had scored nine against Navy two weeks earlier.) Morrill and Webster took turns holding the ball near the center line. The Maryland defense did not come out to play us, and there was virtually no action for seven minutes. Many of the fans, even some of the old-guard Hopkins lacrossemen, were displeased with this tactic. But with two key players on the bench, we felt it was necessary, and it did give us an 11–10 victory. Maryland could have initiated the action by coming out from their defensive perimeter to play Morrill and Webster, as they were behind on the scoreboard, but they did not.

The other item of controversy in 1958 involved the selection of the national champion. A point system was to be used as a guide by the executive committee of the United States Intercollegiate Lacrosse Association. Points were to be awarded according to the three levels of play: 6 points for defeating an A team, 5 for a B team, and 4 for a C team. Realizing that we had only scheduled six A teams, compared to Army's seven, Marshall Turner contacted the president of the association just before the season opened and asked if we should make a last-minute attempt to schedule another A team. He advised us against doing so because he didn't foresee a problem. But the problem did arise, as both Army and Hopkins went undefeated, and Army accumulated 42 points to Hopkins' 41. Ironically, Army's seventh A win was over a Duke team that had won only one game all season. Our B-team victory was over a good W & L team that had beaten Duke and given close games to both Maryland and Hopkins. Army did not play either Maryland or Hopkins in 1958, but the Cadets did beat Mount Washington in the opening game of the season, and Hopkins lost to the Mounties. However, results of games with club teams were to have no bearing on the determination of the champion. Although it seemed logical to us and many others that cochampions should have been declared, the committee vote was 5–4 in favor of Army as sole champion.

A memorable six-week trip to England and the Continent followed in the summer of '58. The Blue Jays won all eight of their lacrosse games, six played in Manchester and two in London.

In 1959 the third season of the Morrill-Webster era got off to an excellent start. The Blue Jays averaged twenty goals a game in their first seven victories. The Homecoming game with Navy figured to be an easy one. The Middies, under first-year coach Willis P. Bilderback, had close calls in several of their victories and had lost to Maryland 15–8 and to Princeton 9–8. Since Hopkins had beaten Princeton 24–3, almost everyone in lacrosse circles expected Hopkins to win with ease. Unfortunately, our team was carried away with its role as favorite, and Navy pulled the upset of the decade by beating us 13–11. It was a bitter defeat for the seniors, their first collegiate loss in three years after twenty-three consecutive victories.

There was doubt in the minds of many as to whether Hopkins could win its last collegiate game of the season against the undefeated Terrapins, who had already trounced Navy. However, our entire team had complete confidence in its ability, and the seniors went out in a blaze of glory with a resounding 20–8 victory over the Terps at College Park. Mickey Webster had seven assists, Billy Morrill six goals, Al Seivold five goals and Hopkins goalie Emmett Collins had twenty-four saves. The Wingate Trophy was divided three ways, because Army, Maryland, and Hopkins each had one collegiate loss on its record. This was the only fair way to handle the championship. It was somewhat ironic that the executive committee changed its thinking so radically in just one year.

The graduation of fourteen seniors, eight of whom had received All-American recognition during their careers, had its effect on the 1960 team. In addition, cocaptain Larry Becker, who was slated for a key role, broke his leg in a preseason game. Nonetheless, three sophomores (Henry Ciccarone, Jerry Schmidt, and Roy Mayne) teamed with junior Jimmy Ives to lead the team to a 7–1 collegiate record, including a 13–7 victory over Maryland. John McNealy and cocaptain Mike Byrne were outstanding on defense. In 1961, we repeated the seven victories but lost to Navy and Maryland. Cocaptains Mike Byrne and goalie Jimmy Greenwood excelled at the defensive end of the field.

Ciccarone, Schmidt, and Mayne and defensemen Phil Sutley and Bill Flannery were the key players on the 1962 team, which compiled an 8–2 collegiate record. Jerry Schmidt led a high-powered offense, which averaged almost fourteen goals per game for the season. Three of our top opponents were undefeated when we met them. The first was Virginia, which had beaten

Maryland the previous week. The game with the Cavaliers was a battle that featured the play of our Ciccarone and of Deeley Nice, the Virginia goalie, who had thirty-four saves for the game. Chic scored five goals for the Blue Jays and played about fifty-three minutes in the come-from-behind 12–8 Hopkins victory. The Army game featured a 1-on-1 confrontation between the nation's best attackman, Jerry Schmidt, and the nation's best defenseman, Army's Bob Fuelhart. Jerry scored four goals to lead Hopkins to a 9–7 victory over the previously unbeaten Cadets. In the third major contest Navy kept its record unblemished by defeating us 16–11 at Annapolis. The last game of the season was a 16–15 heartbreaking loss to Maryland.

E. Doyle Smith, Jr., entered the lacrosse picture at Hopkins in 1963 and began a distinguished career as team manager. Since all my managers have been such a tremendous help to me (in fact, I would have been considerably less effective in carrying out my responsibilities without their dedicated service and friendship), I would like to acknowledge their importance to our teams and to me in particular. Since it is not possible to mention every one of our managers, I have selected Doyle to represent the entire group because he was manager for six years—four as an undergraduate and two as a graduate student. Like so many of my managers, Doyle was super-efficient. His statistical records were flawless. Although at times players would challenge him about the number of ground balls, saves, and assists for which he credited them, they were able to catch him making a mistake only on rare occasions, if ever. He was a true scholar, a member of Phi Beta Kappa. (Our managers were generally exceptional students.) Doyle and all our managers have been an integral part of the Hopkins lacrosse tradition and have made a valuable contribution to our teams.

Dick Webster captained the 1963 team, which posted a 6–3 collegiate record. Henry Ciccarone began his coaching career at Hopkins as assistant varsity coach. Virginia, Navy, and Maryland posted victories over the Jays. The big win of the season was again over Army, in a nip-and-tuck game. Skip Darrell, our sophomore attackman, was making his first trip back to West Point, where he had been a cadet for a brief period two years before. He was given a good bit of kidding by his old buddies but then proceeded to score

four goals in a 10–9 victory. Jerry Pfeifer scored the winning goal with fifteen seconds to go in the game. It was Army's first collegiate loss of the season. Homer Schwartz and Jan Berzins were outstanding at midfield and defense, respectively.

The 1964 season started out well with five straight collegiate victories, including a 15–5 rout of Virginia, which turned around the following week to beat Maryland 13–3. Prospects were bright until the Army game, when the Cadets rallied from a 6–1 deficit to go ahead 7–6 by halftime. They won the game 13–10, and this loss had a demoralizing effect on our team. We lost the following week to Rutgers 10–9. Two days before the Navy game, our top defenseman, Dave MacCool, broke his leg, and we ended a 5–4 season by losing to Navy and Maryland. Lauren Scheffenacker, Homer Schwartz, and Joe Hahn represented Hopkins in the annual all-star game.

The 1965 team stands out as the one that reached its fullest potential throughout an entire season. Eleven seniors, headed by cocaptains Frank Szoka and Chip Giardina, provided the leadership that guided the team to a 9–1 collegiate record. Stan Fine typified the excellent attitude and hustle of this team and did so as a member of our third midfield unit. This situation could have been difficult for him to handle, because he had been an honorable-mention All-American two years earlier. But Stan accepted his position, never stopped hustling, and was one of our top midfield scorers and ground-ball men. Jerry Pfeifer was our leading scorer. Frank Szoka and Jerry Schnydman controlled the majority of faceoffs. Hank Kaestner and Mike Oidick were outstanding on defense, and John Dashiells excelled in the goal. When Dennis Townsend was injured one week before the Army game, Joe Blattner took his place on the starting defense. Although his playing experience was limited to only one year on the freshman team, under Wilson Fewster, Joe did a superb job in helping to limit the Cadets to three goals, enabling us to win 6–3. Chic and I felt our team was really primed for this game, but when we saw Hank Kaestner throw a body check into an Army midfielder early in the game, we knew it was going to be our day. Hank was not known for using his body.

In the Homecoming game with Navy, the team gave 100 percent effort but just could not contain Jimmy Lewis, and the Midshipmen handed us our only loss of the season, 15–6. In the last game of the '65 season Hopkins met the 11–1 Terrapins at College Park. Although behind by two goals (8–6) with less than ten minutes in the game, the Blue Jays scored five unanswered goals, for an 11–8 victory. Jerry Schnydman scored the winning goal; Herb Better and Lucky Mallonee added two insurance goals.

Jerry Schnydman and Hank Kaestner were the most outstanding players on the 1966 team, which compiled a 5–5 collegiate record. After the third game of the season, Mike Oidick, a third-team All-American defenseman in '65, switched to the attack. Stevan Levy started the season as a goalie but lost out in competition with Geoffrey Berlin. However, Steve had been a reserve defenseman the two preceding years and was moved into Oidick's position on the defense. He did an excellent job, and our defense held the opposition to an average of 5.7 goals per game. Steve was selected for the South All-Star team and was one of the best defensive players in the game at Homewood Field.

At the conclusion of the 1966 season Wilson Fewster left Hopkins to enter business. Hopkins lost a great coach; Wilson had made his imprint on lacrosse at Homewood for thirteen years. He was an expert teacher, and his scouting reports on the opposition were masterpieces. He had no peers when a player needed a reprimand—his expressions were classics. But after practice, he had a special way of soothing the offended player's feelings and making him realize he was only trying to help. Wilson also helped me in many ways, not only in the techniques and tactics of the game but in organizational aspects as well. He greatly influenced my career in coaching.

The year 1967 marked the start of another championship era at Hopkins. Joe Cowan was the superstar, but he had plenty of help. Joe teamed up with veterans Downie McCarty and Phil Kneip on the attack; Mike Clark joined Hank Kaestner on the defense; Charlie Goodell ran with Jerry Schnydman in the midfield; and Geoff Berlin was in the goal. The season opener was with Mount Washington, a team the Jays had not beaten since 1941. But this year it was a different story: Hopkins 10–4. In a close game at West Point, Bobby Carter gave a courageous performance on a heavily taped knee and scored three goals in a 12–9 victory. But *the* game of the season was coming up in two weeks with Navy, a

team we had not beaten since 1958. The Middies were riding a thirty-four-game winning streak. Our plans for the Navy game received a serious jolt when Joe Cowan severely bruised his leg the week before in a game with Syracuse. He spent most of the week before the Navy game in bed and was only able to jog at half speed at Friday's practice. However, he was ready to go on Saturday, even though only at 75 percent effectiveness. It was a psychological lift to our team to have Joe in the game, and he had four assists, three of which were to Phil Kneip, who led the scoring with four goals. The Homecoming crowd went wild when we beat the Middies 9–6.

Unfortunately, this game was such a climax that our team was unable to get back to ground level to prepare properly for our last game of the season with Maryland. The Terps had already lost to Navy 10–8 but had an outstanding team. They upset us 9–5 and caused the championship to be shared by Maryland, Navy, and Hopkins.

In the spring of 1967, Charles E. Aronhalt, a member of the 1962–64 teams, was killed in action in Vietnam. For heroism in combat Chuck received the Distinguished Service Cross posthumously. Another gold star was added in his honor to one of the commemorative service flags.

James M. Benson passed away in the fall of 1967, and Hopkins lost a man who had dedicated himself to the service of our athletes for forty-two years. As athletic trainer Jimmy patched up countless numbers of lacrosse players and got them ready for game day, even when the odds were strongly against so doing. Jimmy also helped many high-school athletes when they had injuries. He did have his favorites on the Hopkins teams, and if you were one of his boys, you received special treatment. He didn't tolerate any horsing around in his training room, but he was a friend to many athletes, and coaches as well, and often acted as a sounding board to hear out problems. He was especially good to me, and I cherish his friendship.

Hopkins was fortunate to replace Jimmy with LeRoy J. Brandimore. Brandy came to us with excellent credentials as a trainer at the Naval Academy for ten of his twenty-five years in the navy. He had a wealth of knowledge in training techniques and was readily accepted and appreciated by our athletes. He runs a tight ship in his training room but works tirelessly to minister to those with ailments. He has followed, and even expanded, Jimmy Benson's service to high-school and club athletes. In fact, his training room is almost always filled with Hopkins and community people receiving treatment. He makes excellent use of a staff of four student trainers who work under his supervision.

After losing the opener to Mount Washington in a free-scoring 16–14 contest, the '68 team, led by cocaptains Geoff Berlin and Wes Bachur, was as overpowering as any of my teams. The margin of victory was seven goals or more in every game except the final one with the unbeaten Terrapins. We outshot the Terps by fifty-three to thirty attempts, but Norman VanderSchuyte's twenty-four saves held the final score to 10–8 in Hopkins' favor. The key personnel move of the season was the switching of Charlie Coker to the midfield after he saw only limited action against the Mounties as an attackman. Charlie became a great midfielder for us. After being shut out in the Princeton game, Downie McCarty came back with a four-goal effort against Virginia, and then five goals each in the games against Army, Maryland, and the North-South All-Star game, where he received the Most Valuable Player Award. Buzzy Budnitz deserves the lion's share of the credit for working with Downie as a volunteer assistant coach. McCarty, Kneip, and Cowan formed an attack that was comparable to the Morrill-Webster-Jory combination of ten years earlier.

During the '68 season, Dr. W. Kelso Morrill died suddenly of a heart attack. Kelso loved lacrosse as much as he did teaching mathematics. He was devoted to the game and continually strove to develop excellence in the play of the Hopkins teams, both during his days of active coaching and in his later years in an advisory capacity. Hopkins and the game of lacrosse lost a great man.

The '69 season paralleled the '59 season in several respects. Hopkins won all its collegiate games but one. And again the team that caught us napping was Willis Bilderback's Navy team. Before the Navy game we had beaten all collegiate opponents and defeated Mount Washington 10–4. The most exciting game was a 14–11 victory over previously unbeaten Army at Michie Stadium. However, our team was not mentally ready for Navy two weeks later. After all, Navy had lost to the Carling Club and Princeton, a team that we defeated handily. They barely edged Vir-

ginia, 6–5, and we had beaten the Cavaliers 15–4. Sure enough, Navy upset us by a 9–6 score. But like the '59 team, the Blue Jays bounced back and beat the Terps 14–8, as Joe Cowan and Charlie Goodell led the scoring. Mike Clark, the best defenseman in the country, was given considerable help from his defensive teammates, John Cardillo and Paul Weiss, and goalie John Kelly. We shared the championship with Army.

The 1970 team, cocaptained by Doug Honig and Russ Moore, has a rather special place in my memories. Not only had we lost four All-Americans, including three members of the Hopkins All-Time team (Cowan, Clark, and Goodell), but we lost Henry Ciccarone, who had been working with me as my cocoach since 1963. Chic left coaching on a full-time basis to enter the business world. However, with coach Hal Grosh helping, we put together a team that surprised many people. Charlie Coker was our star player, but he received excellent support from his teammates in the midfield—Honig, Bill Donovan, Gary Handleman, and Eric Bergofsky. The turning point of our season was our rebounding from a 4–0 deficit near the middle of the second quarter to beat Mount Washington 10–9 at Norris Field. After our only loss of the season—to Virginia, 15–8—we faced the unbeaten West Pointers. We moved out to a commanding 8–3 lead, with three minutes remaining in the third quarter. Army then scored five unanswered goals to tie the score 8–8 with six minutes to go in the game. Many felt Army had the momentum to win, but with seven seconds showing on the scoreboard clock, Doug Honig fired the ball into the Army goal for a 9–8 victory. In the final two games, the defensive play of Rob MacCool, Paul Weiss, and Joe Cieslowski, along with goalie Ken Dauses, was outstanding, and we beat Navy 9–7 and Maryland 7–4. Paul Wallace was our leading scorer on the close attack.

Although our 1971 team was limited in talent and won only three games, it gave a good account of itself throughout the season. We were inches away from pulling off the upset of the decade as we battled Virginia even-up in regulation time but then lost 9–8 in overtime. It was the first time since 1958 that we had used the slow-down (stall) offense. The highlight of the season was a trip to the Astrodome in Houston to play Navy and promote the game in that sports-minded state. Close to 20,000 spectators witnessed an exciting game, which Navy won 9–6.

Ralph O'Connor, Hopkins class of 1951, was primarily responsible for this successful venture. Today ten club teams are playing the game in Texas. We closed the season with an 8–5 loss to Maryland. Danny Hall, Bill Donovan, and Ken Dauses played in the North-South All-Star game at Tufts University.

The backbone of my last three teams as Hopkins coach was the class of '74, headed by Jack Thomas and Rick Kowalchuk. In the second game of the 1972 season, Mount Washington held a 5–2 halftime lead, but the Jays shut out the Mounties in the second half and posted a 9–5 victory. The following week we beat Princeton 16–8. The big game of our regular season was with Virginia. The Cavaliers were unbeaten in collegiate play, as they had been during the entire regular season the preceding year. On a rainy day in Charlottesville, we again used the slowdown offense and upset the Cavaliers 13–8. Just before halftime, our defenseman Bob Barbera cleared the ball over the center line, shot from about the restraining line, and scored. Our players on the field and the Hopkins spectators in the stands were jubilant. But most of the players on the bench, one of the officials, and I knew that the goal was not going to count. I had made the mistake of calling for a time-out (to set up a scoring play) several seconds before Barbera shot the ball. In the ensuing time-out, all I could do was to ask his forgiveness. Two weeks later we went to Annapolis to face Navy, which had just beaten Virginia 12–10. It was one of those days when we could do nothing wrong and Navy could do nothing right. Billy Nolan had a four-goal performance in his hometown, and the defense—led by Jim Head, Jim Ferguson, and goalie Les Matthews—was superb. The final score was 17–3 in Hopkins' favor, and I really felt for my good friend Bildy, who was retiring after a brilliant fourteen-year career as varsity coach at the Naval Academy. The next week Maryland gave us our only loss of the regular season, 13–12. In our debut in the NCAA tournament, we beat Washington and Lee 11–5 and then surprised the Terps at College Park with a 9–6 victory in the semifinals. In the finals, Virginia had regained its stride and played like champions in edging us 13–12. Our 1972 record was eleven wins and two losses.

The script was almost identical in 1973; the Blue Jays had another 11–2 season and a one-goal loss in the NCAA finals. The first big game of

the season was with Cornell, which had won the NCAA championship in 1971 and had been the Ivy League champion for five consecutive years. In our first meeting since 1940, Jack Thomas scored five goals and Les Matthews had twenty saves to lead us to a 17–8 victory at Ithaca. Virginia was unbeaten in seven games when it traveled to Homewood. Don Krohn scored four goals in our 14–9 win over the Cavaliers. In the final game of the regular season at College Park, the Terps humiliated us by a 17–4 score. On that afternoon I fully appreciated what Bildy had experienced the year before when we routed Navy. Nonetheless, we recovered from that defeat and beat Army and Virginia, each for the second time of the season, in the NCAA quarterfinal and semifinal games. In the finals we did an excellent job in executing a slowdown offense against the high-powered Terrapins. We held a 5–2 halftime lead and a 9–7 lead with six minutes remaining in the game. But goals by Frank Urso and Doug Schreiber sent the game into overtime. The only goal (by Frank Urso) of the two overtime periods gave Maryland a 10–9 victory and the NCAA championship. As the team walked off the field at the end of the game, a standing ovation from the Hopkins fans helped to ease the sting of defeat. Matthews, Thomas, and Kowalchuk were first-team All-Americans for the second year in a row.

In 1974 the Jays, again led by Thomas and Kowalchuk, won twelve games and lost two, just as they had in the previous two years. But the two losses did not hurt as far as the NCAA championship was concerned. In fact, they helped. In the opener at Charlottesville, our players were somewhat overconfident because we had beaten Virginia twice the year before. The Cavaliers helped to straighten our thinking by trouncing us 15–10. We won the next eight games. Two freshmen were featured in the 20–10 victory over Washington College—Tommy Myrick scored six goals and Richie Hirsch four. Hirsch also had four-goal performances against Cornell and Army. Mount Washington was played under the lights at Homewood Field, and Franz Wittelsberger and Jack Thomas directed a 19–12 victory. Jack again put on a tremendous show at Annapolis, figuring in ten of our twelve goals, but it wasn't quite enough to beat Dick Szlasa's fired-up Navy team. The Middies upset us 13–12. At the time, I felt this loss would help us gain an edge for the battle with the undefeated Terps the next week. Maryland had been averaging almost eighteen goals per game and had rolled over Virginia, 25–13, and Navy, 12–7. But our team was ready for the Terrapins, and I must say it was a great thrill to beat Maryland 17–13, in my last Homecoming game as coach. There were many heroes in the game— Kevin Mahon had eighteen saves in his first varsity game; Rick Kowalchuk had four goals (two were our team's fifteenth and sixteenth goals, which stymied Maryland's rally) and Jimmy Cahill had two solo goals; and Bob Maimone was very effective on faceoffs and Harry Stringer on ground balls.

The team was in high gear for the NCAA playoffs. Hofstra University, coached by Howdy Myers, was our first opponent. Howdy had recruited me when I was a senior in high school, and I had gone to Hopkins primarily because of him. When he removed several of his star players from the squad on the day before our game for violating rules, our players and coaches relaxed a bit, thinking we would have an easy time. I joked with our coaches before the game about Howdy's giving me my start at Hopkins and how he had a chance to end my career in coaching on his first visit back to Homewood Field. Hofstra led at halftime 6–4, and when the score was tied 8–8 with one minute remaining in the third quarter, my little joke about Howdy's return started to stick in my throat. However, Rick Kowalchuk's goal broke the tie, and we scored eight goals in the fourth quarter, the most important being Bill McCutcheon's goal, which gave us a two-goal lead. We won the game 18–10, and Franz Wittelsberger led the scoring with seven goals.

In the semifinal game at Homewood Field, Washington and Lee had our backs to the wall by virtue of a 10–7 lead with twelve minutes remaining in the game. Billy Nolan got us rolling by scoring our eighth goal; Richie Hirsch followed with a score; then Dale Kohler tied the game with his second goal of the game. Kowalchuk scored the big goal with less than two minutes showing on the clock to give us an 11–10 victory. Steven Muller, president of the university, was completely wrapped up in the game. When Wittelsberger scored a goal just before halftime, Dr. Muller jumped to his feet and threw his hands in the air triumphantly, accidentally striking the press-box window. A panel of glass fell out and cut the hand of one of his guests, the attorney general of Puerto Rico. College presidents have

been known to sit on a team bench before, but Dr. Muller's name goes down in the record book as the only college president known to cheer with such fervor as to smash a press-box window.

The stage was now set for the NCAA championship game at Rutgers University with the University of Maryland. Although Hopkins had won the first meeting with the Terps, many felt that their offense was still too powerful for us, but our team was confident, and the seniors, in particular, were especially determined to win a gold medal.

Everyone on the squad gave his best; no one person could be singled out as the hero. With the Terps leading 2–0 early in the game, Rick Kowalchuk broke the ice and scored our first goal. We then jumped to a 10–4 halftime lead and then to 14–6 with five minutes to go in the third quarter. At this point Maryland scored five goals in five minutes to bring the score to 14–11 early in the fourth quarter. Rick countered with his third goal of the game, and this allowed us to breathe easier. Wittelsberger scored our last two goals (he had five for the game), and we won 17–12. Thomas and Hirsch each had three goals, Nolan two, and Barbera one. I think I was probably as happy as Barbera when he scored, because I felt I was finally taken off the hook for denying him a goal in the '72 Virginia game. Kevin Mahon was outstanding in and out of the goal and was given strong support by Mike Siegert and Dennis Gagomiros, who had shut out Maryland's All-American attackman, Pat O'Meally, for the second time that season.

The victory had a special meaning for me. It was a lot easier to bow out of the coaching ranks with the gold medal rather than a third silver one. But more important than my own feelings, the eleven seniors, who had never won a championship, finally made it. They were a fine group of lacrosse players, with two of Hopkins' best, Jack Thomas and Rick Kowalchuk, as their leaders.

Looking back on my twenty years as Hopkins' coach, I realize that scores, goals, assists, and saves don't tell the whole story. Some of my clearest and most prized memories are of the courage and self-sacrifice that spectators never saw. Here are a few examples from recent seasons.

Players do drop from athletic squads, sometimes for good reasons but often simply because they are disappointed in being substitutes. When there is sharp competition, a good player may have to sit on the bench for a long time. This is not easy for a competitive person to accept.

Bill Barton, a junior, faced this situation during the 1970 lacrosse season. He had worked hard to prepare himself for the season, especially because he had undergone arm surgery the preceding summer. When practice started in March, he and Stu Kahl were battling for the starting position at crease attack. Stu won the job. In the first three games of the season, Stu played most of the time and scored five goals. Bill saw only limited action. He was very discouraged and felt he was going to spend most of the season on the bench. He came into my office on the Monday after our third game to say he intended to quit the team.

I assured him that we would give him every opportunity to prove he was better than Stu. But the clinching point was that a team needs two creasemen because there was always the possibility of one getting hurt. He decided not to quit. The coaches watched both players closely in practice but still felt Stu was the number-one man. So for the next three games, Bill continued to "ride the bench." In the seventh game we played an undefeated, powerhouse team from West Point. Bill Barton was again on the bench until the latter part of the first quarter, when Stu Kahl suffered a severe ankle sprain. Bill took his place and was ready in every respect. He scored four goals in our last-second 9–8 upset win. He remained in the starting lineup for the last three games of our season and played extremely well in each. Bill could have let adversity get the best of him but he didn't. Instead, he fought back and was ready when called upon.

There was another member of the 1970 Hopkins team who almost did not play that year. Rob MacCool was an excellent high-school defenseman but was only the fourth defenseman on our 1968 championship team. It was a blow to his pride to spend a major part of the season on the bench, and so he decided not to play for Hopkins in 1969, his junior year. Instead, he played for the Mount Washington Club. When his senior year rolled around, Rob still was not planning to play for Hopkins. However, after receiving encouragement from our players, he came to see me. We buried the hatchet, and he joined our team. He had an outstanding season and was a first-team All-American. Not bad for a player who almost ended his college career at the end of his sophomore year as a fourth defenseman.

Among many recollections of our championship 1974 season I remember with special satisfaction the way two of our players responded to difficult situations. The first was Mike Godack, a sophomore who was competing for the starting job in the goal. As a freshman he had ended the season as the backup goalie to Les Matthews. Mike had a knack for getting his body in the way of the ball and was fearless in stopping it. Shots would bounce off his chest, his legs, his arms, his head. But his stick work was rather stiff and he had little speed, so that his clearing and maneuvering out of the goal were somewhat weak.

In the fall of 1973 Kevin Mahon, an All-American high-school goalie, entered the freshman class at Hopkins. After watching him in our fall workouts, we anticipated his being our starting goalie in the spring. However, during our preseason scrimmages in early March, although Kevin excelled in his clearing and play out of the goal, he just didn't stop the ball as well as Mike. The coaching staff decided to start the season with Mike in the goal. In our opener, with Virginia, Mike was brilliant, making twenty-five saves, some of them spectacular. His clearing was still uncertain, but his overall play was outstanding. He remained in the nets for eight straight victories and did well enough to be on the list of seven goalies being considered for the All-American team. In our tenth game of the season, an upset loss to Navy, Mike's play was certainly acceptable; he had fourteen saves. But in the staff meeting on the Sunday evening following the Navy game, we decided to make a change in the goal. In recent practices Kevin had been stopping the ball more consistently than at the start of the season, and if we were to upset the undefeated University of Maryland, we needed Kevin's speed out of the goal.

On Monday afternoon before our first practice for our game with Maryland, I asked Mike to come into my office. I told him that in the best interest of the team, Kevin was going to start in the goal against the Terps. Mike was obviously crushed with disappointment, but his comment was, "If you really feel the change will help the team, I can accept it. I respect your decision." Although hurting inside, Mike hustled during that Monday-afternoon practice and every day that week. He was going to be ready both mentally and physically if he got a second chance. He did not quit on himself or the team.

One of the beautiful things about this entire episode was Mike's complete support of Kevin. He gave Kevin more encouragment than anyone else on the team, because he knew Kevin had to be a little nervous as he prepared for his first varsity game. Kevin played extremely well in that game and the three playoff games to help lead us to an NCAA championship. Mike never did get the chance to start in any of those games or even to play in a pressure situation. But he was ready and would have come through with flying colors if needed. The Mike Godack story is a classic example of an individual player's placing the well-being of the team ahead of his own personal feelings.

Phil Calderone, also on the 1974 championship team, was placed in the frustrating position of being a substitute in each of his four years at Hopkins. Phil was a fine high-school player, but he was just not quite good enough to ever break into our starting lineup. I am certain he would have been a regular and a high scorer on 75 percent of the college lacrosse teams in the country. Instead of sulking and griping, Phil was always giving encouragement to the players in the game and keeping spirits high on the bench. He never stopped hustling himself during practices, and when he played in the games he did an excellent job. When our players returned to our Athletic Center at 1:00 A.M. after the NCAA finals at Rutgers, the first thing they wanted to do was to strip the mannequin in the Lacrosse Hall of Fame and put on the Columbia-blue uniform of our championship Hopkins team. (The championship team's uniform is placed on the mannequin for the ensuing year.) But they were persuaded to wait until Monday to make the change. Instead of selecting the jersey of either cocaptain, Jack Thomas, number 30, or Rick Kowalchuk, number 34, both three-time All-Americans; our coaches thought it would be appropriate to place jersey number 47 on the mannequin. When our players looked in the Hall of Fame on Monday afternoon and saw Phil Calderone's jersey in the honored position, their approval was spontaneous. Phil Calderone gave 100 percent of his ability, supported his team with enthusiasm, and was proud to be a part of it, even in the role of a substitute.

I could cite a number of other such incidents from my own experience, and I feel sure that coaches of many other colleges could recollect similar examples.

Several weeks after the 1974 championship game, our team traveled to California for a three-week good-will tour. The Hopkins alumni of the state and the California Lacrosse Association were gracious hosts. It was all fun and games for our team, especially for me, because I officially turned the team over to Henry Ciccarone when we arrived in California. Chic is one of the game's best coaches, and he has a wonderful way with people. I know he will keep Hopkins lacrosse in the top ranks of intercollegiate competition.

My coaching career ended in 1974 and so did my playing career. Chic put me in the goal for the second half of the game with the University of California Lacrosse Club. (He felt we had a safe-enough lead of 18–1.) I had eight saves and cleared the ball like an "old pro." With my career ended on the field, it is now my good fortune to have become one of the All-American Blue Jay fans.

index